The American History Series

SERIES EDITORS

John Hope Franklin, *Duke University*
A. S. Eisenstadt, *Brooklyn College*

Donald R. Wright
STATE UNIVERSITY OF NEW YORK—CORTLAND

African Americans in the Colonial Era: From African Origins through the American Revolution

HARLAN DAVIDSON, INC.
WHEELING, ILLINOIS 60090-6000

Library of Congress Cataloging-in-Publication Data

Wright, Donald R.
    African Americans in the colonial era : from African origins
 through the American Revolution / Donald R. Wright.
 —2nd ed.
        p. cm. —(American history series)
    Includes bibliographical references (p. 203) and index.
    ISBN 0-88295-955-7 (alk. paper)
        1. Afro-Americans—History—To 1863. 2. Slavery—United
    States—History. 3. United States—History—Colonial period,
    ca. 1600–1775. I. Title. II. Title: American history
    series (Wheeling, Ill.)

E185.W94 2000
973'.0496073—dc21   99-086389

Cover illustration: Introduction of slavery into Virginia colony.
Courtesy North Wind Picture Archives

Manufactured in the United States of America
04 03 02 01 00 1 2 3 4 5 VP

In memory of Marilou B. Wright

FOREWORD

Every generation writes its own history for the reason that it sees the past in the foreshortened perspective of its own experience. This has surely been true of the writing of American history. The practical aim of our historiography is to give us a more informed sense of where we are going by helping us understand the road we took in getting where we are. As the nature and dimensions of American life are changing, so too are the themes of our historical writing. Today's scholars are hard at work reconsidering every major aspect of the nation's past: its politics, diplomacy, economy, society, recreation, mores and values, as well as status, ethnic, race, sexual, and family relations. The lists of series titles that appear on the inside covers of this book will show at once that our historians are ever broadening the range of their studies.

The aim of this series is to offer our readers a survey of what today's historians are saying about the central themes and aspects of the American past. To do this, we have invited to write for the series only scholars who have made notable contributions to the respective fields in which they are working. Drawing on primary and secondary materials, each volume presents a factual and narrative account of its particular subject, one that affords readers a basis for perceiving its larger dimensions and importance. Conscious that readers respond to the closeness and immediacy of a subject, each of our authors seeks to restore the past as an actual present, to revive it as a living reality. The individuals and groups who figure in the pages of our books appear as real people who once were looking for survival and fulfillment. Aware that historical subjects are often matters of controversy, our authors present their own findings and conclusions. Each volume closes with an extensive critical essay on the writings of the major authorities on its particular theme.

The books in this series are primarily designed for use in both basic and advanced courses in American history, on the undergraduate and graduate levels. Such a series has a particular value these days, when the format of American history courses is being altered to accommodate a greater diversity of reading materials. The series offers a number of distinct advantages. It extends the dimensions of regular course work. It makes clear that the study of our past is, more than the student might otherwise understand, at once complex, profound, and absorbing. It presents that past as a subject of continuing interest and fresh investigation.

For these reasons the series strongly invites an interest that far exceeds the walls of academe. The work of experts in their respective fields, it puts at the disposal of all readers the rich findings of historical inquiry, an invitation to join, in major fields of research, those who are pondering anew the central themes and aspects of our past.

And, going beyond the confines of the classroom, it reminds the general reader no less than the university student that in each successive generation of the ever-changing American adventure, from its very start until our own day, men and women and children were facing their daily problems and attempting, as we are now, to live their lives and to make their way.

John Hope Franklin
A. S. Eisenstadt

CONTENTS

PREFACE TO THE SECOND EDITION AND ACKNOWLEDGMENTS

"She came out of a violent storm," writes Lerone Bennett, Jr., in *Before the Mayflower: A History of Black America* (5th rev. ed., 1982), "with a story no one believed, a name no one recorded and a past no one investigated." The "she" to which Bennett refers is the Dutch vessel that brought the first persons of African descent to the British colonies of mainland North America in 1619. Captain John Smith's notation of this event in his *General History of Virginia* (1624)—"About the last of August [1619] came in a dutch man-of-warre that sold us twenty Negars."—was the first scrap of evidence that many remember of early African-American history. For a long time Bennett was right: no one knew much about the vessel or its human cargo. Because Jamestown planter John Rolfe recorded that the ship had come from the West Indies, the general belief was that the "twenty Negars" came from the Caribbean and were a generation or more removed from Africa. Since most people believed that further investigation of these twenty individual human beings was futile, for more than three centuries their story remained just a few sentences long.

On the eve of the twenty-first century, all this changed. That was when historians Engel Sluiter and John Thornton dug into the past of the vessel and the men and women on board and published their findings (in 1997 and 1998, respectively) in the *William and Mary Quarterly*. From work in Spanish archives, Sluiter learned that the Dutch ship, while privateering in consort with an English corsair, had robbed a Portuguese slaver of part of its human cargo off Campeche, west of the Yucatan Peninsula, in late July or early August 1619, and that the Portuguese captain previously had purchased the cargo of 350 men, women, and children along the coast of West Central Africa, at Luanda, Angola. The "twenty Negars" came directly from Africa. Thornton took this information and ran with it, establishing the slaves' most likely ethnic background and circumstances of enslavement. They were probably Kimbundu-speaking subjects of the Angolan Kingdom of Ndongo, captured in a Portuguese-led military campaign in 1618 or 1619; they were likely urban, people who carried a sense of a common identity; and they knew at least the rudiments of Christianity. Those who survived the Virginia "seasoning" for a year or more may well have met more men and women from the same region, thus adding, as Thornton writes, "a certain Angolan touch to the early Chesapeake."

I call attention here to these historical investigations not to begin a discussion of the nature or character of early African Americans, but to show to what depth, and in what speed, our knowledge of black history in the colonial period is moving. The issue of the *William and Mary Quarterly* containing Thornton's article may still have been in some mailboxes when two of the most important books on African Americans in the colonial era burst upon the scene. One of them, Ira Berlin's *Many Thousands Gone: The First Two Centuries of Slavery in North America* (1998), provides a wholly new, but marvelously comprehensible schema for understanding the evolving nature of African-Americans' lives in the colonial period. The other, Philip D. Morgan's *Slave Counterpoint: Black Culture in the Eighteenth-Century Chesapeake and Lowcountry* (1998), offers the greatest detail yet, in comparative perspective, of nearly every aspect of these lives. And these studies merely sit atop a huge outpouring of highly regarded, relevant scholarship in the 1990s. The bibliographical essay of this book refers to nine books on one or another aspect of the topic that have been published through the first two-thirds of 1999—and ten in 1998, sixteen in 1997, and so on. Fortunate is the student entering the subject today. The advantage over a similar person just a decade ago is enormous.

That said, consider the poor historian who has taken on the task of keeping up with this body of monographic and journal literature—and mastering it sufficiently to craft an up-to-date synthesis. For the last three years I have been scurrying about like a person possessed, buying books to read and use before the library can process them and moaning audibly with the arrival of each new numbered journal portending to contain notice of yet another new monograph or an article revising some argument I was clinging to or shining light on some corner of the topic that I was ready to leave obscure. All of this has forced me to change things in every part of the book.

And, of course, this has rendered a better book than the 1990 edition. But if the second edition offers readers clearer understanding of and deeper insight into the early history of persons of African descent in what would become the United States, the credit must go to the Sluiters and Thorntons, the Berlins and Morgans, and the scores of others who have done the careful investigation, have lived with the primary sources, and have written the studies throughout the decade that underlie this synthesis. It would be a mistake for one to read this book without looking carefully at the bibliographical essay and noticing the wealth of very good historical study upon which it is based. As in the first edition, my biggest debt, by far, is to the authors of these books and articles.

Since writing the first edition of *African Americans in the Colonial Era,* I have had experiences that have altered my perspective on early African-American history in particular and on life in general. After completing a second volume in this series, *African Americans in the Early Republic, 1789–1831* (1993), I returned to the subject of my original historical interest, Africa, and wrote *The World and a Very Small Place in Africa* (1997), which attempts to portray how events in an ever-widening world affected the lives of people living in a tiny spot, a place called Niumi, along the Gambia River in West Africa. Niumi's elite families participated in some of the slave trading that brought Africans to North America, and some of its underclass counted among the enslaved. Working on this book convinced me all the more how the history of mainland North America during the colonial era is part of a larger Atlantic history that brought together Africans, Europeans, and Native Americans, mixing and melding these peoples' thoughts and ways.

One simply cannot understand early American history in any general or specific way, or the historical experience of any subgroup of early America, without placing that understanding in the larger Atlantic context and without knowing something of whence each group came and what each brought to the mix that was colonial America. More so than its predecessor, this edition of *African Americans in the Colonial Era* reflects that conviction.

As I was completing the African book, my wife Marilou was diagnosed with cancer, and eight months later she died. There were no good parts to that story, but the experience brought me much closer to the reality of human suffering and death, making it possible to realize on a deeper level how all the writing about enslavement and the middle passage and "seasoning" and punishment and human misery and death through cold statistics and chilly generalizations masks what in every case was the most painful, individual, human experience. Recognition of this fact can bring some of us in the present to try to do something—in this case, study and think and write—to attend to the pain that is still involved with the African-American past. The further into the future we go, the more we recognize the common humanity of all. It seems increasingly important in 2000 that we look back and pay proper attention to the periods, not long into the past, when we lacked that recognition.

I am grateful to several people for helping me in various ways with this project. Joseph Douglas was an exceptional research assistant. Graham Hodges made arrangements for me to see his newest book, *Root and Branch,* in proofs before publication. Douglas Egerton is my regular inspiration and oracle on matters relating to American history. Abraham Eisenstadt has been an important source of encouragement and wise counsel. Andrew Davidson is a careful and skilled editor who has been ferreting out my clunky sentences for some time now. Perhaps my greatest joy in writing in this series has been the continuing opportunities to mix business with pleasure with Andrew and Linda Gaio-Davidson. I also wish to thank Tim Shannon, Judy Van Buskirk, Sandy Gutman, John Wright, Ben Wright, C. J. Carter, and Doris DeLuca. I trust each knows why.

An advertisement of a cargo of slaves aboard the Bance-Island, *anchored off Chareleston, during a plague of smallpox.*

INTRODUCTION

A decade ago, in 1990, it seemed evident that the study of the lives of African Americans in slavery was far out of temporal and geographical balance. Chattel slavery existed as a legal institution in this country for about two hundred years, roughly from the middle of the seventeenth century to the middle of the nineteenth century. Most of that time—about two-thirds of it—was the colonial period of American history. From before 1650 to after 1790, slavery was a viable American institution mainly on the plantations and smaller farms around the Chesapeake Bay in Virginia and Maryland, throughout the coastal Low Country of South Carolina and Georgia, and along the lower Mississippi River. In only the last fifty years of its existence in this country did slavery move into the lands of the Deep South and undergo a switch from use predominately in tobacco and rice production to that of cotton. Yet the focus of the study of American slavery—and indeed of the history of all African Americans before the Civil War, back to the time of Ulrich B. Phillips's *American Negro Slavery* (1918)—had been on the institution as it operated in the Cotton South between about 1830 and 1860. As late as a decade ago, the best-known books on slavery or slave society in America were such classics as Kenneth Stampp's *The Peculiar Institution: Slavery in the Antebellum South* (1956), John Blassingame's *The Slave Community: Plantation Life in the Antebellum South* (1972), and Eugene Genovese's

Roll, Jordan, Roll: The World the Slaves Made (1972), which were examinations of antebellum slavery with its center in the Deep South.

Naturally, this had skewed the presentation of American slavery in high school and college textbooks and, consequently, the image of slavery that most educated Americans held. It all lacked perspective of time and place. When considering slavery in the country's history, most Americans thought of enormous plantations in Alabama or Mississippi, of black men and women living in quarters resembling small villages, of slaves working in gangs picking cotton, and of their efforts to escape toward the free states in the North. All of these were concepts pertinent to the Deep South in the middle of the nineteenth century. But they did not reflect the lives of African Americans during the two hundred years before the rise of the Cotton Kingdom.

Thus, the first edition of this book was an effort to right this seemingly timeless imbalance by examining the experience of African Americans throughout the colonial era. To a large extent, ten years later the situation is different. Now, thanks largely to a group of American and Atlantic-focused historians who come out of an increasingly respected historical tradition going back to the work of Benjamin Quarles, Winthrop Jordan, and Peter Wood on the one hand, and Philip Curtin on the other, the imbalance is not nearly so great. Finally, not only in college and high school textbooks, which have come a long way in their own right, but on such elaborate television productions as the five-part *Africans in America,* which millions of Americans watched on PBS in 1998, the experience of persons of African descent in America's earliest centuries is getting its due. And is it not a sign of the maturation of the subject that two of the most highly regarded historical studies published in this country in 1998 were about the African-American colonial experience: Ira Berlin's *Many Thousands Gone: The First Two Centuries of Slavery in North America* and Philip D. Morgan's *Slave Counterpoint: Black Culture in the Eighteenth-Century Chesapeake and Low Country*? So it is meaningful—and positive—that this second edition need have less of a corrective tone about it.

Nonetheless, this revised edition still has an important role to play. The heart of my effort in its preparation concerned the integration into the narrative of fresh ideas and new perspectives from the large amount of quality recent scholarship on the topic. Of the books and articles referred to in this book's bibliographical essay, which, by necessity, is a selective one, 122 (plus one CD-ROM) have been published since 1990! These publications make up the body of work that has done the most to right the imbalance in our perspective on slavery.

Thus, while this book's organizational framework remains essentially unchanged, each chapter's content is different— largely a reflection of the new scholarship. But, as before, the book begins in Africa, for the African heritage continues as one of the most important factors in shaping the lives of African Americans. The first chapter examines the variety of living conditions and social relationships in Africa that formed the basis for African-American culture. Then, in some detail, it addresses a topic that still receives too little attention in works of American history, the institution that brought Africans to America, the Atlantic slave trade.

The book then examines the lives of African Americans primarily in the English colonies of mainland North America, but also in the Spanish and French colonies of Florida and the lower Mississippi, from their first arrival to the last decade of the eighteenth century, when the infant United States was getting on its feet and black chattel slavery was further entrenched in the country's legal system. In its coverage of the black experience in America through roughly one and two-thirds centuries, the study focuses on three major topics, which reflect the chapter divisions. One is the origins and development of slavery and racism in the colonies. How could race-based slavery come to exist in a land that simultaneously developed ideas about personal liberty? The answer is that it began in different ways and at different times in the Chesapeake Bay region, the Carolina and Georgia Low Country, the lower Mississippi, and New England and the Middle Colonies. Some degree of racism existed before the first Africans were sold into colonial Virginia, but the fact of having persons of African descent and no one else in the legally defined, debased position of slavery broadened and strengthened the existing racial prejudice.

A second topic is the beginnings and early manifestations of African-American culture. The process of culture formation varied, too, according to time and place. Blacks in America first had to have extensive social contacts with other blacks—they had to exist in black communities—before they could develop group values, ways, and beliefs. And because of demographic configurations and living and working conditions, it took a long time for black communities to exist in the mainland colonies, and their nature differed from place to place. Once formed, black communities were perpetuated by the African-American family, the integral conduit for passing down and thereby preserving manifestations of black culture.

The third topic is the considerable changes African Americans experienced during the tumultuous quarter century of the Revolutionary era. The Revolution raised basic questions over the morality of slavery, for, after all, the Founding Fathers justified their break with England on the self-evident truth that all men are created equal. The Revolutionary era led to the ending of slavery in states north of Maryland and considerable manumission in the Upper South and lower Mississippi, while making slavery more strongly entrenched and the lives of all blacks more restricted in the states where slavery remained. The Revolutionary era also brought new strength to the racist justification for slavery and a second-class citizenship for African Americans that would plague them and their descendants for more than two centuries after the conflict had run its course.

Beyond this, several ideas form the foundation of, or emerge from, this newer study of African Americans in the colonial era. One is simply that a wide variety of experiences characterized the lives of blacks between the time of their existence in Africa and their living as African Americans in the United States near the end of the eighteenth century. These experiences differed considerably over time and across space. Where possible, this study emphasizes the temporal and geographical variety of these experiences. Still more than before, it directs attention to the fact that it was a broader Atlantic context, rather than only a mainland–North

America one, in which colonial African-American history took shape.

Another basic idea of this study—no longer so new now but still good to point out—is that blacks in West Africa through the slave trade years and blacks in America through colonial times were different sorts of people than the older racist or romantic portrayals led people to believe. These Africans and African Americans were neither candidates for the objective case, always being done unto and never doing, nor wily calculators, forever thinking of ways to dupe their masters. They were normal human beings with varying personal qualities, who made rational decisions under varied and difficult circumstances. Simply knowing this enables one to recognize, as never before, the fact that blacks had a hand in many of the good things, and some of the bad things, that happened to them and to others throughout their history. We remain fortunate to be at a stage in the continually evolving study of African-American history when we can step away from stereotypes, exaggerations, and oversights and emphasize black humanity and agency.

Two more somewhat-related ideas come from recent scholarship by Douglas Egerton, James Sidbury, Graham Hodges, and Marcus Rediker. One is that both the character of individual black men and women and the nature of African-American culture as it existed in varying forms around the North America mainland were far more complex than previously recognized. The other is that race was an important determinant for the experience of blacks in Colonial America, but only one of many. The more we consider these matters, the more it becomes apparent that an overriding focus on race was more characteristic of the thinking of wealthy white men than it was of common folk of whatever physical makeup and women. That we have emphasized the importance of race in colonial African-American history may speak more about American society today than American society over two centuries ago.

A final idea is that through the long period of evolution of slavery and black society in the colonial period, much of the course for the subsequent history of African Americans was set. By 1790 the basic American institutions and attitudes concerning slavery and racism were established, and by that time the forces were in motion that would lead to the expansion of slavery, the struggle that would fuel sectionalism and help bring on the Civil War, and the rapid move toward second-class citizenship for African Americans following the legal demise of slavery in 1865. Also, by 1790 the most important elements of African-American culture—family, religion, a spirit of resistance, and a host of truly African-American ways of living—already underlay a stable black community. From this base, African-American community and culture would evolve through the next two centuries, over which time they would provide African Americans a group identity and help them cope with a hostile world. Thus, in the broadest sense, the colonial era encompassed the truly formative years of the African-American experience.

CHAPTER ONE

Atlantic Origins

In the spring of 1727 an English barque, the *John and Betty,* sailed up Chesapeake Bay and into the mouth of the Rappahannock River with 140 African slaves on board. The ship's master, William Denton, brought the vessel to anchor off the main wharf of Robert "King" Carter's enormous plantation. Denton called on Carter, and the planter agreed to manage the sale of the slaves.

For three weeks Carter rowed daily to the barque, where he held forth with fellow planters dealing for the slaves. The human cargo was smaller than many straight from Guinea, so it was not of extraordinary value. Still, it was early in tobacco-growing season and demand for labor was high. Also, a number of the Africans aboard were from Senegambia and the Gold Coast, the regions Virginia planters favored most. So on typical days Carter sold half a dozen slaves, often in pairs, at from £12 to £20 each. When he finished he was wealthier from his percentage of each transaction, and he was convinced that he had performed a service for his peers, the white planters who dominated the export economy of tidewater Virginia.

Less noticeable than the Carters in the historical record, the 140 Africans, who ended up scattered about the area, proceeded to learn their work and seek the keys to getting by in their new situation. They now were part of the labor force of the eighteenth-century British colonies on the North American mainland. If they survived long under the difficult conditions of their new environment, they would begin the lengthy process of acculturation that would lead to their descendants being African Americans.

What occurred on the Rappahannock in 1727 took place in varied fashion over four centuries along the Atlantic side of the New World, from the British colonies of mainland North America to Brazil. The colonies were part of an enormous economic system that linked the continents bordering the Atlantic Ocean. The system relied on European management, capital, and shipping, and it involved New World production of staple goods, mostly sugar, for European consumption. By the seventeenth century those in control of the system preferred African slaves as the colonial labor force.

The idea of importing labor from some distance for intensive work on export crops was an old one. Romans had done this on a grand scale two centuries before the Christian era, when slaves made up perhaps 40 percent of the population of the Italian peninsula and large gangs of enslaved men and women worked the agricultural estates of the Roman grandees. Although slavery declined gradually as an important European economic institution following the Roman Empire's collapse, populations around the Mediterranean heart of the old empire and in much of continental Europe continued to accept the Roman legal status of slaves, which considered such humans as chattel, the property of another. Much later this would help provide a legal basis for Crusaders to enslave their captive enemies—as Muslims had been doing to Christians for some time—and to sell such captives off to the rural agricultural enterprises that were popping up in the eastern Mediterranean after the eleventh century.

By the end of the thirteenth century a plantation system had come into being, one centered on the island of Cyprus and geared to provide sugar to a European market. Like the Atlantic plantations of half a millennium later, these Mediterranean concerns relied on European capital, management, and shipping. Some who worked in the cane were free and some were serfs, but increasingly sugar production came to be identified with slave labor. Mediterranean shippers brought in workers from the Balkans and southern Russia (people who spoke Slavic languages; thus the word "slave," from "Slav") along with others from Asia Minor and North Africa. Some of the men and women purchased in North Africa had been marched across the Sahara Desert from their original homes in the Western Sudan. For over two centuries the Mediterranean plantations made profits and the institution of slavery spread, first to Crete and Sicily and then to coastal Spain and Portugal. By 1450, on the eve of European expansion into the south Atlantic, slave-based sugar plantations existed in the western Mediterranean and even on nearby Atlantic islands.

Most of the men who ventured away from their European homelands after the middle of the fifteenth century and established outposts or acquired vast lands on both sides of the Atlantic had some motives less selfless than spreading Christianity or increasing geographical knowledge. European rulers sponsored many of such enterprises to garner wealth for the state, and most individuals involved had an eye out for personal gain as well. Some state-sponsored enterprises found wealth in the parts of Africa or America that held gold or silver, but most of the lands bordering the Atlantic did not hold such obvious riches. So in the coastal and insular areas the newcomers tended to turn to export agriculture, with sugar as the focus. A model for doing so already existed. Thus developed, at a slow but regular pace, an agricultural economy along the tropical Atlantic rim, first on some islands off West Africa, with São Tomé becoming the leading sugar producer by the beginning of the sixteenth century, and then, by the end of that century, in northeastern Brazil. By 1640 a staple-export economy had spread to the great sugar islands of the Lesser Antilles in the Caribbean and, on a smaller scale and outside the tropics, to English tobacco-growing colonies on the North American mainland. As the Atlantic economy expanded, the plantation model, on a larger scale than ever before, became the accepted way of making profits from the great expanses of land.

But establishing plantations in distant territories had a hitch. Although sugar remained in great demand, the land was productive, and the technology to process sugar cane existed and regularly improved, finding adequate numbers of workers to grow this most labor-intensive of crops became difficult. Those native to America, the so-called Indians, never worked out as field workers as the landowners had hoped they would. Once in captivity or even in close proximity to Europeans, Native Americans died rapidly from the Old World diseases of smallpox, mumps, and measles that the newcomers had brought with them. Those Indians who did not perish after having been enslaved proved remarkably able to resist pressures to adapt to strict work regimes, partly because they could run away relatively easily—their homes and extended families being close by and their knowledge of the surroundings often superior to that of their captors. Bonded Europeans, either criminals sentenced to labor or men willingly under indenture to gain passage to America and, with luck, opportunity, were not a great deal better at performing regimented work in many New World locales. White laborers fell victim to a different host of diseases, these mostly tropical, such as malaria and yellow fever. And should they run away, white servants might pass themselves off as members of the ruling society. Just as important, rising opportunities for poor Europeans at home, either with armies during the almost continual warfare of the era or in jobs paying wages that rose steadily over the seventeenth and eighteenth centuries, limited the number of those willing to make the arduous passage to the New World for the sketchy promise of economic or social gain.

Africans, however, performed effectively as plantation workers under the regimented conditions in the Americas, and European planters soon recognized this as fact, even if they did not understand why it was so. The African homelands of black slaves were places where Old World and tropical diseases were endemic. Africans who survived into adolescence had already acquired some immunity to smallpox, mumps and measles *as well as* to malaria and yellow fever. So in the fresh mix of diseases up and down the Atlantic rim of the New World, even under the difficult conditions of the plantation environment, Africans lived longer—

three to five times longer than their white counterparts. They were also more productive workers. Finally, Africans could not run home or be mistaken for a member of the society of planters.

None of this, of course, would have made any difference had African laborers been in short supply or too expensive for New World planters to obtain. But through most of the years of the Atlantic trade, prices for Africans remained favorable in relation to the price of the crops they produced. (For example, an English planter on the Caribbean island of Jamaica in 1690 had to pay £20 for a "prime" male African, direct from Guinea. That laborer could produce about 500 pounds of sugar in a year. The planter could sell that 500 pounds of sugar for £20, and thus in a year recover the original cost of the slave.) In short, African laborers turned out to be the best deal in economic terms, which were the only terms of real interest to the landowners, shippers, financiers, and merchants involved in the plantation system.

Atlantic Africa

Slaves came to the British mainland colonies over one of two general routes. One was from the West Indies and normally involved shippers of general merchandise, who topped off their cargos with slaves as opportunities offered. Many ships came to the colonies so laden, especially in the earlier years of slave trading, but they brought relatively few slaves—around 15 percent of the total brought to the area that would become the United States before the trade's abolition in 1808. The overwhelming number of slave imports, roughly four of every five, arrived directly from Africa. With notable exceptions, especially in the early years of settlement, these newcomers were unacculturated, raw, frightened— Chesapeake planters characterized them as "outlandish"—persons not long away from their homes in Africa.

Nearly all slaves brought to English North America came from the coast and interior of West and West Central Africa. A few came from the Mozambique coast or Madagascar, around the Cape of Good Hope. English traders brought 85 percent of all slaves arriving in the mainland colonies, and because they never developed close, long-standing links with merchants of specific

African regions, the masters of English slavers purchased captives all along about 3,500 miles of African coastline, from Senegal in the north to Angola in the south. Yet some African markets were especially important as sources for English slaves through the years of the heaviest importing into North America. About a quarter of slave imports to the colonies directly from Africa came from the hinterland of the coastal region normally designated "Congo-Angola," the portion within 500 miles north or south of the Congo River. Portuguese merchants dominated the southern part of this trade and carried most of their slaves to Brazil, but English and Dutch slavers frequented the ports north of the Congo and brought many persons, whom they identified as Kongo, Tio, and Matamba slaves,[1] to North America. Later in the eighteenth century more slaves came to English colonies from the Portuguese ports of Luanda and Benguela and were identified as Ovimbundu and Kwanza. Another quarter came from the coast of southeastern Nigeria, primarily the lands where the Ibo and Ibibio languages were spoken. About 15 percent each came from Senegambia, the land between and around the Senegal and Gambia rivers (where Europeans identified Africans as Mandinka, Fulbe, Serer, Wolof, Bambara, and Jola); the Gold Coast (Ashanti, Fanti); and the coast between and including Sierra Leone and Ivory Coast (Vai, Mende, Kpelle, Kru).

The lands of West and West Central Africa's Atlantic zone are among the continent's most livable. The population of these lands was light by comparison to recent times, and it certainly diminished or grew with droughts and famines or periods of abundance, but it seems generally to have been substantial back through the centuries. At the heart of the region are the rain forests of the Guinea Coast and Congo River basin. Here proximity to the equator keeps the land under the influence of tropical convergence zones that generate regular and often bountiful rainfall. Vegetation

---

1 Where referring to African ethnic groups, it is important to recognize that the ethnic designations are Europeans' notions of who Africans were rather than Africans' ideas of their own and others' identities. It is far from certain that Africans held such a clear sense of ethnic identity as did Europeans.

Africa in the Era of Atlantic Trade,
Seventeenth and Eighteenth Centuries

is lush in spite of the region's compact soils. Palms and hardwoods abound, overshadowing smaller plants that compete for sunlight filtering through the trees. As one moves away from the equator, rainfall diminishes, as does plant life. North of the Guinea Coast, forests give way gradually to wooded savanna, the ground cover becoming less dense the farther north one travels. Across the central belt of West Africa stretch the enormous sky and seemingly endless horizons that make up the broad reaches of the Western

Sudan. This is the land that inspired British colonials to write home about "miles and miles of bloody Africa." Most of the population here sustains itself through a combination of farming and herding. Farther north still, rolling grasslands peppered with trees become drier until vegetation grows sparse. North African Arabs called this dry zone the *Sahel,* the southern "shore" of the Sahara Desert. It sustains a small population of pastoralists who move their herds with the rainfall, sometimes over considerable distances.

Similarly, to the south the Congo forests blend gradually into the southern savannas, and even into desert below Angola. Rains come to both savanna areas seasonally, through their respective summer months, when vegetation takes on new life and crops thrive. Human life is not so healthy during the rains, however, for disease-spreading mosquitos come out in profusion, with standing ponds and puddles for breeding grounds. Back through time it was in the dry season, when crops were in and lands dried out, that the savannas saw more travel, long-distance trade, and, no doubt, warfare.

Any broad discussion of the lives of Africans prior to their enslavement and shipment to America has to misrepresent the way things were. Individual and localized African societies differed greatly to begin with, and they changed over time. The peoples of West and West Central Africa spoke several hundred mutually unintelligible languages (or dialects thereof) and practiced social customs that, in some extremes, were as different from one another as they were from those of Europeans. Furthermore, the English colonies of North America imported Africans for nearly 200 years, and African societies changed as much over this time as did the American society the slaves entered. Life in, say, Angola in 1650 was different in many ways from life in Senegal at the same time, just as it was different from life in Angola in 1800. So the task of describing the "African background" of African Americans seems even more difficult than describing life in America from 1607 to 1787.

Still, in a broad sense, black Africans from the slave-trading area exhibited some elements of cultural homogeneity through the seventeenth and eighteenth centuries, much as they did before and after. Most identified primarily with family and descent groups. An extended family occupying a section of a village was a group that lived and worked together. West Africans tended to trace descent through the male side of the family while West-Central and Central Africans followed matrilineal descent. Most practiced polygyny; men exhibited their wealth with the number of their wives and the size of their families. Security was in numbers of kinsmen, sometimes distant, upon whom one's family could rely in times of need, and in stores of food or animals on the hoof. Although large centers for trade existed, particularly in some of the interior river towns and certain ports on the Atlantic coast, small villages were common throughout the whole region. Villagers worked out a sense of community and cooperation that enabled them to gain the most security and pleasure from their varied situations.

The vast majority of these African men and women also relied on one of two basic modes of subsistence: pastoralism or agriculture. Herdsmen kept cattle, sheep, or goats on the northern and southern extremes of the Atlantic's slave-gathering area, where rainfall was not sufficient for growing crops. Farmers of the savannas north or south of the equatorial forests grew rice, millet, sorghum, or maize—the latter introduced from the New World by the Portuguese before 1600. Those of the more heavily wooded areas nearer the equator grew yams and manioc (another New World import) or harvested bananas, plantains, or palm products. Some of these distinctions are not so important when one considers that Senegalese millet farmers, Nigerian yam farmers, and Angolan maize farmers used similar methods of cultivation, mostly variations of slash-and-burn, or that herders of the savannas often lived in close, symbiotic relationships with grain farmers, exchanging products from their animals (including dung for fuel and fertilizer) for foodstuffs for themselves and their livestock.

Students of African-American history have been among those pointing out some of the cultural principles and assumptions that most West and West-Central Africans shared. Mechal Sobel in *The World They Made Together: Black and White Values in Eighteenth-Century Virginia* (1987) calls attention to common African concepts of space, time, home and the afterlife; Philip D. Morgan in *Slave Counterpoint: Black Culture in the Eighteenth-Century Chesapeake and Lowcountry* (1998) mentions shared assumptions of work, personal interaction, and aesthetic expression, among others. Both authors note these commonalities in the broad range of African cultures to show the basis for the African-American subculture that would come into existence in America—and Sobel argues there is much from these African thoughts and ways that entered into American culture generally.

Still, it is important to note that in many places local identity, local customs, and different local or regional languages tempered any broad sense of unity. Modern maps that show large language families spanning great stretches of the savannas and forests fail to give a complete picture of black Africa's linguistic diversity. Many African languages were spoken only by small groups, and some of the most widely spoken languages were divided into dialects that far fewer people spoke and understood. There were even greater political differences among localities, a fact that the large conquest states or "empires" of earlier or later times often mask. In no sense of the word did black Africans identify themselves as members of a "tribe" and thus take their place in a large sociopolitical realm of "tribal Africa." Colonial officials, early anthropologists, museum curators, and other makers of "tribal" maps have created that false sense, and it is one that dies hard. Individual allegiances were normally to the extended family and the village. Sometimes these allegiances carried more broadly, and nebulously, to a descent group or clan; sometimes they extended further, especially when forced to do so, to a larger political unit—a state or an empire. Certainly relations existed among and across political and language boundaries. Long-distance traders moved across political boundaries, religions and secret societies spread and provided a commonality in larger areas, and momentous historical events united groups of Africans. But most frequently blacks from West and West Central Africa had a restricted definition of their own group. In general, outlooks were local. "We" included the people of the lineage, the village, the small political unit. "They" included everyone else.

Among many of the pastoral and agrarian societies of West and West Central Africa, slavery had long been an established social and economic institution. There is no longer any real doubt concerning slavery's importance in much of precolonial Africa: in some regions of West Africa in the nineteenth century slaves made up from two-thirds to three-quarters of the population. Why this was the case and what slavery in precolonial African societies was like are questions that have perplexed outside observers for a long time.

John Thornton provides a clear and logical discussion of slavery's existence in Africa's Atlantic zone in *Africa and Africans in the Making of the Atlantic World, 1400–1800* (2nd ed., 1998). "Slavery was widespread in Atlantic Africa," he writes, "because slaves were the only form of private, revenue-producing property recognized in African law." Land was owned communally and parceled out to families for their use according to need; need was based on the number of laborers the family could marshal to work the land. So to increase production, certain groups needed to obtain additional laborers outside their lineage. On the one hand, they could do this by paying the brideprice—the exchange of wealth that was part of most African marital relationships, integral to the maintenance of the extended kinship network that held together society—for having sons marry and then waiting for the offspring of the marriage to mature. This explains at least partly the widespread African proclivity to have large numbers of children. But this investment might never pay off because of high infant and childhood mortality, and it took years to rear productive offspring, even in the best of circumstances. On the other hand, they could invest in a slave, one who could be put to work almost immediately and bring a rapid return on the investment. Women slaves also could bear children, who eventually would further augment the size of the labor force. Thus, writes Thornton, slavery was "possibly the most important avenue for private, reproducing wealth available to Africans."

Who owned or sought to acquire slaves? Simply all with sufficient wealth and prestige who wished to preserve or increase their status. Farming families obtained slaves to step up crop production; herding families used slaves to help manage the livestock. Rulers owned slaves to perform their routine work, guard their courts, grow their crops, tend their horses, weave cloth, mine ores, and more. When societies became more militaristic and required larger armies for protection or to launch offensive raids, rulers obtained slaves to make them soldiers of the state. Traders used slaves to provide foodstuffs for them and their families, freeing them to indulge in nonagricultural pursuits, and to serve as porters on commercial enterprises. Persons specializing in religious work kept slaves who produced food while they and their offspring conducted religious training or performed any of a variety of supernatural activities for their clientele.

Although slavery in Africa differed in many ways from the chattel slavery of the Western world, it is difficult to point out the generalized differences between the two systems because slavery in Atlantic Africa varied considerably from one place or circumstance to another. One thing that seems to have varied less than others was the role prescribed for women. Indeed, the majority of slaves in West and West Central Africa during precolonial times were women, and typically they brought a higher price than did men. This stemmed from the obvious reason that women could produce useful offspring, but also from the fact that in many ways women proved to be the main producers in African societies. Women also were more easily assimilated into a new society and less likely to escape from it. Also, slaves associated with a family often performed the same variety of tasks as did other family members, though sometimes individuals specialized in a single craft, such as weaving. Over several generations, and increasingly with marriage and childbirth, slaves might become recognized members of the household, no longer liable for sale and forced relocation. Slaves of royal lineage might serve in offices of state, as soldiers or administrators, and become particularly important personages. The key difference was that slaves and their descendants always remained outsiders, making them perpetually vulnerable to exploitation by the insiders, the original family members. Although slaves' fortunes rose with the wealth and position of the family, they never entirely lost their personal status as persons other than kin.

As in most places where slavery existed, in African societies slaves were obtained by more or less violent means. Warfare—including raids, banditry, and kidnapping—was the most common method. Even wars not fought explicitly to garner slaves often bore such results, for prisoners of war were usually enslaved and sold or put to work locally to help defray the costs of waging the war. Even if ransom was out of the question, there were other considerations. Young boys could be trained as future soldiers; girls and women could be made concubines; and slaves of either sex could be given as gifts to elders in charge of religious shrines. But generally captives were not especially valuable, in any capacity, near their place of capture. Those close to home were likely to escape. Wise captors, therefore, moved prisoners rapidly and sold them away quickly were there no pressing needs for their labor. And even if the local need for labor was strong, it was often better to sell off local captives and buy slaves from some distance away. For these reasons African armies often had a following of merchants eager to buy prisoners at low prices and then march them off to distant markets where their value would be greater.

Less violent methods of enslaving people involved condemnation through judicial or religious proceedings for civil crimes or supposed religious wrongdoing. West Africans did not put people in jail for long periods; instead they relied on physical punishment or enslavement. As Atlantic slaving grew heavy, slavery probably became a more common punishment for an increasing number of offenses to these African societies—for adultery, kidnapping, witchcraft, and theft. Even enslavement for indebtedness seems to have occurred more frequently as time went on. And, finally, there is even some evidence of individuals voluntarily enslaving themselves, almost always because they could not feed or otherwise take care of themselves or their families. In the worst of times, some people chose this extreme form of dependence over starvation.

African societies that regularly acquired slaves were also accustomed to trading them. In fact, export of slaves from black Africa had roots far deeper than the earliest individuals exported via the Atlantic. Various groups across West Africa sold slaves into the trade that led to and across the Sahara to North Africa. The trans-Sahara slave trade out of black Africa lasted longer than the Atlantic trade, from before A.D. 700 to the eve of the twentieth century; over this time it was the means of exporting between 8 and 10 million slaves. The Atlantic slave trade did not surpass that of the trans-Sahara routes until the seventeenth century. For about the same length of time, Central Africans sold captives eastward toward the Indian Ocean. All of this is part of what historians now recognize as the African Diaspora—the movement of peoples from their sub-Saharan African homes to permanent locations in lands covering half the world.

So the onset of the Atlantic slave trade did not signal something altogether new for the men, women, and children living in West and West Central Africa. Once the European demand for slave labor appeared along the Atlantic coast, Africans already had social and economic institutions in place to provide slaves in exchange for commodities they wished to obtain. Little was different about trading slaves coastward instead of inland—just the buyers and their destination. Europeans via the Atlantic even brought most of the same products that African traders had long received in exchange for slaves: cloth, decorative items, metalware, horses, weapons, and more. What proved to be most novel about the Atlantic trade, however, was its scale. No other exporting of slaves, at any time or place before or since, came close to the massive, involuntary movement of people out of West and West Central Africa to the New World over the four centuries following 1450.

The Atlantic Trade

The enterprise that brought African men and women to the New World, and after 1619 to the areas of the North American mainland largely under English control, was what most people now call the Atlantic slave trade. It was an undertaking of massive proportions in terms of duration, area, and numbers of people involved. It began shortly before 1450, with the export of African slaves to continental Europe and sugar plantations on the Atlantic islands, and lasted until after the middle of the nineteenth century. Over the course of more than 4 centuries it caused the greatest intercontinental migration in world history to that time—more Africans arrived in the New World than Europeans before the latter part of the nineteenth century—and it affected people and the destiny of their offspring on all lands bordering the Atlantic.

For many years, historians' estimates of the numbers of Africans transported across the Atlantic as part of the slave trade varied widely. Some thought in terms of a total of 20 million or more; others considered the figure to be barely a quarter of that. Most agreed it was hard to determine. Records were sparse, in several languages, and difficult to come by. But in 1969 Philip D. Curtin, a historian who had used many of the existing shipping records of the Atlantic trade, produced a monumental work, *The Atlantic Slave Trade: A Census,* which began by showing the shoddy chains of evidence for previous estimates—most spiraled back to guesses made by persons in no position to know—and then attempted to estimate the volume of the trade over time based on existing records. Although Curtin's estimates generated a debate that is not yet completely resolved, many now agree on some approximate numbers that are only a slight upward revision of his original figures. In rough terms, over 11.5 million people were exported from the Atlantic coast of black Africa and nearly 10 million of these people arrived in the New World.[2] Annual averages of Africans brought to the New World grew from not quite 4,000 in the late 1500s to a peak of 75,000 in the 1780s. No enterprise of such proportion could have existed through casual contact or chance capture. The Atlantic slave trade was carefully planned and organized, big business.

Study of the Atlantic slave trade sometimes involves more numbers and percentages than one might wish to consider, but the numbers and percentages have their role. They are particularly important for putting parts of the trade in temporal and spatial perspective. (Historians have been making more valuable studies as

---

2 Curtin's figures or their slight, upward revisions have never been accepted popularly. It is an ironic turn that on the morning I write this, May 22, 1999, the Syracuse, New York *Post-Standard* published a submission from a former Syracuse minister presently on a year-long walking tour in West Africa to retrace the slave route. Writing from Elmina in Ghana, the minister informs Central New Yorkers, "most believe it was somewhere between 30 million and 60 million ground up in this colonial visit of death [the Atlantic slave trade]." The writer is correct in that most *do* believe such numbers, scholarly treatments with a basis in evidence notwithstanding.

records have become available over the last few decades, and the recent publication of David Eltis et al, *The Transatlantic Slave Trade, 1562–1867: A Database CD-ROM* (1998), a compilation of data on some 27,000 slaving voyages, suggests still more will be published.) Only a small portion of the Atlantic trade brought captives to the English North American mainland. Of all the Africans who crossed the Atlantic as part of the slave trade, less than 5 percent of the total (fewer than entered the island of Cuba) came to the mainland colonies. However, because the heaviest trade to the North American mainland lasted only from about 1680 to 1808, that trade accounted for some 7 percent of the volume crossing the ocean through those years, and it was a much greater portion, about one-fifth, of the English slave trade at the time. In fact, through several decades after 1740 the British mainland colonies ran a close second to Jamaica as Britain's leading slave market. Thus, in spite of the relative insignificance of the total number of people transported, during the heaviest years of trading in the eighteenth century the mainland colonies were important markets for British slavers.

From 1650 to after 1800, demand for slaves varied at ports all along America's Atlantic and Gulf seaboard, from Salem in the Massachusetts Bay Colony down through Savannah in Georgia and around the northern Gulf of Mexico to New Orleans. In some years such ports as Philadelphia or New York might have imported Africans in the several hundreds. However, three zones along the Atlantic coast served as the colonies' major markets for slaves. They differed in demand and, hence, volume of imports as years passed. The earliest big market was the Chesapeake Bay that touched the coasts of Virginia and Maryland. Slaves began entering there by the shipload after 1680 and the numbers swelled into the thousands in certain years after 1720. South Carolina did not begin importing persons directly from Africa in any number until after 1700, but once it began to do so it quickly grew to become the colonies' largest importer—at that time and eventually for all time. By the 1730s South Carolina was importing, on average, over 2,000 slaves each year. The third market of significance, coastal Georgia, was a late emerger. Demand for workers appeared there after 1755, when planters opened new lands on which they wished to use slave labor. But Georgia relied strictly on the re-export trade from the West Indies for its slaves until 1766, when the first vessel arrived in Savannah from the African coast. Thereafter direct and much larger shipments became the norm.

The first persons of African descent to set foot on land that would become the United States did so long before the English so much as thought of establishing American colonies. Ira Berlin in *Many Thousands Gone: The First Two Centuries of Slavery in North America* (1998) identifies "Atlantic creoles," persons of mixed African, European, and eventually American ancestry, as products of the intercultural experience that occurred with the waxing Atlantic commerce. Atlantic creoles emerged first around the European outposts along Africa's west coast, but they soon gravitated to Iberian ports and then accompanied the earliest European explorers and settlers of the Americas. "Familiar with the commerce of the Atlantic," Berlin writes, "fluent in its new languages, and intimate with its trade and cultures, they were cosmopolitan in its fullest sense."

Such noted Spanish explorers as Ponce de León and Hernando de Soto were accompanied by blacks who served as everything from cultural broker to soldier to scout; one African, the celebrated Estévan, survived Pánfilo de Narváez's ill-fated 1528 expedition in Florida and with the other survivors embarked upon an eight-year trek across the continent to the Pacific Coast, picking up native languages and negotiating for his small party along the way. By this time, African slaves were pouring into Spanish possessions in the Caribbean and South America. Once Spain established a military outpost at St. Augustine in Florida in 1565, blacks worked on fortifications and participated fairly continuously in garrisoning the fort.

Atlantic creoles arrived soon after the English who settled Jamestown, too. A Dutch ship brought the first Africans to the English North American mainland in 1619. In January 1620 Jamestown tobacco planter John Rolfe described the event in a letter to Sir Edwin Sandys:

About the latter end of August, a Dutch man of Warr of the burden of a 160 tunnes arrived at Point-Comfort. . . . He brought not any thing but 20. and odd Negroes, wch the Governo^r and Cape Marchant bought for victualle. . . .

Dutch merchants continued to play the biggest role in the relatively meager mainland slave trade through 1650. Thereafter English-owned and operated vessels took over and carried the lion's share of slaves to British North America. London and Bristol were important English ports participating in the trade, but Liverpool surpassed them both as the eighteenth century ran its course. Also entering into the trafficking of slaves after the middle of the seventeenth century were colonial merchants. Beginning with New Englanders but growing to include entrepreneurs from New York, Philadelphia, and Baltimore, American shippers increased their share of English slaving to a high of perhaps one-third through the quarter century before the American Revolution. Rhode Island became the colony fitting out the largest number of vessels. Through the fifteen years prior to the American Revolution, 271 vessels cleared Rhode Island ports for the African trade, eventually bringing to the Americas over 32,000 persons.

For the first seventy-five years of the colonies' existence, slaves imported into English North America were mostly "seasoned." These men and women came from one of the islands in the Caribbean, principally Barbados or Jamaica, where they had made it through the difficult adjustment to a new disease environment and had learned enough English and enough of what their situations required of them to get by. Importation of Caribbean slaves was not so much the result of the preference of the mainland planters for seasoned workers as it was a function of the nascent mainland market being insufficiently strong to draw vessels with larger numbers of captives directly from Africa—and of the fact that English vessels were not yet carrying many slaves directly from Africa to the New World. But buyers in Virginia, Maryland, and South Carolina eventually recognized the tendency of island planters to unload "refuse Negroes" and "rogues" on the mainland. They also realized that slaves straight from the African continent were cheaper and, because they were unacculturated, less likely to band together with other blacks and rebel. Thus, over the half century from 1680 to 1730, the source of mainland slaves changed. By 1720 the balance between "outlandish" Africans and "seasoned" West Indian imports was about equal. After 1720, four of every five slaves imported into Virginia, Maryland, the Carolinas, and Georgia arrived on a ship directly across the ocean from Africa, increasingly in English vessels. Almost none of the men and women arriving from Africa in the eighteenth century were Atlantic creoles—individuals with linguistic and cultural experience in Africa that would help them get along in their new experience in America—as were the first Africans imported into the mainland colonies a century earlier.

In addition to the Spanish and English, French entrepreneurs brought African slaves to the North American mainland. Employees of the *Compagnie des Indies* imported 500 Africans into the French colony of Louisiana in the summer of 1719, and over the following decade the company brought in over 5,000 more, nearly all arriving directly from Africa. The importation of slaves into Louisiana practically ceased from 1731 to the 1760s, but nearly 4,000 more arrived there between 1763, when Spain took control of the colony, and 1785. Most of these came from Africa with short stopovers in the West Indies.

Of course, the magnitude of the whole African trade into the Atlantic world, or even that of the trade to mainland North America, makes it impossible to describe the way it operated in simple generalities. Trading differed considerably along the African and American coasts. Operations often were different a few hundred miles apart. Ease of procuring captives or methods of doing so could change from one year to the next, let alone over periods of half a century or more, and various African and American ports matured as slave markets at different times. Yet, through the centuries and across the boundaries of cultural areas, certain broad modes of operation persisted from shortly after the opening of the trade through the eighteenth century.

Trading slaves into the Atlantic world was always part of a larger body of exchange. Persons in Europe fitting out vessels for Atlantic trading did so with economic gain in mind and did not limit their considerations of profit to human cargo. Thus, slaves were but one African export commodity among a variety of trade goods. For the first two centuries of Atlantic commerce, until after 1650, Europeans exported a combination of other commodities in greater amounts (by value) than slaves, including gold especially. Around 1700, slaves became the principal African export into the Atlantic colonies and remained so until after 1850.

From the beginning, Europeans realized they were not seeking slaves from a vast, undeveloped wilderness where savages spent their days in idleness and their nights in levity. That white traders believed such misinformation is a notion that came about long after the fact—during the persistent wave of pseudoscientific racism of the late nineteenth century. The western coast of Africa was the outward edge of a commercial network of considerable size and scope that had thrived in one or another form since long before Europeans came nipping at the waterside for commodities to exchange. Long-distance trading was an occupational specialty that West and West-Central Africans held in high regard. The Atlantic hinterland of black Africa contained a grid of trade routes dotted with commercial settlements. These formed a network that permitted traders to travel widely among communities where they could employ local associates as their aids and agents. Taxes and tolls kept village and clan heads or rulers of states amenable to the enterprise. For hundreds of years before the coastwise trade in slaves, itinerant merchants had funneled gold, kola nuts, and slaves to the port cities of the Sahel for transport across the great Sahara. In return they had carried goods from North Africa, including salt, metalware and glassware, figs and dates, back from the southern edge of the desert to locales across the western savannas and into the coastal forests. Central Africans had traded copper, hides, and ivory toward the west coast for palm cloth, palm oil, and salt. Once demand for slaves and other products—some of which, such as foodstuffs, were ancillary to the slave trade—became evident along the coastal periphery of the commercial network, it did not take long for the traders to extend operations to the sailing ships and then the newly sprouting European outposts at the mouths of rivers and on Atlantic beaches and islands. Thus, fairly rapidly, a commercial system was in place to supply products Europeans wanted and to distribute goods Africans desired in exchange.

Great temporal and regional variance characterized African products in European demand. At different times Europeans sought gold, gum, hides, ivory, and beeswax from Senegambia; gold and peppers from Sierra Leone; gold from the Gold Coast; palm products from the Niger Delta; copper, ivory, and dyewoods from the Congo basin. In addition, throughout the length of the coast Europeans obtained African products, kola nuts or palm cloth, for instance, to exchange elsewhere on the continent for other locally produced commodities. But all along the 3,500-mile coastline slaves were in fairly constant and growing demand after 1650. In some areas, Angola for example, slaves were almost always the principal item the Europeans wanted.

Africans were no less careful in designating the products they wanted in exchange.[3] Meeting their varied and changing demands was a necessity for the ship captain who wanted to obtain slaves at a good price. The ships that sailed down the Guinea Coast thus had to serve as something akin to floating hardware and drygoods stores with spirits in the cellar, and fitting out these ships with the proper variety of goods, often imported from distant parts of the globe, was the largest expense of the total voyage, averaging more than the costs of the ship and its crew. Items of apparel and personal decoration made up almost half of all imports, with preferences shifting from beads to cloth and sometimes including semiprecious stones. As nearly everywhere today, dress and personal decoration were important ways West Africans displayed their wealth or indicated their social status. In addition, cloth was an

---

3 It remains necessary to expose what a quarter century ago Philip D. Curtin referred to as "the gewgaw myth" in *Economic Change in Precolonial Africa: Senegambia in the Era of the Slave Trade* (1975): "that Africans foolishly bought articles of adornment or luxuries that served no basic human need, and in return for a basic resource—human beings." Stanley B. Alpern points out, in "What Africans Got for Their Slaves: A Master List of European Trade Goods" in *History in Africa: A Journal of Method,* 22 (1995), that ideas about Africa being "a dumping ground for European rubbish . . . ignore the business acumen of African merchants who . . . knew good commodities from bad, and how to play off one European trader against another to their own profit." Along the West African coast during the years of the Atlantic trade, writes Alpern, "it was, indeed, a seller's market."

important element in payment of brideprice, and European traders needed to keep current on preferred types and styles. Africans in many locales also wanted metals and metalware—these constituted another third of all imports. Spirits, normally in the form of brandy or rum, also were in considerable demand. (Following a visit to the Gambia River in 1764, Abbé Demanet wrote, "Without iron and alcohol one cannot live there, much less trade.") Horses for cavalry use (which, because of sleeping sickness, bred with difficulty in areas infested with the tsetse fly), cutlery, firearms, and gunpowder were also in greater or lesser demand, depending on local supplies and, in some areas, regional hostilities. But variety remained the key: an inventory by Dutch traders in 1728 revealed 218 types of merchandise stored at Elmina Castle on the Gold Coast for use in the acquisition of slaves.

Whether exporting or importing, it was the mesh of the organized commercial networks that made the magnitude of the exchange possible. It is obvious that without European shipping and a considerable demand for labor on the plantations of the New World the Atlantic slave trade could not have taken place. It is less obvious, mostly because of old and incorrect notions of African incapacity or the related lack of knowledge of Africa and its history, that without the existing commercial operations in the hinterland of Africa's Atlantic coast and without sufficient *African* demand for European products, the supply of slaves could never have reached the massive proportions that it did.

The first Europeans to sail down the northwest coast of Africa were the Portuguese. They were the vanguard of what would be, in African eyes, a long line of men with sharp noses, straight hair, and light skin who wedded a capitalist economic system (with special desire to invest in long-distance trade) to advanced maritime technology, and it was they who dominated foreign trade with black Africa for the first two centuries of European contact. The earliest encounters the Portuguese had with coastal-dwelling Africans below the Sahara taught them lessons about cross-cultural trading they would not forget for centuries. In the 1440s, Portuguese "adventurers" along the Atlantic coasts of Morocco and Mauritania began putting ashore and capturing local residents, taking them by surprise and sending them back to Lisbon. Below the Sahara, "surprise" was harder to effect. In 1446 Nuno Tristão sailed into the Gambia River in search of "prisoners" for the pleasure of his patron, Dom Henrique [the often-noted "Henry the Navigator"]. With twenty-two armed men in two boats, Tristão was closing in on a populated settlement along the riverbank when eighty Africans in many more, and much larger, vessels gave chase and rained poisoned arrows on the intruders. Tristão lost three-quarters of his crew, and those who survived were fortunate indeed to have made it back to Lisbon to tell their story.

   Such misfortune did not have to recur often before Europeans in their seagoing ships, far from home and few in number, came to realize what should have been obvious from the beginning: that Africans were not going to wait passively until the next vessel full of marauders arrived to fall upon their dwindling numbers; that Africans were not different from others in their interest in and willingness to exchange human beings for products they needed or wanted; and that Atlantic sailors could, therefore, more easily and safely acquire slaves by trade than by capture. (Only nine years after Tristão's disastrous voyage, Portuguese merchants were coming peacefully to the Gambia and trading with Africans along the river. In the words of a Portuguese court chronicler, after the middle of the fifteenth century, "deeds in those parts [thereafter] involved trade and mercantile dealings more than fortitude and exercise of arms.") Eventually it would become still more apparent to most European traders that some African groups were powerful and would not allow European raiding on land in their vicinities, and it would be clear (though not accurately understood that the agents of death were the various diseases endemic to the tropics) that Europeans could not live long enough in the area, generally speaking, to be able to maintain an effective raiding force over the long term. However, these latter issues did not bear on the initial decision to acquire slaves through exchange of goods. Thus, within a few decades of Portuguese contact with black Africa, a broad pattern of European-African trade came into being that, with minor changes, would be the standard way of trading for slaves from north of the Senegal River to south of Angola until the last years of the Atlantic trade.

With rare exceptions, the Europeans stopped at or stayed close to the waterside, leaving to the Africans the conduct of their own political and military affairs. The Europeans had little choice. Africans were insistent on remaining as middlemen in the trade to the interior. Any white person who marched inland or went far upriver usually paid dearly for that temerity. But Europeans had their hands full just manning their coastal outposts because of the overwhelming loss of life in these places to disease. Death rates varied, but before the use of quinine to temper malaria, after about 1850, European mortality rates in tropical Africa ranged from 250 to 750 per thousand per year. In some locales over certain years it was worse. "The stench of decay and death was everywhere," writes Joseph C. Miller of the eighteenth-century trading port of Luanda, Angola, in *Way of Death: Merchant Capitalism and the Angolan Slave Trade, 1730–1830* (1988). "Only the fortunate left alive."

Following the model of the successful Dutch and English East India companies, European governments sought initially to conduct slaving through the granting of monopolies to private, joint-stock companies. In the ideal, a single company would carry out its nation's African trade. These companies would use their inordinately large profits from the monopoly to offset the high startup costs of the trade and those of maintaining fortified outposts on the coast. England attempted two such ventures, first with the Company of Royal Adventurers for nine years after 1663, and then with the better known and somewhat more successful Royal African Company from 1672 through the end of the century. But by the onset of the eighteenth century it was clear that the state-sanctioned monopolies could not hold their own. There were too many "interlopers" trading with anyone out of gunshot of the company forts, too many Africans willing to sell slaves without regard to nationality, and too many planters across the Atlantic wanting to pay bottom prices for workers, regardless of seller. Exclusive trade for any nation's carriers was doomed. After 1700, independent shippers carried the bulk of the trade, and the competition grew fierce with the rising demand for slaves in the New World.

The end of monopolies did not mean the end of European outposts or "factories" on West Africa's small islands, riverbanks, or ocean beaches, however. Masters of vessels straight from Europe needed persons on the spot with knowledge of local conditions and customs, and residents of the outposts, sometimes having marital and social ties to important African families in the region, sold their services as cross-cultural brokers. It was the original intention also of several European nations to have places along the coast where slaves were bulked—that is, purchased from African sellers and held to await arrival of one of the nation's slaving vessels for shipment to the New World. Many thought it would be in the ship captain's best interest (thus prompting him to pay a hefty markup) to be able to appear; purchase slaves on hand; obtain food, water, and firewood; and be off within a short time for American markets. This was based on the correct notion that waiting to load slaves not yet arrived from the interior or coasting along from market to market in search of a cargo was profitless downtime for the slavers—while crew and captives still had to be fed at the owner's expense. It was based, too, on the knowledge that time spent on the coast meant time spent in the tropical disease environment where crew and human cargo were most likely to sicken and die. In an extreme situation in the mid-eighteenth century, a ship slaving in Loango Bay north of the Congo River needed nine months in port to acquire 348 slaves. By the time the vessel was ready to sail for the Americas, 83 of the Africans on board had died.

But the coastal forts and factories never did much bulking of slaves, largely because of the impracticality and expense of doing so.[4] Rare was the outpost that produced its own food; most purchased grain, fish, and meat from neighboring Africans. This meant there was little work for slaves to engage in while awaiting

---

4 It is probably useful in this age of technology to call attention to new sources of relevant information that were not available when the first edition of this book appeared. At *http://www.h net.msu.edu/~africa/threads/goree.html* one can read arguments from subscribers to the H-Africa discussion network about the French outpost on Gorée Island off Cape Verde. As most European outposts, the one on Gorée never held—or bulked—nearly as many slaves as some contend. The "House of Slaves" on the island, visited by such foreign dignitaries as the Pope and the President of the United States, never held many slaves. Its importance has grown over the last third of the twentieth century as a symbol of the evils perpetrated on African men and women as a result of the Atlantic slave trade.

shipment, and holding slaves on hand meant increased demand for food and water, which might prompt local suppliers of both to raise prices. African merchants and rulers developed ways to put bulked slaves to work in agricultural production until slavers arrived. Sometimes they held slaves only until enough slaving vessels arrived to provide competition and drive up prices. Thus, it is largely myth that the relics of European forts on Africa's Atlantic islands and beaches—such places as Goreé, James Island, Elmina, or Cape Coast Castle—housed vast numbers of the slaves in dungeon-like enclosures before their loading aboard vessels for the voyage to the Americas. "In the overwhelming majority of cases," writes Herbert S. Klein in *The Atlantic Slave Trade* (1999), "it was the Africans who controlled the slaves until the moment of sale to the captain."

From Saint Louis, at the mouth of the Senegal River, to Benguela on the Angola Coast, whether under English, French, Dutch, Danish, Swedish, or Portuguese flags, the outposts were similar in operation if not in form. They might be large, walled castles like the English Royal African Company's center for operations at Cape Coast on the Gold Coast; they might be smaller stone forts like James Fort on a little island twenty-five miles up the Gambia River; or they might be thatched-roof dwellings along a high-surfed Guinea beach. Most were fortified to protect against attacks from pirates and national enemies by sea. Inside the typical fort were living quarters for a garrison, a warehouse for trade goods, and a store for food and water. Residents of the forts usually had to pay Africans for occupancy of their territory as well as for food, water, and firewood. Once the outposts were established and manned, African merchants from the near and more distant interior brought slaves and other commodities for exchange. Sometimes, in Congo-Angola especially, caravans left a particular outpost for the interior laden with trade goods obtained on credit, charged specifically to return with slaves. In all locations the residents of European outposts worked hard at keeping good relations with Africans, regularly giving gifts to and entertaining visiting merchants and local potentates. Their job was to grease the wheels of trade and to tap into the commercial and political intelligence of the hinterland.

Around the European outposts, up and down some of the major rivers of Africa's Atlantic coast, developed small but important commercial communities that took part in the dealings. Philip D. Curtin in *Cross-Cultural Trade in World History* (1984) calls attention to such hybrid communities that have always tended to grow up around the nodes of contact in "trade diasporas." When the Atlantic trade came into being these communities formed around European establishments. Their commercial influence usually spread up rivers as far as fair-sized vessels could navigate, along Atlantic beaches, and to smaller outposts of their own short distances away from the major points of cross-cultural contact. In these communities were groups of people, sometimes whole families and sometimes larger groups that included aids of chiefs and rulers, who served as intermediaries—cultural and commercial brokers—between European shippers and African sellers. A number of these intermediaries were the offspring of more or less formal unions between European men (who normally came to the coast, had a child or children, and died or returned to Europe) and African women. With attachment to each cultural milieu, these Afro-Europeans—some of the earliest "Atlantic creoles" in Berlin's terms—were in some places the key links in the chain of production, transportation, and acquisition of slaves on the coast. In a few areas where Portuguese influence was considerable—south of the Gambia River in Upper Guinea, for instance, or south of the Congo in Angola—Afro-Portuguese communities of long duration controlled much of the trade and used their commercial positions to try to influence local politics. Individual members of this culturally-hybrid, Atlantic creole group spread about the Atlantic rim of all four continents and helped facilitate trade and cultural interaction as they dealt and mixed with persons indigenous to their new homes.

Of course, not all slavers chose to sail to government-subsidized or company-affiliated outposts, where the most thoroughly integrated commercial communities existed. Some sailed to reputed slaving locations along the coast and carried on much less formal dealings shipboard. The appearance of a vessel anchored off the coast might bring one or several traders out in longboats to talk with captains about slaving prospects or to deal for slaves on hand. These traders were sometimes Europeans and sometimes Africans, though most were Afro-Europeans, renegades of a kind who had struck out on their own to make a profit in the thriving commerce. Some of these traders were dirt poor, barely scratching out an existence, without capital, trade goods, or credit worthy of note. Others, some of the mulattos in particular, had been in the business for several generations and were the masters or mistresses of organized "trading houses" who had connections, often through marriage, with important African political and commercial leaders, their own store of goods and foodstuffs, and advanced credit to Africans and other Afro-European traders.

Along the coast of Sierra Leone in the middle of the eighteenth century, one could encounter traders at both extremes of prosperity. Near the Sherbro region was Irishman Nicholas Owen, who ventured to Africa to recover his family's lost fortune. Of his operation, Owen admitted, ". . . if any of the blacks comes I buy their commodities at as cheap a rate as I can, which enables me to trade aboard the ships once or twice a month, which just keeps me from sinking in the principle stock."

But from Owen's location a slaver did not have to sail far to encounter one of his rivals, the mulatto Henry Tucker, a man who had traveled in Europe and lived "in the English manner." Tucker had six wives and many children who participated in his operations. He even maintained his own fields with slave labor to grow provisions for slave ships. Owen describes his wealthy competitor:

His strength consists of his own slaves and their children, who have built a town about him and serve as his *gremetos* [aids in commercial dealings] upon all occasions. This man bears the character of a fair trader among the Europeans, but to the contrary among the blacks. His riches set him above the kings and his numerous people above being surprised by war; almost all the blacks owe him money, which brings a dread of being stopt upon that account, so that he is esteemed and feared by all who have the misfortune to be in his power.

Meshing with the European system in the vicinity of the outposts and ports was an African economic network of equal complexity. Throughout the hinterland of sub-Saharan Africa's Atlantic coast there developed, over time, slave-gathering, delivery, and marketing systems that were organized, systematic, efficient, and competitive. These systems were integrated with the movement of other goods to the coast and with the dispersal of European wares brought in exchange. If no two systems were alike, they fell within general patterns of operation according to region and time of trade.

Across the western savannas, from Senegambia to Lake Chad and as far south as the central Gold Coast, slave caravans tended to be under the control of specialized Muslim African merchants. These politically neutral international traders, themselves slave owners and users, relied on ethnic relations, personal connections, and a broad sense of occupational solidarity throughout the dispersed commercial communities of the trading network to ease the movement of their caravans and get the most from their trade. When Englishman Richard Jobson was trading some distance up the Gambia River in 1620, he dealt with such an African trader, who appealed to Jobson's feeling for fellow merchants. "In our time of trading together," Jobson writes,

if it were his owne goods he bartered for, he would tell us, this is for my self, and you must deale better with me, than either with the Kings of the Country or any others, because I am as you are, a Julietto, which signifies a Merchant, that goes from place to place, neither do I, as the Kings of our Country do which is to eate, and drinke, and lye still at home among their women, but I seeke abroad as you doe.

Caravans of hundreds of persons and scores of pack animals trekked across hundreds of miles of West Africa's savannas. Islamic religious wars along the upper Senegal River and in the Futa Jalon highlands to the south, and secular warfare among the Bambara of the upper Niger, provided captives for such caravans at different times in the eighteenth century. The caravan leader was responsible for the arrangements—the dispensation of credit especially, but also supplies of food and water, protection, and local trading. Agents in towns along the way lent assistance. Such aid was vital to the success of a large caravan, in which problems of provisioning might rival those of a small army and which encountered local officials charging variable tariffs and tolls. When known agents were not available, caravan leaders relied on West Africa's centuries-old, institutional custom of hospitality and reciprocity, the "landlord-stranger relationship." Under such tacit agreements a villager of means saw to arranging for providing the needs of the caravan, and in return the caravan leader, on leaving, would give gifts commensurate with the services rendered.

When large caravans neared the coast, leaders exercised options on how and where to proceed with the sale of slaves. Prices offered, goods available, and local political circumstances affected decisions concerning which routes to take or markets to seek. Throughout most years of the trade, slaves from the Muslim network were marched all the way to the Atlantic ports in Senegambia, and they began reaching coastal markets between Guinea and Ivory Coast directly, without sales through middlemen, after 1720.

In the early years Muslim merchants brought slaves to the Gold Coast and the Bight of Benin. After the mid-seventeenth century, however, strong African states gained control of trade between European forts on the Gold Coast and the Niger Delta, and another pattern of slave marketing arose there. Early slaving in this region brought new military technology—firearms to the Gold Coast and horses to the savanna hinterland of the Slave Coast— and that technology enabled states to arise. Asante and Oyo were the most powerful and thus are best known, but other states existed at various times and became tributary to or incorporated into the larger entities. These states had the military power to prevent Muslim traders from penetrating their northern limits and to contain Europeans in their coastal outposts. In between, they controlled slave procurement and marketing, favoring their own government traders and restricting foreign and local merchants. For a time one of these states, Dahomey, even limited exchange on its coast to a single trader, the state agent, the Yovogon at Wydah.

Throughout the interior of the Bight of Benin, inland marketing centers existed where itinerant merchants met with representatives of outlying chiefs who had acquired slaves in a variety of ways—purchase, capture, tribute payment, or gift. After making sure their own labor supplies were adequate, chiefs exchanged slaves for luxury goods or military equipment, especially horses, that might help them capture more slaves. In larger markets special brokers fed slaves and provided them shelter before sale. Once the merchants acquired slaves, some marched them directly to the coast, using them as porters to carry leather goods, textiles, foodstuffs, or other items to exchange in local or regional trade. Others moved only a short way before selling their slaves, who then underwent passage through a chain of traders with smaller caravans, generally heading coastward. On the edge of communities lining major routes of slave movement were *zangos,* designated resting places where merchants and their slaves and pack animals could get food and water and take shelter. Once on the coast, merchants exchanged slaves and other trade items for goods to take back into the interior. The traders sometimes retained some slaves to use as porters on the return trip.

Farther east and south, inland of the Bight of Biafra where the Ibo and Ibibio lived, a private system of marketing control prevailed. Absence of centralized states here did not lessen the ability of traders to produce slaves. On the contrary, the trade from the Bight of Biafra grew greatly after 1730, and by mid-century it provided one-third of all the slaves carried in English ships. What developed with the increase in demand were clan-based commercial associations that competed for slaves from the interior and for markets at such infamous ports as Bonny, Brass, and Calabar. These associations often were tied to Ibo, Ijaw, Igala, and Aro religious shrines. Over time the Aro won almost complete control of slave procurement and delivery. By the mid-eighteenth century regular Aro markets operated across a series of trading routes in the interior. In some places Aro associations organized mercenary forces to conduct slave raids northward toward the Benue River valley. A thoughtful article by Paul E. Lovejoy and David Richardson, "Trust, Pawnship, and Atlantic History: The Institutional Foundations of the Old Calabar Slave Trade," *American Historical Review,* 104 (1999), points out the elaborate, institutionalized, social, and commercial relationships between European and African merchants that made possible the slaving operations. When European captains came to the Biafran coast they visited port towns near the mouths of the many rivers and extended credit in trade goods to one of the local, English- or Creole-speaking commercial families (or "trading houses"). These families sent armed parties in enormous boats up the rivers to the Aro markets where they exchanged the goods the British merchants had advanced them for slaves; then they returned with the men and women captives to the coastal towns. Guaranteeing a return on the advanced goods were human pawns, relatives of the trading families whom the British captains detained until the families repaid the debts in slaves. In one of the trade towns, Old Calabar, the local male secret society, the Depe, became an agency of local government to regulate commerce and collect debts.

Below the Bight of Biafra, along the Atlantic coast from roughly the equator to the southern border of modern Namibia, an area referred to for convenience as Congo-Angola, African states on the one hand and the Portuguese centered in Luanda on the other tried mightily to control trade as rigidly as they could, but competition from private African traders made long-term monopoly impossible. Thus prices remained low. Within this structure developed a network of perhaps unequaled efficiency that in the eighteenth century was able to deliver for export over 2 million slaves.

North of the Congo River were three major harbors (Loango Bay, Malomba, and Cabinda) where, particularly after 1680, masters of English, Dutch, and French ships met with representatives of the Vili kingdom to acquire slaves. Ship captains had to obtain licenses to trade, which allowed them to construct temporary shelters for the Africans they would acquire. Royal Vili officials negotiated customs fees and supervised brokers who helped Vili merchants and European buyers agree on prices. From these ports to the interior was a Vili trade diaspora. Rulers organized heavily guarded caravans that ventured to markets several hundred miles away bearing salt, palm oil, and cloth. Merchants from farther inland brought slaves and ivory to these markets for exchange.

In contrast to Vili control of the coast north of the Congo, Portuguese crown officials, almost all Afro-Portuguese, dominated slave acquisition and marketing for several hundred miles into the interior to the south of the great river. For half a century after 1650, governors and *capitaes mores* based in Luanda exploited and abused the nearby populations. These officials provided recognition to African chiefs and then charged them tribute payments in slaves; they raided more distant African settlements for slaves, hiring their own soldiers for such work in violation of orders from Lisbon; and they granted sanction to private raiding parties organized by Afro-Portuguese entrepreneurs. Then, around the beginning of the eighteenth century, government-organized slave raiding diminished and private Portuguese, mulatto, and African merchants took over. As happened farther up the coast, these traders left Luanda or Benguela with trade goods that commercial firms on the coast advanced them and headed for one of several major interior trading centers. There they exchanged their goods for between a score and one hundred slaves and brought them back to the port for holding. As demand on the coast increased, important slaving markets developed in the near and far interior. In a sense, the system of the coastal region reproduced itself in stages toward the interior, where African states sent their own agents farther inland to markets and fairs that drew slaves from their own hinterlands. By the end of the eighteenth century slaves were coming to the Angola coast from beyond the upper Kasai River, seven hundred miles into the interior.

The variety of marketing systems that existed between Senegambia and Angola affected how European merchants acquired slaves but meant little to the humans who were the products of the systems. The hardships Africans encountered from the time of enslavement to the point of sale are frequently overlooked because of popular emphasis on the horrors of slaves' shipboard experience between Africa and America. In *The Atlantic Slave Trade,* Klein draws attention to the fact that the voyages to the New World averaged one to two months, whereas six months to a year elapsed between the time a slave was captured in West Africa and the time he or she boarded a European slaving vessel for the Atlantic crossing. Even eighteenth-century British abolitionists, who focused their attack on the evils of the ocean passage to America, argued that over two-thirds of all human mortality associated with the slave trade occurred in Africa. Mungo Park, the Scottish physician who explored the upper Niger River at the end of the eighteenth century, experienced the difficult march to the Senegambian Atlantic coast when he traveled with a Muslim-organized slave caravan. Some of the slaves had been taken in raids and held for three years before their sale. Once on the march, Park writes, the slaves

are commonly secured, by putting the right leg of one, and the left of another, into the same pair of fetters. By supporting the fetters with a string, they can walk, very slowly. Every four slaves are likewise fastened together by the necks, with a strong rope of twisted thongs; and in the night, an additional pair of fetters is put on their hands, and sometimes a light iron chain passed round their necks.

Shelter for slaves was normally like that provided the pack animals—a stockaded area of bare ground. The men and women on the march ate cheaply of whatever the local fare. Corn, millet, or yams were staples, depending on location. Any cooked food the slaves consumed they themselves prepared. The caravans were largely self-contained, the slaves being forced to carry items to meet the caravan's needs. On the march to the coast following his capture near his home in Guinea, six-year-old Broteer Furro (who took the name Venture Smith in America) had to carry on his head a twenty-five-pound stone for grinding the caravan's corn. Most slaves enhanced the profits of the traders by carrying trade goods as well, men sometimes being required to tote over 50 pounds of goods and women over 30 pounds.

Another difficult time for slaves was the period of waiting in port. On average the wait was three months. Food was scarce in some seasons. Caravan leaders, buyers, sellers, and ship captains were all eager to skimp on supplies to reduce overhead. Again, where possible, merchants rented slaves to local people for work, especially during the planting or harvesting season of local crops.

Overlooked for many years were the epidemiological difficulties slaves experienced when marched from one African disease environment to another. Men and women brought up in the savannas contracted sleeping sickness in the forests; those reared in drier or higher areas caught malaria or yellow fever in the wetter lowlands; and different strains of influenza and other diseases often lurked in regions even closer to their original homes. Death rates varied across the slave-trading area and through time; they are impossible to estimate with accuracy. It is clear, however, that the African man, woman, or child sold to a ship captain for conveyance to the New World was already a survivor.

The Slaving Voyage

By the time English planters began importing slaves directly from Africa into mainland North America in good-sized numbers, the Atlantic trade had been in operation for over two centuries. Enough word had passed through the shipyards and docks of Liverpool and London from experienced traders to make most English captains wise to the business. Within broad parameters they knew where to go along the African coast, what types of trade goods to take along with them, and how to get by under usual conditions. Although they always hoped for good winds and rapid transactions, they knew it would take three or four months to reach the farthest slave marts in Angola with necessary stops to take on fresh water and supplies; they knew loading was unpredictable but that having to stop at different ports over several months to procure slaves in small bunches, as well as to secure provisions for them, was likely; and they figured on another one to two months, with decent winds, in the Atlantic crossing to North America. They were also aware of other key factors. The healthiest time of year for Europeans to sail close to Africa's tropical shores north of the equator was during the English winter months, vice versa for lands south of the line. They knew how disease could decimate a ship's crew and its human cargo. Finally they knew that the market for slaves in Virginia or South Carolina was greatest, and prices the highest, during the cropping season of late April into early November, when it would also be easiest to obtain a return cargo of colonial produce. For these reasons, it seemed wise to leave the British Isles with designs of landing in the colonies in the early summer. This required planning for layovers at different ports of call and was always open to disruption from the vagaries of slave supply, the availability of food and water, proper sailing winds, and more. However, records show how good their planning was: less than 1 percent of all slave ships entering the Chesapeake in the first three quarters of the eighteenth century arrived between November and April; and only 9 percent of all slavers entering South Carolina did so over those late fall and winter months.

By the time English shippers began coming to the North American mainland directly from Africa, they had settled on an optimal size and design for their vessels. Slavers tended generally to be smaller than vessels carrying nonhuman cargo, and those coming to British North America were smaller still than those sailing to other locations to the south. After 1680, most slavers weighed between 100 and 200 tons, with the size increasing gradually through the eighteenth century, and the typical vessel arriving in Virginia or South Carolina straight from Africa through that time carried about 200 slaves. Such ships differed from most others of the time in their having more decks, some temporary platforms that carpenters built for the specific purpose of carrying humans in the prone position, and side ports, grated bulkheads, and lattice hatches, all of the latter fashioned to direct fresh air into the lower decks. In addition to equipment particular to the slaving voyage—shackling irons and ropes mainly, but also nets to prevent escape when near land—the slaver had to carry an inordinately large number of casks for food and potable water. A ship with 404 slaves and a crew of 47 left Africa with 13,000 pounds of food. The English slaver *Brookes* on a late-eighteenth-century voyage with 600 Africans and 45 sailors carried 34,000 gallons of water. More space still had to be allotted for firewood for cooking.

Crews aboard slave ships were larger than normal, usually one member for every seven to ten slaves, because feeding and controlling the captive humans posed special tasks and risks not associated with inanimate cargo. And it naturally followed that African duty was more dangerous and less popular than any other. Paid little and often crimped or taken from jail for service, slaver crews were generally hard men, victims themselves of the economic system that employed them. Exceptions were the captain, who often had a stake in the slaving venture, the ship's surgeon, present as much to assure the purchase of healthy men and women in Africa as to maintain their health aboard ship, carpenters, and coopers.

Captains usually stuck to one of two modes of trade along the African Coast: ship trade or shore trade. However, most traded both ways depending on the necessities of the location. Good harbors, roadsteads, or river estuaries that appeared relatively free of disease brought buyers to shore. Rough surf, seasonal unhealthiness, or merchants willing to come out to the ships to barter led to shipboard transactions.

Shippers coming south from Europe found they had to deal, sometimes extensively, with local African political authorities. Those who wanted to take advantage of established outposts and of the enterprise of the surrounding communities almost always had to satisfy local African officials with payments of custom before trading could begin. Custom sometimes proved onerous in cost and time. In the Gambia River, where English-chartered companies maintained a fort and garrison on James Island, slavers coughed up goods simply for the right to trade in the river and lost precious time in what today one might call "red tape." Captain Charles Heatly, master of an English vessel trading for slaves in the 1660s, described the procedure:

When a ship arrives in the River Gambia she comes to an anchor at Gillofree [Juffure] Port, in the Kingdom of Barra, opposite James Fort on James' Island. . . . You send your boat on shore to acquaint the Alkaide or Mayor of the town of your arrival; he in common returns with the boat, and receives from you an anchorage-money. Ten gallons of liquor for the king, value 30s., and two iron bars for himself, value 7s., and perhaps presents, a few bottles of wine, beer, cyder, etc. He immediately despatches messengers with the liquor as above to the king, informing him that such vessel is arrived, and only wants to pay his Customs, intending to proceed up the river. The king consults his councillors for a proper day to receive the same, and sends word to the alkaide accordingly. After a detention of four, five, six and seven days, he sends his people to receive his Custom, 140 bars in merchandise, amount sterling on an average £16.

If slaves were on hand in nearby villages, the slaver might procure them and sail on to another location. Almost never did one spot provide enough slaves to fill the holds of even relatively small vessels. The captain could opt to remain anchored at a particular spot on the prospect that more slaves would soon be brought forth from the interior. This was not always a huge gamble, for intelligence of such activity was surprisingly good, and at big markets caravans arrived with regularity. News of the approach of large numbers of slaves traveled fast and far. Commanders at outposts or captains themselves could send word inland of desirable trade goods on board or the immediate demand for slaves on the coast in hopes of luring African traders to the factories or ships. Caravan leaders were well aware of relative demand and competitive prices.

At times during the trade's heyday, from the 1740s through the rest of the century, competition at slaving markets on the coast grew exceptionally keen. A vessel that sailed to the Loango Coast north of the Congo in 1742 found fourteen other European vessels there, and it took four months to purchase a cargo of 362 slaves. Many ships simply failed to get a full load and crossed the Atlantic with a partial cargo.

Considering everything from the cost of trade goods and transportation to customs duties, broker fees, food costs, and markups by middlemen, slaves were generally a good value for European buyers. Prices in the English market in the Gambia River were typical of those along the coast, rising steadily from the early years of the trade. In the 1680s one healthy adult slave cost an English buyer on average £5.47, but that price rose gradually to £9.43 in the 1720s, £10.05 in the 1740s, £14.10 in the 1760s, and £20.95 in the 1780s. Profit in the enterprise is evident in prices for slaves in the American market. A healthy adult slave in Virginia in 1690 brought £15, in 1760, £45.

At the point of sale the English buyer, usually in the company of a surgeon or an experienced hand, examined the available slaves. Parties figured slave values in a standard unit of labor, "one good slave," which was originally one young male slave between eighteen and twenty-five years old and in good health, but later came to represent women as well as somewhat-older men. Slaves below this standard counted as a fraction. With the assistance of a broker, English buyer and African seller bargained until they agreed on a price for the lot of the people for sale. Bargaining was usually in a fictitious currency of the region. They dickered in "bars" (from the original iron bars imported into West Africa) from Senegambia to the Ivory Coast, in "trade ounces" (based on an ounce of gold dust) on the Gold Coast, and in "manilas" (bracelet-like pieces of brass), cowrie shells, and cloth currency elsewhere. The currencies fluctuated, sometimes widely, and separate rates of exchange existed for different African exports, usually depending on the bargain struck by the individuals. But the bargaining was not as simple as the buyer agreeing to provide so much cloth, for example, for so many slaves. African merchants were interested in an assortment of goods they could resell, and the shipper with the proper mix of imports in his possession saw the value of each rise accordingly. No English merchant with just a few different commodities to exchange could expect a good deal on slaves. A typical assortment of goods exchanged for 180 Africans in the Gambia River in 1740–41 included 1,178 silver coins, 164 guns, 119 gallons of rum, 1,140 lbs. of gunpowder, 150 pieces of linen, 430 iron bars, 92 cutlasses, 450 gunflints, 66 lbs. of carnelian beads, 2,556 lbs. of salt, 63 pieces of Indian textile, 4,391 lbs. of glass beads, 219 yards of woolen cloth, 35 lbs. of lead balls, 288 lbs. of crystal, 102 brass pans, 662 lbs. of pewterware, 71 pairs of pistols, 37 lbs. of cowrie shells, 30 pieces of Manchester textiles, 398 lbs. of fringe, 47 reams of paper, and 2 copper rods.

The meeting of African captive with English shipper was fraught with trauma for the slave. Notwithstanding the deep shock of initial enslavement, forced removal to the coast, and holding (and perhaps working) on the spot for several months, the African now confronted frightening new forces: an alien group of sharp-nosed Europeans occupying the strange construction of a sailing ship, afloat on the saltwater expanse of the unfamiliar Atlantic Ocean. Miller in *Way of Death* describes the experience at port towns along the Angola coast:

All the slaves trembled in terror at meeting the white cannibals of the cities, the first Europeans whom many of the slaves would have seen. They feared the whites' intention of converting Africans' brains into cheese or rending the fat of African bodies into cooking oil, as well as burning their bones into gunpowder. They clearly regarded the towns as places of certain death, as indeed they became for many, if not for the reasons slaves feared.

Olaudah Equiano (in *Interesting Narrative of the Life of Olaudah Equiano, or Gustavus Vasa, the African, written by himself,* 1789, edited by Paul Edwards, 1967), from southern Nigeria, recalled the experience vividly:

The first object which saluted my eyes when I arrived on the coast was the sea, and a slave ship which was then riding at anchor and waiting for its cargo. These filled me with astonishment, which was soon converted into terror when I was carried on board. I was immediately handled and tossed up to see if I were sound by some of the crew, and I was now persuaded that I had gotten into a world of bad spirits and that they were going to kill me. Their complexions too differing so much from ours, their long hair and the language they spoke (which was very different from any I had ever heard) united to confirm me in this belief. Indeed such were the horrors of my views and fears at the moment that, if ten thousand worlds had been my own, I would have freely parted with them all to have exchanged my condition with that of the meanest slave in my own country. When I looked round the ship too and saw a large furnace or copper boiling and a multitude of black people of every description chained together every one of their countenances expressing dejection and sorrow, I no longer doubted my fate; and quite overpowered with horror and anguish, I fell motionless on the deck and fainted.

It is difficult to assess the psychological effect of the entire experience on the captive because of the lack of evidence, but some witnesses described what one might assume—a continued state of chronic depression was the norm for Africans through much of the time following their enslavement and movement. Surgeons on board slaving vessels noted "a gloomy pensiveness" on the visages of Africans. As we know now, such mental states probably had adverse effects on the captives' abilities to ward off illness, and in a number of cases their situations prompted men and women to commit suicide.

Not all slaves boarded a vessel at once. A person sent aboard just prior to departure for the Americas might be joining others who had been on the ship for a matter of weeks or months. The treatment the Africans received at initial boarding did not lessen their sense of trauma. Some masters had crews wash down and shave slaves, ostensibly for reasons of health. Shackles were common for all slaves while close to shore and for adult men even longer. When a vessel was in sight of land, an experienced captain would gird it with nets to prevent escapes overboard.

As with most topics relating to the Atlantic slave trade, assessing the voyage from the African coast to ports in America, the so-called middle passage, is difficult to do in a fair, accurate way. No more than a handful of the African men and women who experienced the trip left records, and those who did were not altogether typical. Some voiced or wrote their accounts in an effort to end the slave trade. Englishmen who left written accounts of their experiences as masters or crewmen on slavers, or who testified before parliamentary committees investigating the traffic, usually did so for a reason. Some wanted to justify slaving, so they likely underplayed the horrors of life on board ship; others wanted to have Parliament outlaw the African trade, so they amassed evidence and emphasized the worst parts of the slaving voyage. When considering the raw inhumanity of the whole episode, it is not easy to examine the middle passage and weigh its effects dispassionately, but recent studies, increasingly able to focus on the statistical evaluation of the thousands of voyages, aid one's attempt to do so. These studies show that efforts toward more or less humane treatment of the captives mattered little in the way the uprooted Africans coped with the voyage. Random influences, or at least factors largely beyond the control of even the most experienced and skillful captains, had the greatest effect on slave health and mortality between Africa and the Americas.

In demographic terms, in only one way—general age—was the typical shipload composition of Africans coming to the British North American mainland different from the makeup of other ships transporting Europeans to the New World. Two times as many African men as women crossed the Atlantic; fewer than one in ten slaves transported were under ten years old or approaching middle age. Students of the trade long thought the larger number of adult men was a result of planter preferences in the Americas, but studies suggest that supply factors might have been just as im-

portant in dictating the composition of the cargo. The demand for
women was high in the colonies, for they did most of the same
work as men; prices for men and women were not always the
same, but often they were close. However, the Africans controlling
who entered the slave trade were apt to retain women slaves,
whom they valued more highly—as agricultural producers primarily, but also as bearers of offspring—than men. Young children
and older adults were simply less economical to trade. They cost
as much to enslave and transport, yet they brought lower prices because of their inability to work as productively as young adults.

Basic elements of the voyage are easy to establish. Africans
had little room—between five and seven square feet of deck space
per person. This was less than half the space accorded contemporary European shipboard convicts (like those who made the voyage to Australia), emigrants (like those indentured servants set-
tling the same English mainland colonies), or soldiers (like those
hauled over to fight in the American Revolution). Slave decks
were usually four or five feet high, but sometimes they were lower,
and the space was confining. One person sold off a slave ship in
Charleston remembered, "It was more than a week after I left the
ship before I could straighten my limbs." Captains allowed the Africans to remain topside through much of the day as weather permitted. It was better for the people, cooler with fresher air and
more room to move, and it enabled crews to go below and make
feeble efforts to swab out. Most men remained connected to one
another with leg irons that were fastened to chains running along
the deck. In spite of such fettering, slaves were encouraged into
movement and activity. On occasion, captains forced adult men to
perform the least popular tasks needed to keep the ship afloat and
on the move. "Coerced by threats and kicks, if occasionally enticed with the promise of more food and momentary release from
irons," writes W. Jeffrey Bolster in *Black Jacks: African American
Seamen in the Age of Sail* (1997), "Africans aboard ship hauled
halyards and manned windlasses. They pumped eternally, the most
onerous of sailors' tasks."

Ideas of hygiene on shipboard were primitive. Captains made
a reasonable effort to guard food and water from contamination

and to isolate the sickest slaves, but sanitary facilities were inadequate under the best of conditions, and bilges quickly grew foul. The worst times were when bad weather forced people below for long periods. In tropical and subtropical waters the temperature could become stifling, augmented, as it was, by the heat and sweat given off by the confined humanity. Grates and canvas airfoils admitted some fresh air, but below decks it still could get downright fetid. Alexander Falconbridge, who served as surgeon on slave ships (and who in 1788 wrote *An Account of the Slave Trade on the Coast of Africa* to acquaint the English public with the abuses of the trade), tells of one such occasion:

Some wet and blowing weather having occasioned port-holes to be shut and the grating to be covered, fluxes and fevers among the negroes ensued. While they were in this situation, I frequently went down among them till at length their rooms became so extremely hot as to be only bearable for a very short time. But the excessive heat was not the only thing that rendered their situation intolerable. The deck, that is, the floor of their rooms, was so covered with the blood and mucus which had proceeded from them in consequence of the flux, that it resembled a slaughter-house.

Whether one could actually smell a slaver before sighting it, as was often said, depended on wind speed and direction, but the very idea suggests the unpleasant and unhealthy conditions for the persons on board. Dr. Alexander Garden, the Charleston port physician, who was often the first person to come on board a slaver upon its arrival from the Atlantic crossing, encountered the "Filth, putrid Air, putrid Dysenteries" and remarked, "it is a wonder any escaped with Life."

Captains normally purchased food for the crossing on the African coast. What the slaves ate depended in part on where they left Africa. Corn, millet, and rice were staples for vessels leaving the less-forested coasts (Senegambia, Angola). Yams were standard fare from the Niger Delta to the Congo River. English captains often brought provisions from home, too, and these included biscuits and dried beans for their ease of storage and general acceptance. All of these items, sometimes in combination, tended to be supplemented with peppers, palm oil, or bits of salted meat or fish. In the latter part of the eighteenth century captains added lime juice to the diet to prevent scurvy. "Three meals a day" is a modern convention that concerned slavers little. Slaves normally ate twice, morning and evening, in small groups out of communal tubs. Whatever the crew fixed usually turned out to be a soup or stew-like concoction without much variety. Each African on board consumed daily, on average, about 2,000 calories.

Daily intake of water was more important. Each person received about a pint of water with a meal, which, even augmented by the food's liquid, was not enough to meet normal bodily needs, let alone the enhanced requirements of persons confined in the heat and humidity below decks and likely suffering from diarrhea. Dehydration was thus an enormous problem for the men and women on board. It produced the condition that the British termed "fixed melancholy" and the Portuguese knew as *banzo*—the sunken eyes, weakness, emaciation, apathy, inability to eat, and delirium that accompanied water and electrolyte loss and the ensuing fall of blood pressure—that slaves often exhibited before their death.

It is not clear to what extent the density of slaves on board—whether shipmasters packed the men and women loosely (in relative terms) or tightly—affected mortality in any great way. In *Way of Death* Miller argues that "tight packing" meant heavier mortality on Portuguese slavers plying the trade between Angola and Brazil. However, studies of the English trade show that despite the growing tendency of slavers to raise the number of captives on board through the eighteenth century, probably the result of rising prices paid for slaves in the Americas, mortality rates generally declined. What affected mortality more than anything else may have been the simple factor of time at sea. This varied according to the length of the voyage (Senegambia to Virginia is just over four thousand miles; Angola to Virginia nearly six thousand miles) and the ship's speed, which the vessel's configuration and existing winds dictated. Most captains planned for a voyage of from forty to sixty days and they figured, as insurance, on carrying twice as much food and water as the slaves would consume on such a trip.

Longer voyages had higher rates of mortality, mainly because of water shortages and the contamination of existing food and water supplies that brought on dysentery, the dreaded "flux" that heightened dehydration and was regarded by many contemporaries as the biggest killer.

Another curious factor in mortality on the voyage was a slave's region of origin in Africa. Persons from the Bight of Biafra seem to have had the highest mortality rate; those from the Loango Coast, immediately south of Biafra, among the lowest. Why this was the case is puzzling, but the individual's health at embarkation seems to have been keenly important. Such uncontrollable factors as the length of the march to the port, regional drought or famine, or strength of demand on the coast (prompting Africans to sell weaker persons when prices were higher) affected health and, consequently, mortality on the voyage.

Mortality rates on the middle passage in the eighteenth century were, on average, between 12 and 15 percent, an astronomical figure given that slaves on Atlantic vessels were almost all of prime age—older adolescents and young adults—and thus not at all likely to die over a one- or two-month period under normal circumstances. The mortality rate for slaves was higher than that for prisoners, soldiers, and America-bound immigrants on ocean voyages at the same time. All death rates dropped considerably in the second half of the eighteenth century, but those of slaves less so. Yet, the simple percentage figure is misleading for consideration of the typical slaving voyage, for most individual slave vessels crossing the Atlantic had a lower mortality rate. Captains wanted it so. If they were paid according to the profit of the voyage, which was tied to sales, they strove to keep slave deaths at a minimum. The average is skewed upwards by a small number of vessels that experienced astronomical mortality, almost always because of an uncontrollable epidemic of measles or smallpox on board. It is skewed, too, by the results of perils at sea that were common to all at the time: shipwrecks, sinkings, pirate attacks. Shipboard slave revolts (such as that on the *Amistad* in 1839, which gained popular attention following the 1997 Steven Spielberg film) occurred occasionally and resulted in loss of life, but they were not frequent occurences—once for every fifty-five Rhode Island vessels making the middle passage between 1730 and 1807, for instance, which is one revolt during every four and one-half years of slaving.

Middle-passage mortality was, as mentioned, heavier in the earlier days of the trade. After 1750 mortality rates in the passage declined noticeably. Reasons for this are several. The speed of ships increased with new designs and such innovations as copper sheathing, thus cutting the important element of time at sea. New ship configurations also allowed vessels to carry more water and catch more from the rains. Also, in addition to learning more about preventing smallpox, only after the 1760s did captains learn that they could prevent scurvy by feeding people citrus fruits, and they learned then, too, that one could produce fresh water by boiling and evaporating salt water. Reducing dehydration of the men and women on board meant lower death rates. But, again, regardless of these innovations, a considerably higher percentage of Africans died in transit to America than of any other group.

Dangers of the voyage were not over with landfall. Africans who had become inured to a host of diseases endemic to their tropical homes were once again thrust into a new disease environment, one with new foods and different water as well. Some ports required several weeks' quarantine of arriving slaves, and it took days or weeks to arrange for sale. This was always a time of further slave mortality. In colonial Virginia between 1710 and 1718, for example, over 5 percent of the captive Africans died between the time they reached America and their sale and dispersal. Half a century later, South Carolina's governor complained about the "large number of dead negroes, whose bodies have been thrown into the river [and] are drove upon the marsh opposite Charles Town." For that matter, the entire first year and more in America would be precarious for African immigrants: perhaps one-fourth of all newly arrived slaves in the Chesapeake and one-third of those arriving in the Low Country died before that initial year was out. Just two years after he arranged for sale of the slaves off the *John and Betty* in 1729, "King" Carter, who kept close tabs on his most recently purchased slaves, complained, "My new Hands are all down in their Seasoning Except one. I must wait with Patience till they recover their strength before I can send them to a distant quarter."

The sale of slaves worked differently in various colonial ports. In the Chesapeake the experience of the *John and Betty* with colonial grandee Carter was typical. Large slave owners in the region were the central figures in most economic dealings; buying and selling slaves was no exception. Captains of vessels entering the Chesapeake with lists of prominent planters who might serve as middlemen cast around for the best deal. Commissions of 7 or 8 percent were common. The planters evaluated buyers' credit, helped obtain return cargoes, arranged for provisions, and sometimes made deals for leasing slaves. They carried out transactions shipboard, where the Africans remained quartered, or at nearby wharves. After the middle of the seventeenth century—perhaps as profits from investing one's time in agricultural pursuits were less promising—some planters would buy lots of slaves from a ship's master and then march them around to settlements and crossroads, selling them in small bunches. All of this took time: on average it was two months between arrival and final sales for slavers entering the Chesapeake.

It was different for slave ships going to Charleston. With its smaller neighboring ports of Georgetown and Beaufort, Charleston was an enormous slave mart, the major port of entry for Africans on the British colonial mainland, importing one-quarter of all slaves brought into the mainland colonies from Africa through 1775. African men and women arriving in Charleston were sold more rapidly and in larger lots than those arriving up the coast. Many South Carolina planters had financial interest in merchant firms, and slaving captains who called regularly established relations with one or another of these firms for everything from slave acquisition in Africa to marketing in America. Eighteen such firms did 60 percent of the slaving business in Charleston. Individual merchant houses might at one time have a consignment of several hundred slaves to sell. They did the advertising and most often sold the slaves at public auction for cash or commodities. Some provided credit for needy buyers. If the market was not promising, the firm might hold the Africans until prospects improved, but the costs of food and shelter had to be weighed in the decision. Through it all—quarantine, advertising, auctioning—things happened quickly in Charleston, averaging twelve days between ship's arrival and date of final sale.

From one of the main points of entry, buyers transported slaves across an increasingly wide part of the colonies' southern Atlantic hinterland. From Charleston, large numbers of slaves moved on into Georgia after about 1750, smaller numbers went to North Carolina, and coasting vessels moved slaves northward to other British mainland colonies. This movement tended to be swift, since the sooner an African man or woman arrived on a farm or plantation, the sooner his or her new owner could begin to recoup the investment and begin to profit through the person's labor.

Arrival on a plantation or a small farm in America meant part of a test for the Africans was completed. Being alive was a victory of sorts. From the time of enslavement in Africa, through passage to the coast, across the Atlantic, and to a location of some permanence in America, more than one-third—perhaps half—of all the victimized Africans died. But now the black men, women, and children had to do more than survive—they had to learn to get by and eventually to acculturate to necessary degrees in a new land under radically different circumstances. Above all, the newest forced immigrants to America had to learn to perform their new work as their owners directed, for the vast Atlantic slaving system brought them to the colonies as a commodity of labor. This fact would play the biggest role in directing the lives of the slaves and their offspring in the new land for generations to come.

CHAPTER TWO

Development of Slavery in Mainland North America

When the first English colonists settled Jamestown in 1607, they did not have in mind establishing an economy and society based on slavery. None of the earliest settlers of colonial Virginia and Maryland intended specifically to import African chattel slaves as their workforce. But black slavery appeared in these colonies before the middle of the seventeenth century, and it grew rapidly after 1680. By a little after 1700, over half of all the laborers in the two Chesapeake colonies were of African origin and enslaved.

The institution of black slavery, which already had appeared as close as Spanish Florida, began slowly in Virginia and Maryland; it caught on there and in some other new mainland colonies as the seventeenth century ran its course. In a narrow sense, it began because English colonists with bountiful land were having difficulty finding an adequate, stable labor force to make their efforts, mostly at growing tobacco, pay. White servitude worked for some decades alongside black slavery, but the latter soon proved more economical and fraught with fewer problems for the landowners. But, in a larger sense, black slavery began in the English mainland colonies without much questioning, perhaps inevitably, because the colonies were part of the growing Atlantic colonial economic system that produced staples for the European market and relied on whichever form of labor best fit its needs. In the Atlantic world of the seventeenth century, African chattel slavery was a recognized and increasingly preferred labor supply. Throughout tropical parts of the New World from Brazil to Cuba, black slavery was spreading rapidly. Planters could work Africans harder and control them more thoroughly than they could European servants, and because Africans were inexpensive by comparison with other laborers, they brought owners greater profits. So British colonists in Virginia and Maryland were not trying something radically different when, after 1680, they began buying large numbers of Africans to work their lands. They were following what by then had become a conventional pattern in the Atlantic colonial system.

English settlers came to the North American mainland colonies to prosper, and the way to do so there was tied to trade. Each colony was to find something to produce for the home market and then, with a favorable balance of trade, purchase imports made in England. The main variation among the colonies was in items produced. Virginia and Maryland grew tobacco at first, and then over time they diversified and began producing cereals and livestock for export primarily to other English colonies. Low-Country South Carolina and Georgia moved in the other direction, exporting livestock and timber before establishing plantations for growing rice and indigo. Along the lower Mississippi, French landholders tried desperately to make profits from tobacco and indigo. Northern colonies produced food, including fish, and all the colonies, but especially the northern ones, participated in a carrying trade. In every sense, producing for export fueled a need for laborers. The commodities produced would be the most important determinant of the size and type of labor force that the colonists would require.

But it is always important to recognize that the mainland colonies did not exist alone in these enterprises. They had close ties to the islands in the Caribbean. Shipping out of London, Liverpool, and Bristol serviced English colonies in both areas. Islanders emigrated to the mainland when opportunities seemed greater. Mainland colonists knew well what was taking place in the rest of the Atlantic world but were especially attuned to the Caribbean. By the 1640s, English planters on Barbados and their French counterparts on Martinique were making the change from tobacco and cotton production to sugar cane, and as they did they opted for African slave labor over the white servants they had been using. Jamaica and the other English Leeward Islands (Antigua, Montserrat, Nevis, and St. Christopher) and French-controlled St. Domingue followed suit. By the last quarter of the seventeenth century the plantation model, with owners using repressive force to exact extraordinary amounts of work out of African men and women held in bondage, existed "next door" to the mainland colonies and was still growing in other colonies up and down the Atlantic edge of the Americas. It is not surprising that the mainland colonies began to import African slaves in large numbers. What seems more surprising is that they waited so long to begin to do so.

One historian, Ira Berlin, has made a particularly important contribution to understanding of the development of North American mainland slavery. As early as 1980 (in "Time, Space, and the Evolution of Afro-American Society in British Mainland North America," *American Historical Review,* 80), Berlin wrote about the temporal and spatial differences in slavery's development. Black slavery, he pointed out, came into being at different times in various mainland regions; it began for different reasons (though some factors were similar); and through the seventeenth and eighteenth centuries various forms of slave systems developed in different mainland areas. In his most recent book, *Many Thousands Gone,* Berlin broadens his earlier arguments and provides a carefully organized schematic for studying the first two centuries of slavery in mainland North America that is likely to be central to understanding this complex matter for a long time.

Berlin has clear vision of grand issues and writes about them so simply and directly that he makes the heretofore unrevealed seem obvious. He differentiates societies with slaves (in which slavery "was just one form of labor among many") and slave societies (in which slavery "stood at the center of economic produc-

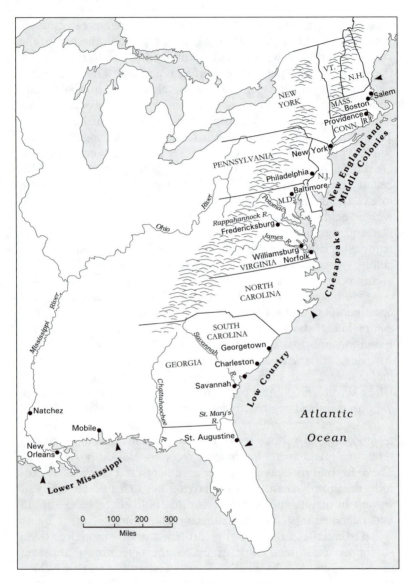

Colonies of the North American Mainland
in the Eighteenth Century

tion") and charts how and when, in particular regions of mainland North America that had different economies and labor needs at different times, societies moved from being one to the other. Berlin considers the mainland colonies by region: *the Chesapeake* (including tidewater and piedmont areas of Virginia, Maryland, and North Carolina); *the Low Country* (of South Carolina and Georgia, along with tidewater areas stretching to Florida); *the North* (New England and the Mid-Atlantic); and *the lower Mississippi Valley* (including West Florida). He groups Africans and African Americans chronologically, by their sets of common experiences, into *charter generations* ("the first arrivals, their children, and in some cases their grandchildren"), *plantation generations* ("who were forced to grow the great staples"), and *revolutionary generations* ("who grasped the promise of freedom and faced a resurgent slave regime"). He emphasizes the over-riding importance of work in slavery's growth and evolution and stresses the effects of the late-eighteenth-century Age of Revolution that roiled the waters of American slavery. Perhaps most important, Berlin points out that the constant struggle between master and slave to determine the nature of their relationship was the primary agitator of these waters from the start. It was a struggle not of individuals of equal power, to be sure, but one between willful humans nonetheless that persisted in every locale where slavery existed and was the major force behind the changing nature of the institution and the African-American society that evolved in each of the regions.

The Chesapeake

The first English settlers in colonial Virginia (after 1607) and Maryland (after 1634) found a temperate climate and land that was abundant, fertile, and thinly populated. "The mildnesse of the aire, the fertilitie of the soile, and the situation of the rivers," wrote John Smith in *A Map of Virginia* (1612), "are so propitious to the nature and use of man as no place is more convenient for pleasure, profit, and man's sustenance." It was a land "overgrowne with trees" that, in Smith's vision, could "soone be amended by good husbandry." This seemed ideal for what the merchants and speculators who paid for the colonial venture wanted: rapid profits.

They hoped settlers could quickly begin producing a staple crop not grown in England, sell it on the English market, and buy English manufactures in return. This early enterprise would prompt more Englishmen to come to the colonies and grow more of the staple; taxes on the exchange would help the crown; and the fields of the American mainland would be places to send the alarming number of landless, often unemployed, Englishmen then posing a threat to a society that suffered from declining real wages, civil war, and social turmoil.

If Virginia and Maryland did not fit the model exactly as the original financiers had dreamed of it, they came close. Within a decade of settlement Virginia colonists were growing tobacco, which the English used more than any other Europeans, and getting good prices for its export while importing a variety of English-made commodities. And there was more land for the claiming—so long as colonists could control the Native Americans who lived on it—and opportunity seemed boundless. As tobacco boomed, demand for laborers grew beyond the expectations of the early colonial planters. Still, England had plenty of poor men wanting work, so it was primarily these young men (median age sixteen) who came to the colonies in the early decades to work the tobacco fields. Unable to afford their own passage, the laborers made arrangements with recruiters in English market centers to repay their fare through work in the new lands. Thus, they came mostly as servants—some as tenants working for shares of their crop, some as bondservants, and some as apprentices. All had fairly long (five to seven years) terms of servitude, or "indenture."

Early colonial planters were not tied solely to English servants, however. For a time there was hope that Native Americans would work in the fields, benefit from "English civilizing tendencies," and develop a harmonious relationship with the colonists. This vision never panned out for a variety of reasons, but largely, it seems, because the Native-American lifestyle was not that of a regimented cultivator. They balked at the work and ran off or literally died under the strain of it.

English mainland colonists imported persons of African descent too, the first in Jamestown in 1619, and they seemed to fit the colonial ideal better. Although their precise status is not clear, these early African arrivals were bound laborers in somewhat the same sense as their white counterparts. Most were probably closer to slaves than to indentured servants, and on the whole they seemed to have served for longer stints than did whites. Still, their condition was hardly that of the chattel slaves of the tidewater plantations a century later. By most accounts their lives were not significantly different from those of English servants in the same place at the same time. Being mostly Atlantic creoles familiar with the English language and the workings of commerce around the Atlantic rim, the early-seventeenth-century Virginians and Marylanders of African descent were not at a disadvantage to the white workers with whom they lived and interacted. Some of them gained their freedom; some eventually owned servants themselves. T. H. Breen and Stephen Innes in a fascinating little book, *"Myne Owne Ground": Race and Freedom on Virginia's Eastern Shore, 1640–1676* (1980), found that in Virginia's Northampton County there was a time around the middle of the seventeenth century when a number of resourceful blacks purchased their freedom and entered into the class of small planters. "They became part of a complex human network," the authors conclude, "and it was their success in dealing with white planters, great and small, servants and slaves, that in large measure explains their viability."

Stories of some of these free blacks stand out in the records. *FREE BLACKS* One Virginia arrival, identified only as "Antonio a Negro" and sold as something approximating a slave in 1621, survived an Indian assault with four others (out of the fifty-six men on their plantation), married an African woman, and by 1650, as Anthony Johnson, had acquired his freedom along with 250 acres and a herd of cattle. Five years later, on advice from his extended family, Johnson successfully sued a white man, Robert Parker, for detaining a slave belonging to Johnson. Part of the Johnson clan moved to Somerset, Maryland, in the 1660s, where they continued to prosper, in a fashion, until the turn of the century. Another free African American, Francis Payne, worked six years to be able to purchase two servants and accumulate 1,650 pounds of tobacco, all of which he traded for his freedom. He then worked seven more years for wages and acquired 3,800 pounds of tobacco, enough to buy his wife and children out of slavery. Yet another black man in seventeenth-century Northampton County exhibited such confidence in his status that he manifested a certain contempt for the law—as administered largely by whites. When approached while working tobacco by a warrant-bearing Northampton County Court official, Virginian Tony Longo told the officer, "shitt of your warrant," and Longo's wife offered up to the official "such noyse that I could hardly heare my owne words." Johnson, Payne, and Longo were not alone. In Northampton County between 1664 and 1677, ten of fifty-three black males were free householders. These free blacks lived like the whites who were not of the wealthiest class. They owned land, grew crops, raised livestock, traded, argued in the courts, and had broad social relationships, some legal and moral and some not. But the number of blacks, free or serving, remained small through mid-century. Out of a Chesapeake population of nearly thirteen thousand black residents, only three hundred were of African descent.

With some exceptions, the early experience of white and black servants in the American colonies was neither a pleasant nor rewarding one. Most wanted to come to the colonies, complete their periods of service, work a few years for wages, and then obtain land, acquire their own servants, and gradually enter the wealthier, planter class. Some were able to achieve their goal. Many did not. Servitude in the colonies was not what they expected, not at all like servitude in England. In order to make the most of the tobacco boom, planters extracted from their servants all the labor they could, far more than young Englishmen were used to doing. As a consequence, discipline grew harsh and servants soon became, in the eyes of those who worked them, less human and more a commodity. If their status was better than that of African slaves on the larger sugar plantations on Caribbean islands at the same time, the difference was not marked. Furthermore, and no doubt more important for those involved, not many servants lived long enough to become planters on any scale. And regardless of race or status, because of typhoid, malaria, influenza, measles, and smallpox, for most who came to the mainland colonies during the first third of the century, the new land was a deathtrap.

Immigrants to the mainland began living longer after the 1640s, though, and for a time opportunity was abundant. However, for several decades tobacco prices had been falling and wages remained low. Large planters and speculators had obtained much of the good tidewater land. Edmund S. Morgan in *American Slavery, American Freedom: The Ordeal of Colonial Virginia* (1975) describes the consequences for Chesapeake laborers. Growing numbers of servants who lived through their indentures were unable to acquire the resources to buy land. Soon there developed a group of young men similar to those feared in England—poor, landless, restless vagabonds living on the margins of wealthier society. Such were especially dangerous in the colonies where all men, for their own protection, were armed. They posed a threat to colonial authorities because they resented and envied the ruling landed gentry. Rebellion was in the air, and it became manifest on several occasions—the best known being Bacon's Rebellion in 1676. Landowners tried several methods of preventing the growth of these poorer classes, including lengthening terms of servitude. They also saw to the passage of laws preventing the propertyless from voting. Still, the problem remained. Servitude had provided a labor force, but it had brought with it a disruptive class of hard-to-control young men, similar to the mother country's. By the end of the 1670s some prosperous tidewater landowners involved in governing Virginia and Maryland might have recognized that a switch to another form of servitude might afford them more, and more permanent, control over the labor force.

In any event, it was not planter fears of rebellious former servants that cut importation of English bondsmen into the Chesapeake. It was a combination of declining numbers of young Englishmen available and willing to venture across the Atlantic, waning opportunity for such men in Virginia and Maryland, and competition from other new colonies for the limited supply of white laborers. Dropping birthrates in England after 1630 cut the number of potential American migrants after midcentury. So did war. The English Civil War disrupted the flow of servants to America, and rising real wages in the mother country following the war rendered fewer unemployed and footloose men eager to listen to colonial recruiters. A generation later, King William III's

War followed closely by Queen Anne's War left England only five years of respite between 1688 and 1713, led many potential servants to find military employment or take the jobs abandoned by those in service. Opportunities in the Chesapeake no longer tempted white servants so much after 1680, either, when a long depression in at least a portion of the tobacco market began, making it still more difficult for poor immigrants to acquire enough money to obtain their own land and labor force. By comparison, opportunity appeared greater in New York (which England took over from the Dutch in 1664) and Pennsylvania (established in 1681). Many of the remaining young Englishmen willing to venture across the Atlantic preferred to pursue their lives in these colonies rather than in the Chesapeake, and some whites already in Virginia and Maryland left to join them. Through the course of the 1690s more whites left the Chesapeake colonies than entered them, and by 1700 white servant immigration had almost completely ceased.

That Chesapeake planters continued to prefer white servants to black slaves is evident through their labor-seeking activities. When they could not acquire enough young Englishmen, they sought young Englishwomen, then young Irishmen. Still, there were not enough whites available, even at the higher prices planters were willing to pay for them. So out of necessity, it seems, they made the same switch to African slaves that their counterparts on sugar plantations in the Caribbean had done almost half a century earlier.

It was good fortune for the planters that large numbers of English shippers had begun to participate in the carrying trade of slaves from Africa in the last third of the seventeenth century, a fact the 1672 organization of the Royal African Company signified to Virginia and Maryland tobacco growers. When the source of white servants dwindled, another cheap, abundant supply of workers was available, these black, from Africa, and bound for life. The new laborers struck planters as "outlandish"—much different from the Atlantic creoles generally familiar with European languages and ways—persons with filed teeth and ritual facial scars who spoke languages and practiced customs that seemed to the English brutish and strange. Yet they were comparatively inexpensive and with sufficient force could be made to work hard in the tobacco fields, often better than white servants who preceded them. It was thus a combination of factors that led to a plantation revolution around the Chesapeake Bay, over time turning Virginia and Maryland's society with slaves into a slave society and altering the lives and possibilities for advancement of persons of African descent in the colonies.

The transition to black slavery occurred at a varied pace throughout the Tidewater. The wealthy growers of sweet-scented tobacco in York County, low on the west side of the Chesapeake Bay, bought Africans early. By the 1680s four of every five bound laborers there were black. Areas farther north made the switch more slowly. By 1695, however, the rush to buy Africans was on; by 1700, Chesapeake planters purchased 3,000 Africans, about the same number they had purchased over the previous twenty years. Population figures provide evidence for the switch. In 1660 there were not 1,700 blacks in all of Virginia and Maryland, and in 1680 there were still only about 4,600. But by the end of the century the black population of the two colonies had tripled to almost 13,000, and nearly all of them were slaves. Free whites still made up the majority of tobacco laborers in 1700, but black slaves had become the laborers of choice, and slave labor was rapidly gaining ground on free labor.

Once the institution of black slavery was established, demand took over and pulled slave vessels crossing the ocean from Africa. From 1700 the Atlantic trade would be the major source of labor until the slave population could sustain natural growth, and that would be awhile. Mortality rates for "unseasoned" slaves in English North America remained high through the first two decades of the eighteenth century. Also, from Africa came an imbalance of men, which automatically meant fewer offspring than in a sexually balanced population. Then, too, planters who knew they could obtain young male laborers cheaply through the trade saw no need to import women, and they did not encourage (and probably actively discouraged) childbirth, which hindered a woman's ability to work. So the number of slaves imported annually into the Chesapeake region rose steadily to a peak in about 1740. It was around then that the native-born African-American population achieved a rough sexual balance and began to grow naturally. Once the sexual balance evened out, African Americans showed they could indeed be, as some planters considered them, "a prolifick people." Darrett and Anita Rutman in *A Place in Time: Middlesex County, Virginia, 1650–1750* (1984) write of one "Sharlott," a twelve-year-old girl purchased by Henry Thacker in 1720. Over forty-four years Sharlott had thirteen children of her own, and in 1764 she, her surviving children, and her grandchildren numbered twenty-two persons—all still Thacker's slaves.

The Chesapeake region went through important economic changes as the eighteenth century progressed. Some of the changes were necessitated by the nature of tobacco and its fragile place in the market. Tobacco sapped the tidewater soils of their nutrients. Planters could produce a tobacco crop in the same field for about three years before having to let it lie fallow for perhaps as long as two decades. As long as land was plentiful and the population small, this was practical, but it became less so as Virginia and Maryland grew, and less appealing in the downswings of fluctuating tobacco prices. Some planters began growing winter wheat to complement their tobacco production in the first half of the eighteenth century, but more turned to grain production in the 1750s and 1760s. North Carolina, too, was entering the mix in a bigger way around the middle of the eighteenth century. That colony's slave economy matured rapidly after 1750, resting on production of naval stores, lumber, grains, and provisions. North Carolinians imported the bulk of their slaves later than the Chesapeake colonies to the north, and more of them directly from Africa. By the time of the American Revolution, the region comprising Virginia, Maryland, and North Carolina had a more diversified economy than other staple-producing regions of the mainland, but all had one thing in common: nearly all the work was in the hands of enslaved men and women whose ancestors had come from Africa.

The Atlantic trade into the Chesapeake leveled off and then began a gradual decline toward the last third of the century. But the overall numbers remain startling. Between 1690 and 1770, Chesapeake planters bought about 100,000 slaves off vessels from West and West Central Africa. On the eve of the American Revolution the nearly 200,000 men and women of African descent living around the Chesapeake made up between two-thirds and three-fourths of all Virginia and Maryland's laborers, and they constituted practically the entirety of the agricultural workforce.

The growth of black slavery to fill colonial labor needs necessitated a legal basis for the institution. Long-standing precedent was not relevant because English common law did not allow slavery. In fact, more so than almost anywhere else, individual rights were the basis for much of the law in England. Nevertheless, the economic and social pressures of English planters to create slavery in order to compete successfully with their New World neighbors from Portugal, The Netherlands, and France led to the legal establishment of such an institution in the Americas. Fortunately for mainland planters, English landowners in the Caribbean had worked through the legal difficulties a generation before slavery became an issue in the Chesapeake. Virginia burgesses and Maryland assemblymen could look to Barbados and Jamaica for legal precedent when constructing their own slave codes.

There was a direct relationship between the changing proportion of blacks to whites in a colony and the sense of need a colonial government felt to develop laws regulating the slave population. Tidewater legislators had not bothered to codify slavery until the number of slaves there swelled and problems with their control arose. Before this time, at least some blacks and whites shared escapades and punishments. In 1649, for instance, William Watts, a white man, and Mary, a black servant, performed the same penance for fornication as would any white couple: they had to stand before the congregation in church at Elizabeth River in Virginia, dressed in a white sheet and holding a white wand. But beginning around the middle of the seventeenth century, colonial judges and lawmakers started stripping away the rights of African immigrants. When the erosion of blacks' legal status took place differs by location. In some places courts were treating individual blacks differently from whites by 1640, as indicated by runaway black servant John Punch's sentence "to serve his said master or his assigns for the time of his natural life here or elsewhere." The two white servants who ran away with Punch, "one called Victor, a dutchman, the other a Scotchman called James Gregory," decreed the Virginia court that appeared so careful to record whites' national origins, had to serve their masters an additional year and the colony three years. Colonial records bear no evidence of a white servant in America ever receiving such a sentence as that of John Punch.

In other places blacks like Anthony Johnson held their own in court cases against whites through the 1660s. But the trend was toward the loss of black rights. In the 1640s blacks in Maryland lost the right to bear firearms. In the 1640s (Virginia) and 1660s (Maryland) black women were included in lists of tithables (because those taxed were "all those that worked in the ground," and black women did so, along with white and black men). In the 1660s both colonies meted out stiff punishment for fornication between individuals of the two races. (Maryland decreed in 1664 that all "English women forgettfull of their free Condicion and to the disgrace of our Nation do intermarry with Negro Slaves . . . shall Serve the master of such slaves during the life of her husband.") Recognizing that masters must make slaves fear for their lives—their liberty already lost—to get necessary work from them, and realizing that this required a level of brutality that easily could result in the slaves' death, Virginia in 1669 passed "*An act about the casual killing of slaves*":

Be it enacted and declared by this grand assembly, if any slave resist his master (or other by his masters order correcting him) and by the extremity of the correction should chance to die, that his death shall not be accompted Felony, but the master (or that other person appointed by the master to punish him) be acquit from molestation, since it cannot be prepensed malice (which alone makes murther Felony) should induce any man to destroy his own estate.

Social practice did not always follow the law, so some free blacks, remaining descendants of the Atlantic creole population that arrived during the first half-century of the colonies' existence, continued to be viable and respected members of Chesapeake communities and had all manner of relations with whites into the 1670s. But whatever dike held back the flood of legislation and social practice condemning blacks to slavery and ostracism broke with the importation of large numbers of African men and women after the 1680s. In short order, blacks in the Chesapeake lost most of their remaining rights and found themselves completely set apart from whites on all levels of colonial society.

The most important loss to any hope slaves harbored to attain freedom and any social position was the right to hold property. For everyone in colonial America, property was the basis for freedom and dreams of prosperity. In property all persons had legal rights that gave them confidence in their dealings with others. In property all persons had self-respect that manifested itself in a variety of ways favorable to the individual. Removing African Americans' right to own property took away their ability to accumulate wealth and to participate in the quest for betterment that had once included almost all mainland colonists. The loss of their right to personal property undermined the possibility for blacks to have success in personal relations.

Thus, after the first two decades of the eighteenth century, the Chesapeake colonies were well on their way to becoming slave societies rather than societies with slaves. The economic and social system that existed is sometimes characterized in relative terms as one of "smaller plantations," but that seems to refer to the most evident institutions of the Tidewater and does not describe appropriately the variety of circumstances in which African Americans lived at different times and in different places. Until black slavery caught hold, persons of African descent who lived in the Chesapeake were scattered broadly among white servants and free men. Their public contacts were with as many whites as blacks. There was little segregation based on race. African Americans seldom lived on farms with more than a dozen workers of any kind, and only a few lived with more than a handful of other slaves.

With the increase of slavery after 1700, Chesapeake society grew in a direction of having three broad levels based on land and slave holdings. Most landowners lived on family farms of a relatively small size. In Virginia the more prosperous of these might have owned a slave or two or a hired hand, but family members did most of the work. In Maryland by far the largest group of landowners owned no servants or slaves. There also was a middle level of landowners, those with aspirations of becoming big-time planters, who owned a few slaves. These people normally succeeded in joining the class of big planters, or else overextended themselves and failed. The middling farmers were thus a group that was economically and socially "transient," and its numbers declined as the century progressed.

The class of landowners that remained relatively small was that of the largest planters, who owned nearly all of the African Americans in the two colonies. Gloria L. Main in *Tobacco Colony: Life in Early Maryland, 1650–1720* (1982) searched probate records from six Maryland counties and found that through the period of her study two-thirds of all slaves worked for just 6 percent of the planters. On the largest plantations owners hired overseers from the group of young, landless white men in the vicinity, and these men drove their workers in gangs and practiced harsh discipline.

The farms, crops, and slaves fell into distinct spatial arrangements. The largest plantations were the tobacco-growing holdings along the Chesapeake Bay and its rivers and inlets. This region formed a tobacco core in the two colonies, with wealth and slaves concentrated on large estates. Around the periphery—the Virginia and Maryland eastern shores, northern Maryland, and areas of Virginia more distant from the water—grain farming and livestock raising increasingly were the basic economic activities. Here smaller land holdings and fewer slaves were the norm.

Even on large plantations slaves did not always live together in a single group of communal quarters. Instead, planters often housed their slaves in small clusters of dwellings located in various places around their holdings; this dispersed herds of cattle and hogs, which the slaves tended, and put laborers close to the fields they worked. Tobacco fields tended to be small and separated because the best tobacco-growing soils were seldom found in large patches. Also, as mentioned, tobacco stripped the soil of nutrients and rendered fields barren for long periods, so once-productive fields in one locale might be grown over in brush a few years later. In Maryland a typical grouping of dwellings might house four or five men or women field hands and one or two women to cook, wash, and care for children. Residents of one such cluster might have thirty cattle and twenty hogs to look after and several fields of tobacco to maintain. One of the wealthiest Maryland colonists in 1681, Colonel Benjamin Rozer, owned a workforce of sixty-nine slaves and servants. Of these he kept fourteen at the "dwelling plantation" on Port Tobacco Creek, and he settled the others among half a dozen work sites with such names as "Jack's," "Indian Field," and "War Captain's Neck."

Over about a century the establishment and development of black slavery altered nearly every facet of society in the Chesapeake colonies. In 1680 persons of African descent had constituted just a little over 7 percent of the total population of Virginia and Maryland. A century later blacks made up nearly 40 percent of all the people in the two colonies. As the slave population grew, Virginia legislators stayed busy creating new ways of controlling unruly African Americans in their midst. Punishments grew harsh. Philip J. Schwarz in *Twice Condemned: Slaves and the Criminal Laws of Virginia, 1705–1865* (1988) relates the story of Jacob, a slave of Martha Flint of Lancaster County, Virginia, who stood trial with his owner and another white woman for stealing tobacco and food from several local whites. The white women received whippings. Jacob, who could have been hanged for his actions, was granted "mercy" because he acted in the company of "Christian white persons," including the person who owned him. So instead of execution for stealing what turned out to be six pence worth of goods, Jacob was made to stand for an hour at the pillory, to have each ear nailed to the pillory and then cut off "close to the head," and then to receive a "full whipping."

With the growth of black slavery also came about the almost total disappearance of free blacks among the population, a fact that would have considerable effect on the evolution of African-American culture in the colonies. By the onset of the Revolution, free blacks made up less than 5 percent of the total Virginia and Maryland black population. A century after slavery had become the preferred institution for colonial labor, persons of African descent lived in considerable numbers throughout the Chesapeake; practically all of them were slaves.

The Low Country

If one defines mainland North America's Low Country broadly, as stretching from Cape Fear in the north all the way down past St. Augustine in the south—the area today that makes up the Atlantic littoral of South Carolina, Georgia, and northern Florida, then one recognizes that the English were neither the first Europeans to establishment a permanent settlement there nor the first ones to bring African slaves to the region. As noted, the Spanish were. After Spain decided to establish a military outpost at St. Augustine in Florida in 1565, blacks worked on the fortifications and participated fairly continuously in garrisoning the fort. Over a century later, free blacks and slaves lent their building skills when fear of pirates and rival European nations brought Spain finally to build a huge stone fort on the site, in 1672, and free blacks and mulattos provided six officers and forty-two men to St. Augustine's black militia in 1683. The Spanish outpost at St. Augustine functioned to protect the country's shipping passing between the wealthy colonies of New Spain and the mother country rather than to grow staples for export, as in most of the American settlements. Thus, the population of Africans—or of any persons serving as laborers—in Spanish Florida remained small.

Yet in spite of its size or purpose, the Spanish settlement of blacks, whites, and Indians at St. Augustine would be a thorn in the side of English efforts to create a slave-based plantation economy in southern parts of the British mainland after 1670. For religious and humane reasons, doubtlessly reinforced by political and military factors, Spain's Charles II in 1693 granted freedom to slaves escaping from the English colonies who made it to the Florida outpost. Thereafter, Spanish Florida became a direction for escape and a potential refuge for black men and women fleeing the tightening bonds of English plantation slavery. Initially Spanish authorities reneged on the crown's promise and sold some of the early fugitives back into slavery to benefit the financially strapped colony, but after 1738, when St. Augustine's new governor reinforced the royal edict, prospects for runaways brightened. In that year, with the governor's permission and under the leadership of a black militia captain named Francisco Menendez, thirty-eight fugitives from the English colonies established the first free-black town on the North American mainland some two miles due north of St Augustine. They named the village Gracia Real de Santa Teresa de Mose; it would be abandoned and then rebuilt and occupied until the Spanish lost Florida to the English in 1763. Throughout the village's existence, according to Jane Landers in *Black Society in Spanish Florida* (1999), "the continuing lure of Mose" would draw slaves from England's southernmost mainland colonies while its free black residents would find a way "to shape a village community under extremely difficult conditions."

The slaves fleeing in the direction of Mose and St. Augustine were coming from the thriving slave societies in South Carolina and, later, Georgia. These milieus differed considerably from the Spanish settlements in northeastern Florida, but they differed as well from the English colonies of the Chesapeake.

Early English migrants to the mainland Low Country came from other English colonies, Barbados especially in the beginning, as opposed to the British Isles. Like their counterparts to the north, they came intent on producing for an English market, but the Low Country was not tobacco country. For the first thirty years of settlement these newcomers concentrated on providing livestock and timber for the English in the Caribbean and deerskins for those "back home" in England. After that they turned, gradually at first but then almost totally, to rice production.

The first South Carolina settlers arrived after 1670 with a clear sense of who would be doing the major work of production. African slavery had been thriving in the sugar cane fields of Barbados since the 1640s. Two of South Carolina's Lords Proprietors had been successful Barbadian planters and several others were directors of the Royal African Company, which made its profit off the delivery of slaves to the Americas. The first Englishmen acquiring land along the South Carolina coast noted "the aptnes of Negroes and other servants fitt for such labor as wilbe there required." So black slaves, mostly Atlantic creoles, were present in South Carolina in the year of the colony's founding, and after a generation of settlement persons of African descent constituted a majority of the

Low-Country population. The extension of settlement and agricultural production in coastal South Carolina, then, would mean the spread of an economy and society based on slavery, regardless of what else the founders and first settlers may have had in mind.

Another important difference between the Low Country and the Chesapeake had to do with environment. The lowland region was subtropical, a land of summer heat and humidity, malarial swamps, and pine forests. It was more like the islands of the British West Indies or the homelands of many Africans than any part of the British Isles or the northern mainland colonies. Adult slaves who had acquired in Africa some resistance to malaria or yellow fever had advantages over their masters in staying healthy, and they had the benefit of knowing more than the whites did about how to raise and care for plants and animals in a subtropical clime. This meant that for the early years of Low-Country settlement, English masters were more dependent on their slaves than was normally the case elsewhere in the colonies. It meant also that Africans would be important in bringing their know-how to bear on developing the colonial Low Country and particularly on introducing techniques of stock raising and rice production that would help planters find suitable exports for the colonial market.

From its birth as a colony in 1670 through the first thirty years of its existence, South Carolina was a child of Barbados. Its first settlers were from Barbados, its economy was geared to supply Barbados with provisions, and the model lifestyle of the South Carolina landowner was that of the Barbadian planter. By 1650 the English island in the Caribbean was seriously overcrowded and most of its arable land was under cultivation. Freed servants on Barbados now lacked opportunity and the population needed provisions. So in the last third of the century there was considerable migration from Barbados to other English colonies in the New World. In 1670 a mix of wealthy planters, freed servants, and slaves of African descent left the island to settle on the Ashley River near what is now Charleston. Quickly they began to produce foods, raise livestock, and harvest timber for the island market.

Whether or not slavery was to be part of South Carolina's economy and society was never a question. Its proprietors granted *"slavery as a way of life"*

generous amounts of land to those bringing black slaves with them to the colony: "To the Owner of every Negro-Man or Slave, brought thither to settle within the first year, twenty acres; and for every Woman Negro or Slave, ten acres of Land; and all Men-Negro's or slaves after that time, and within the first five years, ten acres, and for every Woman Negro or slave, five acres." The 1669 Fundamental Constitutions of Carolina, written by John Locke and meant to guide the colonists in their new settlement, accepted slavery as a way of life. It was unequivocal in stating, "Every Freeman of Carolina, shall have absolute power and authority over Negro Slaves, of what opinion or Religion soever."

Taking advantage of the situation were such individuals as John Coming, distant ancestor of Edward Ball, about whom Ball writes in his black-and-white family history, *Slaves in the Family* (1998). Coming was a sailor from Devon in southwestern England, who in 1669 signed as first mate on the vessel taking the first colonists to Carolina. After wintering in Barbados, where they picked up more colonists and their slaves, the group made permanent settlement at the confluence of the Ashley and Cooper rivers, the spot on the welcoming bay that is now Charleston. Coming married an Englishwoman, Affra, on the voyage, set up residence at the new settlement, and then spent the 1670s as captain of a vessel carrying servants from England to Carolina (thereby earning himself a headright to Carolina land) and hauling cargo among England's New World colonies. Ball suspects some of this cargo consisted of enslaved men and women, Native Americans from Carolina taken to Barbados, and Africans purchased on Barbados and taken back to Carolina.

In 1682 Coming retired from sailing, turned in enough warrants for land to obtain a 740-acre plot located twenty-five miles up the Cooper River, and with his wife began building the equivalent of an English farm, on a much grander scale, in America. To perform much of the work, Coming began buying Indian and African slaves. Through the 1680s these men and women built a house for the Comings and African-like quarters for themselves, the latter with earthen walls and thatched roofs. They then felled trees and drained the land, selling off the timber or, later, extracting tar and pitch from it, and raising cattle for the beef or hides on the cleared fields. Coming died in 1695, Affra in 1699, without having had children. Ownership of the estate was split between Affra's nephew, John Harleston, and her husband's half-nephew, Elias Ball of Devon. Ball arrived in South Carolina in 1698, ambitious and profit hungry. Perhaps above the odors from the cattle and the tar kilns he could smell prosperity of a different sort in the balmy breeze. Like most New World endeavors, Ball's would be based on the labor of others; these, increasingly, would be enslaved Africans.

If Coming's experience was typical, then most of the slaves passed on to his and his wife's heirs were persons of African descent rather than natives of the region. Through these early years, between one-fourth and one-third of the individuals coming to South Carolina were enslaved blacks, predominantly men. Their importance to colonial enterprise in the Low Country was considerable from the beginning. Some West Africans were experienced breeders and keepers of cattle. English settlers, who picked up some techniques for keeping livestock in subtropical conditions from practices in the Spanish and British West Indies, relied also on African expertise to develop herds. Therefore methods of tending cattle in South Carolina's free-grazing environment tended to combine techniques of husbandry used across West Africa's savannas, which included seasonal burning to freshen grasses and nighttime penning of cattle for protection, with those in use in the Caribbean. The exceptional knowledge of stock raising of peoples along the Gambia River, the Fulbe, coupled with the importance of producing livestock for the Barbados market in the early years of South Carolina's struggle to establish itself as a viable colony, helps explain Carolina planters' long-standing preference for Gambian slaves.

But if some Gambians' experience with animals was useful for a generation of South Carolina's history, that of others from the same region and other parts of West Arica with the planting and growing of a certain grain crop altered the colony's way of life dramatically after 1700. The beginning of rice production created a demand for labor that would cause South Carolina to import more slaves than any other mainland colony through the rest of the eighteenth century. Ball's ancestors would ride this wave: by the end of the 1720s the Ball plantations would cover 4,328 Low-Country acres, worked by forty-three slaves. "Rice would become the manna of the Balls," he writes, "and the bane of thousands of blacks."

Since Carolina's founding, its settlers had gone through the same search for a staple as had Virginia colonists in the first decades of the seventeenth century. They performed systematic experiments with cotton, silk, tobacco, indigo, sugar cane, naval stores, ginger, and wine. They experimented with rice also, but through the mid-1690s they did not have much to show for their effort. Then, sometime near the end of the century, Carolinians began to succeed in growing and processing rice for the market. The grain was inexpensive, filling, and easy to store, making it popular among poorer European families as well as a preferred grain for feeding armies and gang workers. With the demand for food high and the European population inching upward, in time a "rice revolution" struck the Low Country with effects every bit as profound as tobacco's had been on the Chesapeake.

Africans played a significant role in South Carolina's move to a rice economy (and they probably did so for Ball's ancestors specifically, since Ball suspects "that during the first years after his immigration, Elias had only a vague idea how to manage his copious inheritance, and that he was forced to put himself under the apprenticeship of his slaves"). Fair numbers of men and women from societies having long experience cultivating rice came to South Carolina before 1700. Such coastal groups as the Jola, Papel, Baga, Temne, and Mende from the Gambia River south past Cape Palmas produced wet rice for centuries prior to their contact with Europeans. So did inland peoples, the Bambara and Mandinka of the upper Niger in particular. Their methods of production were similar. They built dikes to catch water; turned the wet soil with long-handled, flat-tongued instruments; planted with a hoe; sang in unison as they cultivated; husked with mortar and pestle; and winnowed the grains with broad, flat, woven baskets. Experienced slaves who were encouraged to produce their own provisions grew rice successfully while their masters were failing to do so. Planters eager to find a staple to market would have been easy to convince of the efficacy of African techniques of rice production. Thus, knowledge of rice cultivation spread among South Carolina planters over a generation beginning in the 1690s.

For a brief time after 1700, South Carolina had one of the most diversified lists of exports in colonial America. Then rice overtook all the others. South Carolina exported 1.5 million pounds of rice in 1710, 6 million pounds in 1720, and 20 million pounds in 1730. By the 1720s rice was the major Low-Country export, surpassing pitch and tar. When around the middle of the century Carolina planters introduced a "tidal flow" method of rice production that regulated water on fields and prevented poor yields from drought, rice, and in particular a strain known as Carolina Gold, had become the Low-Country king. "The only Commodity of Consequence produced in South Carolina is Rice," noted the colony's governor, James Glen, in 1761, "and they reckon it as much their staple Commodity, as sugar is to Barbados and Jamaica, or Tobacco to Virginia and Maryland." By Glen's time the popular grain was accounting for 60 percent of all exports of the region.

Geography limited rice culture and affected the direction of its spread. Rice grew readily only in the lowest coastlands where tidal rivers irrigated the fields. This restricted its cultivation to a strip along the Atlantic seldom more than twenty miles wide. Southward along the Carolina coast, rice culture spread rapidly, but that spread halted at the Savannah River, below which ownership claims with Spain were not clear.

It was along those more southerly coastal lands in 1732 that England chartered Georgia, a colony that was to reform England's dispossessed and criminal elements and be the basis for a society that saw virtue in hard work, temperance, and Christian morals. The Georgia Trustees banned slavery from the colony by legislation in 1734 because they believed slavery would hinder development of the virtuous, egalitarian society of small landholders they expected to create. So Georgia was free of slaves, more or less, through the first two decades of its existence.

Slavery might have come to Georgia eventually no matter what, but its introduction was hurried along because of the failure of the inadequately prepared and poorly skilled white colonists to succeed at producing anything (wine, silk, and more) the trustees wanted. South Carolinians in particular began pressing Georgia's trustees and the English Parliament to make slavery legal in the colony. The trustees experimented with a more humane system of forced servitude in the 1740s, but by mid-century it fell before economic expedience. Thereafter, Parliament rendered Georgia free of restriction on slave holding. Land-hungry South Carolinians were the first migrants into Georgia's coastal regions after 1750. They brought with them their know-how for producing rice and their preferred labor force. Other groups followed and moved southward toward the St. Mary's River following Spanish cession of disputed land after 1763.

Low-Country Georgians got most of their slaves via the South Carolina market until the middle 1760s. After that they began importing slaves directly from Africa. Like other colonies, Georgia had to wait until its market could dispose of entire cargoes before fully laden slavers bothered to put in at its ports. But by 1773 Georgia had a black population of around 15,000, roughly equal the size of its white population. As in South Carolina, in Georgia's rice-producing region blacks outnumbered whites considerably. Because of the confinement of rice culture to the narrow coastal strip and of the difficulties Georgians had finding staple products to grow in the backcountry, slavery in colonial Georgia remained exclusively a Low-Country institution. Georgia's 126-mile-long Rice Coast was also its Slave Coast.

The transformation to rice production in South Carolina and its spread to coastal Georgia brought about plantation agriculture on a scale not before known on the North American mainland, and the large plantation operations affected the working lives of the slaves. More than any other mainland area, the Low Country began to resemble the sugar cane islands in the British West Indies. Small farms were not as efficient as large, specialized plantations, so the latter became the norm. By the end of the century, in spite of disruptions associated with the American Revolution, two Ball brothers owned plantations totaling nearly 15,000 acres and worked by 500 slaves.

If this were not enough, the Low Country developed a secondary staple, indigo, which one planter termed "an excellent colleague Commodity with Rice." The early growth of English textile

indigo

production in the 1740s and the demand for the blue dye that indigo rendered brought a thirty-year-long boom in the crop. Indigo is a delicate plant that requires lots of attention during its growth and fairly extensive processing at its harvest, but it has a short production cycle, just seven months, so planters could integrate it with other operations—production of naval stores, for instance, or even the growing of rice.

Therefore the Atlantic trade was asked to bring in enormous numbers of Africans to provide the workforce needed for these plantation enterprises, but it responded to the demand. Between 1706 and 1776, 94,000 slaves entered Charleston harbor for sale and disbursement throughout the Low Country. By 1740, in the oldest plantation areas north and south of Charleston, black slaves made up 90 percent of the population. The largest plantation owners grew exceedingly wealthy and spent time away from production, in Charleston or Savannah during winter months and perhaps in New England through the heat of the summer. In their absences hired managers and overseers saw to the management of the plantation.

The difficult working and living conditions brought on by the switch to intensive staple agriculture led to rising rates of slave mortality in the Low Country. South Carolina physician Alexander Garden notified the Royal Society of Arts in 1755 of the situation:

. . . Tilling, Planting, Hoeing, Reaping, Threshing, Pounding have all been done merely by the poor Slaves here. Labour and the Loss of many of their Lives testified the Fatigue they Underwent, in Satiating the Inexpressible Avarice of their Masters, [who] . . . pay . . . dear for their Barbarity, by the loss of many . . . Valuable Negroes, and how can it well be otherwise, the poor Wretches are Obliged to Labour hard to Compleat their Task, and often overheat themselves, then Exposing themselves to the bad Air, or Drinking Cold Water, are immediately . . . Seized with Dangerous Pleurisies and peripneumonies . . . which soon . . . End their wretched Being here.

Masters were not particularly mindful of the results. Prices for imported Africans dropped a bit with increased supply, so masters could more readily purchase healthy Africans to replace the deceased. When prices for rice fell, as they did with the rising production, planters' instincts were to clear more land, grow more

rice, increase crop yield, and exact still more labor from the existing workforce—all of which meant worsening living conditions
and greater morbidity for the slaves. Not until the eve of the
American Revolution did the Low-Country slave population begin
to sustain itself, and "salt water" slaves continued to flow into the
region in large numbers.

As in other colonies, when the proportion of slaves to free persons began to rise, or even portended to do so, white anxiety
mounted. The result in South Carolina and Georgia was the steady
erosion of rights for blacks until they faced the strictest laws with
the harshest punishments of anywhere in the English mainland
colonies. The process took place first in South Carolina, where in
the 1690s the Assembly began borrowing from the slave codes
of its "parent" colony, Barbados. White fears rose particularly,
though, after the mid-1720s, when slave imports into the colony
topped 1,000 per year. As the Lords Commissioners for Trade and
Plantations put it, "ye whole Province was lately in danger of being massacred by their Owne Slaves, who are too numerous in
proportion to ye White Men there." "Suspicious gatherings" of
blacks in the streets of Charleston set whites on edge, prompting
the organization, in 1721, of a "Negro Watch" to stop slaves on
sight (with instructions to shoot any black not halting on command) and to confine blacks found on the street after 9:00 P.M. In
the same year the colonial militia took over previously irregular
patrols in rural areas. Powers of patrolmen were arbitrary and almost without limits. They could administer twenty lashes to a
slave found off the plantation without authorization, search slave
dwellings indiscriminately, and kill suspected runaways who resisted or fled. A system of justices of the peace for minor offenses
and panels of justices and freemen for felonies maintained the appearance of formality in the seemingly contradictory realm of
"slave justice." Punishments for those judged guilty were swift,
severe, and frequently inhumane. They included castration; nose-
splitting; chopping off of ears, hands, or toes; branding; or burning
at the stake. Overseers and masters administered their own justice
and punishment on the plantation, and those acts varied from more
reasonable to arbitrary and depraved.

Beyond the law, however, was social practice, which limited slaves' lives and took away from the quality of their existence. Tension between the minority of white workers and the black majority manifested itself in the setting apart of specific jobs for each group. Whites limited blacks in the practice of skilled trades and designated certain jobs as fit only for persons of color. Consequently, blacks, often the young, collected and disposed of all refuse, built most roads and cut canals, served as carters and stevedores, and even had duty as roughnecks to collect debts or settle masters' scores. Tensions mounted between white and black men over sexual relations. White preoccupation with the very notion of a black man raping a white woman grew through the century. The *South Carolina Gazette* tended to overlook the ravishing of black women by white men, as happened with some regularity, but it devoted front-page space to instances of rape committed by black men alleged to have occurred in distant colonies.

Even still, there were hidden social and cultural advantages for blacks living on the isolated Low-Country plantations. Rice production required individual, demanding work on separate, quarter-acre plots; it lent itself to a task system of labor. Overseers gave individual slaves specific tasks to complete for a day's work. When finished the person had free time. This free time, which men and women worked hard to gain, enabled rice plantation slaves to do things on their own, among fellow slaves, and usually away from the eyes of white society. They raised their own crops and poultry, made crafts, hunted and fished, sold their surplus wares or produce, and spent time socializing with their peers. The effects of this intermittent isolation and limited free time were important in the development of a distinct culture among Low-Country slaves—a culture that manifested much more of their African heritage than that of other blacks who were less isolated and had less personal freedom.

The Lower Mississippi

The experience of persons of African descent in the lower Mississippi Valley differed in many ways from that of blacks in other parts of the North American mainland. France and Spain were the major European colonial nations involved in the region through the colonial period (England would control West Florida after 1763), and the lower Mississippi remained marginal in the ambitious New World colonial designs of each. The French tried early on to create a slave-based, staple-producing economy, but it never took hold and thrived as it would in other parts of the southeastern mainland. Thus, what by 1730 was a slave society, where persons of African descent outnumbered whites and where rigorous enforcement of rigid slave laws meant harsh discipline, had become a more open setting by mid-century. What evolved, according to Daniel Usner in *Indians, Settlers, and Slaves in a Frontier Exchange Economy: The Lower Mississippi Valley before 1783* (1992), was a mingling of Indians, whites, and blacks that allowed individuals in each group greater movement, more social and economic interaction, and for blacks some opportunity for freedom, even as it continued to manifest the typical harsh living and working conditions that were a function of slavery in all parts of the New World. After 1763 Spanish control meant more efforts to stimulate plantation production with more white settlers and black slaves, but Spain provided ambitious blacks still greater opportunities to gain and thrive in freedom. All of this led to a greater mixing of blacks, whites, and Indians in the lower Mississippi than anywhere else in the colonial period.

Frenchmen from Canada established the first European settlements in the seasonally-steamy lower Mississippi Valley in 1699, intent mainly on securing a back door to the Indian fur trade. At the time, with slave-based sugar plantations thriving on the French Caribbean islands of St. Domingue and Martinique, French authorities saw little reason to try to duplicate that success along the Mississippi with African or Indian slaves. But following establishment of New Orleans by the French crown in 1718, settlers with an eye on plantation agriculture raised the pressure to allow importation of African slaves, and a year later the government relented. So between 1719 and 1731 the French *Compagnie des Indies* brought nearly 6,000 slaves directly from Africa into Louisiana. A good number of these people came from Senegambia; the French referred to some as Bambaras, not so much an ethnic identifier—as it is now—as a term for captive or soldier from the Senegambian interior. Other African arrivals came from the Bight of Biafra and Angola.

Louisiana was an unhealthy place and many of the new migrants did not live long, but in time Louisiana's African population began to survive—better than the whites in the region. By 1727 blacks outnumbered whites in the colony. Those Africans who remained around New Orleans constructed levees, built buildings, and worked on the farms and plantations that abutted the small-sized town. Outside of New Orleans slaves felled trees, cut roads, constructed levees, built dwellings, and provided the labor to create tobacco and indigo plantations on huge estates lining the Mississippi from New Orleans north to Point Coupée.

French slavery in the New World already had a legal basis in the *Code Noir* that King Louis XIV had decreed in 1685; his successor, Louis XV, merely issued a new and similar code for Louisiana in 1724. Unlike English laws, the French code called for Catholic instruction for slaves and placed church and state in a position to be the guarantors of some meager slave rights, but it never worked that way. Rare was the plantation slave who received sacraments beyond baptism; rarer still the abused slave who resorted to the law for protection or compensation. Reflecting the typical fears of a white minority, punishments of slaves for wrongdoing were as severe in the lower Mississippi as they were anywhere. In *Mammon and Manon in Early New Orleans: The First Slave Society in the Deep South, 1719–1819* (1999), Thomas N. Ingersoll writes of the retribution leveled against slave rebels from 1730s New Orleans: "As late as 1800 there were living whites and blacks who remembered the sounds of bones breaking on the wheel and the cries of the victims as the sun slowly put them out of their misery high above the Bayou Road." Jesuits, who were thought to be present at least partly to look after the well being of slaves and indigenous folk, owned and worked slaves on one of the largest plantations. Thus, in the teeming heat of long summers, in a disease environment that included yellow fever among the other subtropical plagues, and in a budding plantation economy demanding hard work and meting out punishment most severe, the lot of slaves up and down the lower Mississippi was a particularly mean one.

As everywhere else in the New World, blacks in the lower Mississippi Valley were not the only ones maltreated by the European colonists. Indians, some of whom the French enslaved also, were displeased and threatened by the expanding plantation economy. French authorities were continually afraid that runaways from Louisiana plantations would make common cause with the Indians, and small numbers of them did just that. There even existed a handful of maroon settlements where Africans, Indians, African Americans, and African Indians in just about every manifestation organized banditry raids, traded goods stolen from the French colonists, and planned ways to halt the expansion of plantations. In 1729 Natchez Indians aided by fugitive slaves rose up in the districts north of New Orleans and killed over two hundred French settlers, liberating slaves in the process. New Orleans's governor armed fifteen trusted slaves from the city, who joined the Natchez's enemies, the Choctaw, to quell the rebellion. Two years later, a group of fugitives the French called "Bambaras" planned another insurrection with local Indians, only to be defeated by a French force augmented once again by slaves. In such a threatening environment, French authorities rewarded blacks who fought for them with their freedom and then formed a small black militia to protect the colony and ensure the loyalty of its black population in the future. Over the next several decades that militia helped protect the settlement against more groups of Indians and prepared to fight various European enemies when rumors of invasion spread.

The frightening insurrections, coupled with fear of a larger and potentially unruly black majority, brought French authorities to stop importing African slaves into the lower Mississippi after 1733. With that, the expansion of tobacco- and indigo-producing plantations slowed dramatically and the colony began to diversify its export economy. Thus, at the very time that African slaves were beginning to pour into the Chesapeake and Low-Country colonies of Anglo-America, where plantation agriculture was holding its own (in the former) and thriving (in the latter), demands and constrictions on Africans and African Americans in the lower Mississippi Valley began to loosen. As creoles began to replace African-born slaves, more men (especially) and women were finding ways

Africans & Indians

to gain their freedom. Once they did, they joined the broad spectrum of the Franco-American-African-Indian population that exchanged goods and services with one another in a broad, free-wheeling, subsistence-based exchange economy that the French could do little to control. Eventually, slaves participated in the economy, too. In place of providing their bondspeople food and clothing, some masters began allowing them time to work for themselves, and many of them marketed the foods they had grown on their own behalf or game they had trapped and hunted. Some prospered from services they provided as boatmen along the bayous and backwaters. Eventually, masters permitted individual slaves to hire out their own time. Assisting in service as the guardians of society, as well as a police force, in New Orleans and on the remaining plantations were free black militiamen. The more integral their service became in securing the colony's residents against foreign and domestic threats, the more these men gained in individual respect and status. Thus, by 1760 a unique creole society had formed in the lower Mississippi. The slaves in this society had greater independence than their counterparts in Anglo-America, and the smaller number of free blacks within it found more opportunity. Harsh punishment and discrimination continued to exist there, to be sure, but along with such treatment existed opportunity for some and a modest amount of respect for at least a few.

Takeover of Louisiana by Spain and West Florida by England, as dictated by the 1763 Treaty of Paris, altered this arrangement at least in degree. Both new rulers had intentions of trying again to create a staple-producing economy—and they did bring in more settlers and slaves and increased indigo production in particular—but both had their hands full simply maintaining order in their new colonies, so society and the economy remained fluid. The black militia helped authorities put down a revolt by unhappy French planters in 1769 and then stood more strongly than ever as a force to quell unrest in the colony. This prompted Spanish authorities to keep paths to freedom open for Louisiana blacks, who might augment their small number of supporters. It was during the period of Spanish control that New Orleans's population of free blacks increased in number and advanced socially and economically. For the remainder of the colonial period mostly creole blacks, speaking a unique French-African language, worked hard in the lower Mississippi heat, above all, but they also played and mixed in New Orleans and up and down the great river.

Thus, what had begun as a slave society had become a society with slaves, where work in particular and life in general was difficult for the vast majority of blacks who remained in slavery, but where an openness in marketing and movement and a level of white-black-red interaction not known elsewhere—one even including opportunity for blacks in a limited sense—prevailed through the rest of the colonial period. Not until planters began growing sugar there after 1795 would conditions change significantly for African Americans in the lower Mississippi Valley. By that time, New Orleans had the foundations of a unique creole society in its sizable free-black population. Those who remained in slavery, and the many more who followed formed the backbone of a workforce that would turn nineteenth-century Louisiana into a land of commercial agriculture based on sugar cane.

New England and the Middle Colonies

After considering black slavery from the Chesapeake to East Florida and in Louisiana, one tends to think of the much smaller number of blacks in New England and the Middle Colonies as relatively insignificant. After all, in 1770 there were barely 50,000 individuals of African descent north of Maryland, not quite 4.5 percent of the total population, whereas in the same year from Maryland southward some 400,000 blacks made up 40 percent of the total number of persons. Blacks were only 2.5 percent of the New England population and 6.5 percent of the people in the Middle Colonies on the eve of the American Revolution.

But figures alone fail to give an accurate picture of the importance of slavery to the economy of the area north of the Chesapeake and especially to particular regions of the area. In some of the most agriculturally productive rural areas of Connecticut, Long Island, the lower Hudson River valley, and southern Pennsylvania blacks made up as much as half the workforce in the de-

cades after the middle of the eighteenth century. Certain industries—ironworking in Pennsylvania or tanning in New York, for
instance—relied heavily on slave labor, and slaves worked in the
carrying trade and around shipyards in Rhode Island and Massachusetts. In New England, blacks were concentrated near coastal
urban centers and along river systems, with a particularly heavy
concentration in Rhode Island. The Middle Colonies had black urban populations of considerable size, where they moved from
serving the gentry to assisting tradesmen. Thus, in certain areas
the black population was a significant proportion of the total and
critical to the regional economy. In these places blacks did not live
in isolation from others of African descent and the demands and
customs of whites did not totally dominate their lives.

In addition to sheer numbers of people involved, slavery in
New England and the Middle Colonies was different in other obvious ways from the institution found on the mainland from the
Chesapeake southward. Plantations never formed from Pennsylvania northward. If the typical southern African American after 1750
lived and worked with a fair-sized group of other slaves on a large
tobacco or rice plantation, the typical northern slave lived alone or
with one or two others slaves, perhaps in a dwelling with the family of the owner, and worked on a small farm, in a small industry,
as a domestic, or at a trade in an urban area. The origin of most
northern slaves was different, too. Before about 1740 it was rare
for captives to arrive in a northern port immediately after the voyage from Africa. Most of the early imports were Atlantic creoles
who came from the West Indies or one of the southern mainland
colonies. Only between 1740 and 1770 was there direct importation of men and women from Africa into northern markets, and
even then their numbers never approached those in the plantation
colonies.

Reasons for the considerable differences of slavery in the
northern colonies have to do with the region's economy. New England and the Middle Colonies never devoted most of their resources to production of a major staple for export. There was simply not one in demand that they could produce. Instead, over time,
northerners became efficient at a variety of tasks that, when com-

bined, brought them the export credits they needed to keep in check their balance of trade. These tasks included grain and live-stock farming, whaling and fishing, and the carrying trade. None of these tasks involved the same economy of scale that southern planters exercised. Even those northerners producing food for ex-port did so efficiently on small farms. There were exceptions, of course, but most producers relied on their own and their families' labor, and they tended not to gain the extraordinary wealth that would enable them to buy many laborers and considerably expand operations.

Why, then, did settlers of the northern colonies get involved with black slavery in the first place, even in the relatively small numbers they did, and why did northerners continue to purchase slaves all the way to the eve of the Revolution? The answer to the first question has to do largely with their early and extensive par-ticipation in the carrying trade, and to the second with their need for labor and its availability. Both show how much their decisions and actions were bound up in the Atlantic economy in which they operated.

Dutch colonists rather than the English were the first to import slaves north of Maryland. The Dutch West India Company, which carried out settlement of New Netherland along the Hudson River, established posts there in the mid-1620s for participation in the fur trade. The company may have desired development of a stable, ag-riculture producing colony along the lower Hudson as well, but it refused to invest enough to prompt a sufficient number of coloniz-ers from the Netherlands to settle there. Instead, it brought in workers before farmers. Always eager to introduce chattel slavery to New World colonies so it could enhance its brisk carrying trade in slaves, the company began in 1626 to import blacks into its own mainland colony. Most of these people had African, Portuguese, or Dutch names and came from Curaçao in the Dutch West Indies or from the holds of Spanish ships, removed from these by pirates. In addition to building roads and forts and raising food for the Dutch garrison in New Amsterdam, the slaves cleared lands along the Hudson. By mid-century enough slaves had entered the colony and rendered enough land arable to alter the nature of New Netherland. Only then did Dutch colonists arrive intending to settle permanently, using the cleared lands for growing grain and keeping livestock. Farming replaced fur trading as the principal colonial activity. A fair number of the earliest slaves, largely Atlantic creoles, used their knowledge of the Dutch Atlantic mercantile world to their advantage: many gained baptism in the Dutch Reformed Church (believing church membership might help in their quest for freedom), established families, accumulated property, and pushed for their rights under law. Some obtained their freedom from the company and gained title to farmlands on lower Manhattan Island. Thus, the 1640s found free-black men and women trading at a weekly market and frolicking in taverns with Indians, Dutch, and Walloons, resulting in a melding of cultures.

But access to freedom closed quickly to persons of even partial African ancestry in New Netherland. Dutch authorities used the promise of the availability of slaves as a lure to attract more white farmers, settlers who would need labor—and who recognized the economics of the situation. In the 1640s a "seasoned" slave from the West Indies cost about the same as the wages, provisions, and lodging for a free worker for a single year. Thus, from coastal African ports newly opened to Dutch shipping and from older, established markets in the Caribbean came many more slaves. The Dutch Reformed Church helped move along acceptance of slavery in the colony by halting slave baptism and curtailing emancipation there. By the 1660s one in eight citizens of New Netherland owned slaves and persons of African descent made up a quarter of the colony's population.

The takeover of New Netherland by the English in 1664 did not alter the status of slaves there. If the new colonial government took a while to express itself on the prescribed status of Africans in bondage and the future of slavery in the colony, white colonists already knew what they wanted and moved faster to effect it. They continued to seek enslaved men and women to do the variety of tasks needed in the growing urban port on lower Manhattan and to work the farms that were spreading along the lower Hudson. Eventually, English laws in New York recognized slavery as a legal institution at the same time they placed restrictions on white servitude. As they did, demand for slaves increased. The slave trade from the islands and other colonies flourished—if only in imports of a few at a time—and New York's black population grew. By 1700 the colony had 2,000 slaves in a total population of about 19,000 and by 1750 the number of those enslaved had grown to 10,000 out of 75,000 total—more than any other mainland colony north of the Chesapeake. Many of these Africans lived in the vicinity of New York City, where 43 percent of whites in a rough 1703 census owned one or two slaves. Because of their use as domestics in the city, black women outnumbered black men among this slave population.

New York was not the only Middle Colony to which the Dutch West India Company brought slaves. Its ships carried blacks in small lots to settlements along the Delaware River after 1639 and to the west bank of the Hudson that became part of New Jersey in 1664. English proprietors of New Jersey eventually authorized slavery and encouraged the importation of slaves by offering prospective settlers up to sixty acres for each slave they brought to the colony. By the end of the century, Perth Amboy became one of the main ports of entry for northern slaves.

There were slaves in Pennsylvania, too, even before there were Quakers. A handful of farmers owned and worked blacks along the Delaware River as early as the 1660s, and the arrival of English, Irish, and Welsh with William Penn in 1682 did not change that. The English slave trade was just picking up to meet the growing mainland demand as Penn and those joining him in his "holy experiment" settled along the Delaware's western bank, and the new migrants took advantage of the situation. While still living in temporary housing, in 1684, Philadelphia Quakers snapped up 150 Africans off a slaver to work clearing trees and erecting houses. Penn himself preferred black slaves to white servants "for then," he reasoned, "a man has them while they live"; he owned and worked about a dozen black men and women on his estate. Philadelphia carriers in the Caribbean trade soon were bringing slaves as part of return cargos. By 1700 one Philadelphia family in fifteen owned slaves. Pennsylvania laws began treating slaves differently than servants early in the eighteenth century, and in 1726 the colonial legislature codified the laws governing slavery and free blacks. While these laws were "less rigorous than legislation regulating the activities of slaves in most other colonies," write Gary B. Nash and Jean R. Soderlund in *Freedom by Degrees: Emancipation in Pennsylvania and Its Aftermath* (1991), they formalized a caste system on the basis of skin shade." Through the first two-thirds of the eighteenth century, as Pennsylvania more clearly became a major port city and cosmopolitan center distinguished from its rural hinterland, so did slavery take urban and rural forms. Bonded black workers were more important in Philadelphia's early years, as they helped build the city, labored in and around the bustling port facilities as well as on ships, and worked for the city's artisans, merchants, and professionals. Other slaves grew increasingly important as agricultural workers on the farmlands of southeastern Pennsylvania after 1750.

New England had fewer African Americans than any other region of the mainland colonies. Black slaves had been in the region since before 1640, however, and in some places they were important elements of the economy and society. Most black men and women came there because of coastal New England's interdependence with the West Indies and its heavy participation in the Caribbean trade. Ships arriving in New England ports from the British West Indies often carried half a dozen slaves. Some were "refuse" slaves (the infirm or ailing, who could not be sold profitably in the island markets), exiled offenders of various sorts, or those purchased to work the voyage northward and then sold upon its termination. More New England slave imports were African by birth than this implies, however. A slaver sometimes used the Caribbean islands as way stations, selling some of its captives and then passing on to New England with a partial load of Caribbean produce and the remainder of its slaves. New England masters seemed to care less than Tidewater planters about receiving the "bad lot" of slaves from the Caribbean, just as they showed less concern for place of origin of the Africans they purchased. They believed they could train blacks individually and instill proper Yankee traits in even the most reluctant slave. Thus, although most ships carrying slaves to the region through the first third of the eighteenth century came from the West Indies, a portion of the slaves imported into New England once had a home in Africa.

After about 1740, northern slavery took on a much greater African cast. In a fashion similar to what happened regarding the decline of servants in the late-seventeenth-century Chesapeake, increasing opportunities in Europe and occasional blocking of European shipping lanes by warfare cut the immigration of white laborers to the northern colonies, prompting the labor-hungry Yankees to purchase slaves. Demand was great enough to entice whole shiploads from Africa, so the new entrants were not predominantly Atlantic creoles, as before, but men and women fresh from the Atlantic crossing and not long out of a West-African society. This change in the nature of the slave trade would affect everything from the ability of black men and women to build families and conduct orderly domestic lives to the marked infusion of African elements in northern African-American culture and the waning of the region's free-black population.

Regardless of where the slaves came from, the distribution of African Americans in the northern colonies was uneven. This was particularly true in New England, where, because of the ties of slave imports to colonial shipping, major ports held concentrations of African Americans. In 1754 three quarters of Massachusetts's black population of 2,700 lived in coastal towns in only three counties. At the same time, blacks made up good portions of the population of Rhode Island's Narragansett ports—20 percent of Newport, 30 percent of South Kingston, and 40 percent of Charlestown.

Slavery in northern towns and cities from Salem to Philadelphia was different from most other forms of slavery in the colonies. Gary B. Nash's "Slaves and Slaveowners in Colonial Philadelphia" in his *Race, Class, and Politics: Essays on American Colonial and Revolutionary Society* (1986) provides a picture of who owned slaves in a northern colonial city and what the slaves did. In 1767 most Philadelphia masters (521) owned only one or two slaves (905 total). For many owners the bondspeople were a symbol of status. Merchants and shopkeepers owned one-third of the slaves, professionals owned 10 percent, innkeepers or tavern owners about 5 percent, and widows and "gentlemen" another 5 percent. Nearly all slaves from this last group were household servants. Artisans and craftsmen or men involved in maritime ventures owned the other half of the city's slaves. Bakers, ropemakers, brewers, millers, shipwrights, blockmakers, sailmakers, goldsmiths, and ferrymen also used slaves in their work. A surprising number of ship captains and mariners (10 percent of all owners) purchased slaves with the intention of having them work on board ship as sailors.

None of this should give the impression that northern slavery was entirely, or even primarily, an urban experience. As elsewhere, the vast majority of northern blacks lived and worked in the countryside. Most were agricultural workers on small or middle-sized farms, with the heaviest concentrations in Connecticut and Rhode Island, on Long Island, and in northern New Jersey. These farms raised provisions and draft animals primarily for export to the West Indies. Even here, white laborers made up a good part of the workers on seasonal crops. Through most of the year, African Americans worked around the masters' houses and stables. As in the cities, owning a slave was a mark of wealth and status.

Because African Americans were in much smaller proportion to the total northern population, control of slaves in most locales was less of a problem than it was in the southern colonies. Absence of laws regulating slavery did not reflect this so much as did lax enforcement of those already on the books. Slave codes in New England were probably the least stringent of all. There, slaves walked a fine line between being persons with certain rights on the one hand, and being pieces of property on the other. The result was ambivalence in colonial statutes. Massachusetts taxed slaves as persons *and* as property; Connecticut and Rhode Island taxed them as they did livestock. New England slaves could own, transfer, and inherit property at the same time their masters could sell and bequeath them. Puritan masters were especially inconsistent in dealings with their bondspeople. To them the slave was part of the family, so Massachusetts Puritans saw to it that their slaves had "all the liberties and Christian usages which the law of God, established in Israel concerning such persons, doth normally require." However, Puritans regarded persons of African descent in Biblical terms, too, which meant, in the words of Cotton Mather, they were "miserable children of Adam and Noah." Strict in their response to all sexual matters, Puritans held particular abhorrence of miscegenation. The Massachusetts law banishing—usually to the West Indies—blacks guilty of fornication with whites was the most severe of such laws in any continental colony.

The increase in the number of slaves with a greater African presence alarmed some northerners by the mid-eighteenth century, prompting some colonies to tighten laws regarding manumission and slave control. In the Middle Colonies, where larger numbers of African Americans tended to congregate in cities, authorities had more difficulty controlling slave populations. Curfews and laws forbidding the serving of alcohol to blacks were common; punishments for those who broke these laws were severe. New York had the most difficulty of any northern city. It experienced panics over slave conspiracies in 1712 and 1741. The latter led to the arrest of 54 blacks and execution of 31 of them.

NYC slave conspiracies

In spite of the body of legislation that governed northern slaves, their lives were not so proscribed as those of slaves in southern colonies. It was difficult in any town or city where slaves worked as deliverymen, errand runners, or hired artisans to restrain their movement and assembly. It was not so much easier in the countryside, where slaves found time to work for themselves and to participate in petty trade at crossroads and in town markets. So urban authorities gradually grew tolerant of curfew violations and gatherings of African Americans that did not appear to presage trouble. Still, lack of enforcement did not reduce the total effect of the northern slave codes. "They cast a shadow everywhere," writes Edgar J. McManus in *Black Bondage in the North* (1973), "reminding slaves they were a caste apart, living on sufferance in a system amply geared for their destruction."

Beyond jurisdiction of the slave codes was a body of African Americans in the North who were free. Numbers of free blacks in the northern colonies were small, on par with the numbers of free blacks in the southern colonies. In material ways, the lives of these free people were not considerably better than those of the slaves in

Free blacks in N.

their midst. In some ways the very presence of slavery hindered free blacks. Slaves who rose to responsible positions under their masters' employ posed no threat to white society, but free blacks who achieved important positions by themselves did. So whites took care to see that northern free black persons remained in menial jobs. Free black shopkeepers had difficulty getting credit. Free black artisans were not always welcome in shipyards or at building sites. For those who were destitute life was more difficult in freedom than in slavery. In Boston in 1742 there were 110 free blacks in the almshouse and 36 in the workhouse, this out of the city's total black population, slave and free, of only 1,500. If other immigrants to the mainland received rewards for hard work, thrift, and steady movement toward assimilation, Africans in colonial America suffered for such behavior at the hands of a white population that saw African-American advancement as a serious threat to the established order.

Slavery and Racial Prejudice

Consideration of the origins of slavery in the English mainland colonies leads to questions about the relationship between slavery and racial prejudice. Was English racial prejudice against black Africans the main reason that slavery began? Or did the enslavement of Africans come first for economic reasons, the condition of slavery then leading to racial prejudice against those enslaved?

Investigation to answer these questions has centered on the Chesapeake, where English mainland colonists made the first legal commitment to black slavery and first practiced slavery on a large scale. The major problem investigators encounter has to do with the lack of acceptable evidence showing clear trends for the period before 1660. Good historians have examined existing evidence and concluded that English landowners treated their black and white servants similarly. Others equally good have used the same evidence to find that the early English settlers had strong feelings of racial prejudice against Africans, concluding that this racism was the basis for the eventual development of black slavery as a major economic and social institution in the colonies. One historian, Winthrop D. Jordan, offers a middle ground in *White Over Black: American Attitudes Toward the Negro, 1550–1812* (1968). Enslaving blacks was an "unthinking decision," according to Jordan. "Slavery and 'prejudice' may have been equally cause and effect, continuously reacting upon each other, dynamically joining hands to hustle the Negro down the road to complete degradation." But not everyone has since agreed with this part of Jordan's book, and the issue remains unresolved.

The intellectual and emotional atmosphere surrounding the early English settlers of the Chesapeake had a considerable effect on the colonists' attitudes and thus bears on questions about the relationship between racial prejudice and the origin of slavery in Virginia and Maryland. For matters concerning race, the first colonists carried strong emotions—less so about Africans than about Indians. Although armed before arrival with ambivalent feelings about the persons they found living in the New World, once settlers craved the Native Americans' land, a hostile-savage-without-civilization image gained acceptance. Colonists assuaged their guilt over taking these lands by thinking of Indians as brutish, uncultured, areligious, nearer to beasts than to human beings. They witnessed Native Americans being violent in the futile—though wholly justifiable—defense of their lands, and this only reinforced English conceptions. By the 1620s, following massacres of encroaching settlers by local Indians, Virginians were describing Native Americans as "by nature slothfull and idle, vitious, melancholy, slovenly, of bad conditions, lyers, of small memory, of no constancy or trust . . . , never looking what dangers may happen afterwards, less capable then children of sixe or seven years old, and less apt and ingenious." Such ideas of a people physically different from the English developed rapidly throughout the mainland colonies.

English ideas about Africans affected settlers' thoughts and actions, too. Before confronting Africans in America, most English already had negative preconceptions of blackness and black people. In the English world, black signified things dark, sinister, evil and foul, whereas white suggested purity and virtue. Most Africans the English encountered were not just darker than they, as were Mediterranean people, but many were among the darkest

[margin handwritten note: stronger prejudice against Nat. Am.]

people in the world, odd-looking individuals with customs the English found strange. They were not only un-Christian but seemingly without religion to an English mentality that found its basis on earth and beyond in Christianity. And Africans were apparently savage folk who dressed in few clothes, ate strange foods without utensils, and lived among odd and ferocious beasts. So no matter where African immigrants arrived on the mainland, they stepped into a narrowly defined world charged with strong feeling toward themselves and others of color, namely those native to the land.

But was it primarily this racial prejudice that led English settlers to adopt slavery as the permanent condition for African immigrants to the mainland? More and more students of the period believe not. They believe, instead (and as argued in earlier portions of this chapter), that the colonists' failure to find elsewhere in North America the long-term, stable labor force they needed to fulfill their economic ambitions, coupled with the availability of large numbers of Africans at inexpensive prices, brought the colonists to opt for black slavery—as other Europeans in the New World had done not so long before. Racial prejudice would help the English justify enslaving Africans some time later when they needed to do so, just as it helped them rationalize taking land from Native Americans, but perceived economic necessity was more the reason for the turn to black slavery.

And once slavery became a permanent condition for Africans in America, its effect on strengthening the existing racial prejudice was considerable. One racial group could hardly keep another in bondage without developing negative feelings about those they had forcibly enslaved. When it proved necessary to punish slaves beyond the limits English law allowed—as when Robert "King" Carter could get an order from the Lancaster County (Virginia) court, as he did in March 1707, to cut off the toes of "two incorrigible negroes of his named Bambarra Harry and Dinah . . . for the better reclaiming the said negroes and deterring others from ill practices"—justification came in labelling the persons of African descent different from the white English. "It was not necessary to extend the rights of Englishmen to Africans," writes Edmund Morgan, "because Africans were 'a brutish sort of people.' And because they were 'brutish' it was necessary 'or at least convenient' to kill or maim them in order to make them work."

Across all classes of white colonial society, negative feelings toward Africans and African Americans grew with their increased enslavement. The very existence of black slavery provided a sense of separateness and unity to whites of gentry, middling, or commoner classes. It gave whites a common identity and then intensified their attitudes toward one of the other major identifiable groups on the mainland. The result within a few generations was a white society manifesting early forms of racial prejudice that would soon intensify and last for centuries, and a black population caught in a labor system that must necessarily keep them at the bottom of America's economy and society. Gary B. Nash summarizes African Americans' plight in *Red, White, and Black: The Peoples of Early America*, fourth edition (2000):

Irrevocably caught in the web of perpetual servitude, the slave had little opportunity to prove the white stereotype wrong. Socially and legally defined as less than humans, African-Americans became a truly servile, ignoble, degraded people in the eyes of the Europeans. This was used as further reason to keep them in slavery, for it was argued that they were worth nothing better and were incapable of occupying any higher role. In the long evolution of racial attitudes in America, nothing was of greater importance than the enslavement of Africans.

CHAPTER THREE

African-American Culture

Frederick Douglass, the gifted African American who escaped from slavery in 1838 and became one of the country's leading abolitionists, was born in Talbot County, Maryland, in 1818. Many know of Douglass and the difficulties he faced as a slave from *Narrative of the Life of Frederick Douglass, an American Slave*, which he wrote in 1845 to further the abolitionist cause. Much of the book concerns his relationship with white masters and mistresses. There is little in the narrative about his family or the black community in which he lived.

In the late 1970s, Dickson J. Preston began investigating Douglass's early life to determine how much of the *Narrative* he could verify with independent evidence. In *Young Frederick Douglass: The Maryland Years* (1980), Preston shows that Douglass

had not sprung full-grown out of nowhere, as his contemporaries seemed to think; his black ancestors, for a century or more before his birth, had been a strong and closely knit kin group with family pride and traditions that were handed on to him by his part-Indian grand mother, Betsey Bailey. His roots were anchored deeply in the earliest American experience.

Douglass's family was part of a black subculture of Maryland's Eastern Shore, itself a variant of a greater Chesapeake African-American culture. Both were set into the broader unity of black culture in America and of blacks around the Atlantic basin. Both were tied closely to the Euro-American culture of whites, among whom African Americans lived, worked, worshiped, and played. Douglass was not unique among mainland North American blacks in his family origins or cultural surroundings. Throughout the mainland for several generations before Douglass was born, African Americans had been living in families and participating in different but related subcultures that were stable products of a long evolution in the colonies—part of a broader cultural mixing and melding occurring up and down the Atlantic side of the Americas and at Atlantic ports in Africa and Europe. The black American subcultures that appeared long before Douglass's birth were the result of interactions among Africans, Native Americans, and Europeans. What emerged were patterns of behavior and social customs that were distinctly African American.

African-American culture did indeed come to absorb many elements from the cultures of Europeans and Indians. But any idea that acculturation in colonial America moved in a single direction—from Anglo-Americans to African Americans or Native Americans without spreading in reverse—is one that treats culture narrowly and fails to hold up to careful examination of the evidence. Not until the last few years have historians begun to realize just how much African Americans have influenced important aspects of Euro-American culture. In *The World They Made Together,* Sobel shows the extent of the interdependence of Anglo-Virginian and Afro-Virginian subcultures in colonial times. The two groups from different preindustrial worlds shared many of the same values and held many of the same ideas—especially in their thoughts of time, space, world view, causality, family ties, and death and the afterlife. In this environment, Africans had considerable influence in the shaping of Euro-American culture. More recently, William Piersen, in *Black Legacy: America's Hidden Heritage* (1993), has argued that the colonial foundation for such cultural interdependence persisted in the southern states in particular. "The evidence is compelling," he writes, that white southerners adopted much from the culture of blacks who raised their children and who lived alongside them. In speech patterns, in traditions of manners and honor, in the region's ways of cooking, work habits, religious styles, in southern 'superstitious beliefs,' holiday celebrations, and music, the white American South developed a distinctive and African-American way of life.

That until recently historians were unaware of this widespread sharing of values, habits, and ways of life between blacks and whites is largely a factor of their sources. White people, who kept most of the records on which historians must rely, simply failed to realize how much black thoughts and values changed their own ways of doing things and looking at the world.

Africans in America

Not all persons of African descent who arrived on slave ships in colonial America were "raw Africans"—persons fresh out of West-African farming or herding communities for whom coming into contact with whites on an American farm or plantation was a shocking experience. As Berlin shows in *Many Thousands Gone,* many of the earliest slaves in mainland American locales were Atlantic creoles, products of the long-standing commercial world of the Atlantic rim of four continents, people familiar with European languages, religions, and ways of living. Some of these individuals used their linguistic facility and cultural knowledge to their advantage. Fitting into the patterns of life in British mainland North America was not easy for them, but it was easier for them than it would be for the Africans who would follow.

And Africans followed in abundance. Atlantic creoles were nowhere in great numbers. Neither were they long in the majority among mainland slaves. At different times in different places, but certainly widespread by the time slavery began growing rapidly in a number of mainland regions after the early decades of the eighteenth century, "outlandish" Africans made up the overwhelming majority on the slave vessels arriving in South Carolina, Virginia, New York, or Louisiana. For them, nothing would be easy.

Africans went through considerable change in the process of becoming African Americans. Slaves just arriving after the grueling Atlantic crossing were stepping into completely new physical, social, and cultural settings. Tired, sore, probably sick and poorly nourished, likely separated quickly from other Africans they had come to know on the voyage, they must have been bewildered and frightened of what was to come. Over a short time they had been forcibly detached from the kinship networks that had been their social, economic, and psychological underpinnings in Africa. Never would they be more alone. Yet by 1770, most African Americans throughout the mainland colonies were living in families with extended ties of kinship in greater black communities, and they were practicing a culture of their own. The development of African-American families, communities, and a common culture took place during the first two-thirds of the eighteenth century in the English mainland colonies. These activities set the basis for black life in America from that time forward.

New African culture arising

Slaves' early experiences were among the most difficult they faced once in America. Simply getting by in the harsh circumstances of their new surroundings was a tall order, and adaptation came but slowly. To help them cope and build new lives, the uprooted Africans tended to cling to their own cultural traditions and ways of doing things. These included a sense of personal identity; a language; a worldview that usually involved a religion; ideas of time and space, family life, and work; social customs; historical traditions; and a good bit of general know-how. Because slaves came from such a broad range of West and West Central Africa, as a group they brought with them a variety of languages, customs, and traditions. So individually they were not able simply to join with others and practice group survival on the basis of a common heritage. However, most Africans held in common enough ideas that they could mingle certain aspects of their respective cultures. For many this process seems to have begun soon after capture in Africa or aboard a ship. Once they arrived in the English colonies they continued this amalgamation even as they began applying "old ways" to new circumstances. This process of clinging to and adapting certain of their traditional customs while borrowing heavily from Anglo-American and Native-American ways would result, over time, in the development of a hybrid African-American culture.

But just how *African* was it? This is a question that has perplexed historians and anthropologists at least since E. Franklin
Frazier expressed doubts about the persistence of African cultural
elements in America in *The Negro Family in the United States* in
1939. Two years later Melville J. Herskovits countered by drawing
attention to New World black culture's African nature in *The Myth
of the Negro Past*. The disagreement flared again in the 1990s,
fanned by two well-received books. John Thornton, in *Africa and
Africans in the Making of the Atlantic World, 1400–1800* (1992,
2nd ed., 1997), argues that the Atlantic slave trade was not so random as widely thought, but instead brought persons of like
ethnicity to particular New World regions, even to particular plantations in these regions, where they formed "a base from which
many elements of African culture could be shared, continued, and
developed in America." Gwendolyn Midlo Hall agrees in *Africans
in Colonial Louisiana: The Development of Afro-Creole Culture in
the Eighteenth Century* (1992), arguing that persons from Senegambia, and from the Bambara group in particular, shaped early
black culture in colonial Louisiana. Still more recently, Michael A.
Gomez has brought together a wider variety of data to make the
same broad argument on the scale of all British mainland North
America in *Exchanging Our Country Marks: The Transformation
of African Identities in the Colonial and Antebellum South* (1998).

The earlier of these 1990s studies set off exchanges on the
Internet and in print, questioning ethnic identification, then and
now, and raising valid issues about determining Africanisms in
American culture. Some were quick to argue that Africans did not
identify themselves with large ethnic groupings the way Europeans did. It was the white slave traders and the men and women
who owned slaves in the Americas who spoke of Africans in ethnic terms—a person was a "Bambara" or an "Ibo" in the eyes of
the enslaver rather than the enslaved. Transmitting their ethnicity
to the New World or uniting with others of some broad grouping
in America to maintain their cultural ways was not necessarily a
high priority of most enslaved men and women from Africa. And
although slaves who ended up in certain parts of America tended
to come from particular regions of West or West Central Africa at
certain times, there *was* a randomizing tendency in the Atlantic

trade—the ports on both sides of the ocean were funnels, bringing together persons with different languages and beliefs from broad hinterlands on the African side and dispersing them in reverse fashion from ports on the American side. The experience of enslavement, separation from kin, and movement over thousands of miles uprooted African men, women, and children from their particular cultural ways, and forces in the Americas worked against survival of many particular (and purely) African traits. "Africans in Virginia found themselves purchased in tiny lots, dispersed onto widely scattered estates, resident on small plantations, soon surrounded by a majority of native-born slaves, and brought into close contact with whites," writes Philip D. Morgan in "The Cultural Implications of the Atlantic Slave Trade: African Regional Origins, American Destinations and New World Developments," in *Routes to Slavery.* "All of this was not conducive to the reconstitution of an African ethnic identity."

Of course, there was a broad African basis for the African-American culture that would emerge by the end of the colonial period, but what resulted was a hybrid sort of cultural creation—one befitting the heterogeneous Atlantic world that involved the mixing of persons from four continents. As with all thoughts of culture change and formation around the Atlantic rim in the seventeenth and eighteenth centuries—whether along the Gambia River in West Africa or inland from the Cape of Good Hope at Africa's southern tip or in the Atlantic hinterlands of northeastern Brazil or on the islands of the Caribbean—when considering African-American culture, Morgan continues, "the emphasis should be on heterogeneity, on fluid boundaries, on precarious and permeable zones of interaction, on hybrid societies, on mosaics of borderlands where cultures jostled and converged in combinations and permutations of dizzying complexity." In the United States the combinations involved broad African and European cultural traits, along with those of the indigenous persons the Africans and Europeans lived among.

The complexity was so dizzying, in fact, that often the tendency has been to see only how Africans acculturated and adopted European ways. But a fresh perspective is that of Sobel and Piersen, who focus on such less obvious cultural traits as ideas and ways of thinking. In this regard, Sobel does not ask "How 'African' was African-American culture?" but, instead, "How 'African' was the broader culture of colonial Virginia?" Her answer, after examining commonly held notions of time, space, world view, causality, family ties, and death and the afterlife, is "more than we might think."

Demography, Community, and Culture

Not all newly arrived Africans went through a process of culture formation in similar fashion or at the same time and pace. For individuals the rate of acculturation varied according to a combination of factors including their local circumstances, the strength of their particular African cultural tradition, and their personal willingness to change. For groups the process varied more widely because individual survival did not require formation of a group culture. However, a single, and simple, principle dominates consideration of the development of African-American culture in colonial America. It is that blacks in America first had to have extensive social contacts with a substantial number of other blacks —they had to exist in black communities—before there could be real development of group values, ways, and beliefs. The conduit for passing these manifestations of culture along to subsequent generations was the black family, in which adults could teach their children ways of doing things and values considered important for survival and good living.

For more than a century of black existence in the English mainland colonies, the obstacles to African-American community development and family formation were myriad. Simple demographic configurations—the number of blacks and the relative numbers of blacks and whites in specific locations—affected African-American social relations. These numbers were determined largely by the nature of the economy and of the slave trade in any given region at any given time. In addition to sufficient numbers of African Americans within proximity with whom to interact, blacks required a certain amount of freedom to interact outside the supervision of whites.

Proximity to white colonists also affected African-American social and cultural development. Contrary to the traditional image of American slavery, in many places in colonial America blacks lived, worked, and interacted daily and fully with whites. This was true not only in New England, but as far south as urban Charleston or rural Virginia. In the latter colony, even the wealthiest masters spent hours each day with their slaves, directing, working, punishing, cajoling, teasing, arguing, relaxing, laughing, and worshiping. African slaves who had such close relationships with whites learned English, accepted Christianity, and practiced Euro-American customs—all with an African cast—more quickly than those who did not. Those living and working with larger numbers of blacks and fewer whites in more isolated conditions—on Low-Country plantations, for example, where blacks were in overwhelming majority—had more extensive social relations among themselves and better retained their African customs. For them, naturally, acculturation toward an Anglo-American "norm" was slower and less complete.

Demographic configurations between American slaves born in Africa (and hereafter referred to simply as *Africans*) and those of African descent born in the New World and partly acculturated (the true African Americans or American *creoles*) also were important for community development and cultural change. Where slave imports from Africa were heavy over several years and a good proportion of the black population comprised slaves born in Africa, the Africans tended to remain separate, keep more to themselves, and retain more of their African ways. Where the trade was light or involved a majority of Atlantic creoles or "seasoned" slaves from the Caribbean, there was more unity among the partly acculturated black population and less adherence to undadulterated African customs.

Demographics and the slave trade also played a role in the ability of black populations to grow by natural increase and to maintain stable families. As long as the Atlantic trade was bringing large numbers of slaves every year to a particular region of the mainland, black men continued to outnumber black women there. Knowing they could more cheaply purchase and train a male adult laborer from Africa than to rear one, owners in these regions often did little to encourage marriage, procreation, and family life among their slaves. They worked women as hard as they did men and allowed minimal time off for bearing or rearing children. Also, slaves suffered in the new disease environment and, with replacements coming so cheaply, many owners cared little for the health of their slaves. So when the slave trade was heavy, slave mortality rates were high and birth rates low. Under such circumstances a slave society could not replace its numbers naturally. And the slave trade continued for some time to bring in twice as many men as women from across the Atlantic. With more black men than black women present and with interracial marriage illegal, it was impossible for most slaves to achieve a normal family life. Through the first half-century of mainland settlement, because of unequal sex ratios and high death rates, few males, black or white, were able to marry. When the slave trade from Africa declined, slave populations began increasing their numbers through natural means and sex ratios became more balanced. Only then could families provide the foundation of slave communities.

Different circumstances for living and working affected community development, too. Slaves living on isolated plantations that functioned as self-contained production units had less contact with Anglo-American culture than such persons on small farms growing provisions for local markets. Plantation slaves working under the task system had more control of their lives than those working in gangs under more watchful eyes, and this degree of autonomy enabled them to hold onto more of their African culture. Over time, in certain regions, plantation life grew settled and slaves enjoyed mobility among plantations. Once this happened, even those African-American communities centered on one plantation could broaden to include others in the vicinity.

Urban slaves generally enjoyed greater autonomy than their rural counterparts, but they also lived more closely with whites. Some were permitted to attain skills, live on their own, and hire their own time. In the urban atmosphere, where work requirements led to laxness in enforcing controls, black men and women mingled with white men and women at work and play. For them acculturation—or, actually, cultural borrowing, in both directions—took place regularly. James Sidbury in *Ploughshares into Swords: Race, Rebellion, and Identity in Gabriel's Virginia, 1730–1810* (1997) shows that in the rapidly growing, more open, urban Chesapeake settings—late-eighteenth-century Richmond is his example—black perceptions of individual and community identity involved not simply race and status in bondage, but gender, skill, religion, and current ideologies. The worlds of black and white, enslaved and free, woman and man in the urban Chesapeake overlapped and grew snarled. In the welter of cross-cutting influences, personal and community identities came to be remarkably complex.

And, finally, some groups of blacks found themselves in situations that offered them a unique existence that affected their acculturation. A group with as much autonomy as urban blacks, or perhaps more of it still, was that of African Americans working as boatmen and seamen. Not many did so through the first third of the eighteenth century, but from the 1740s on through Revolutionary times and beyond blacks, many of them slaves, worked the lighters and river craft that carried goods in the colonial economy and served on civilian and military ships at sea. Some of these individuals had an Atlantic creole heritage. Most of them were accustomed to the ways of whites, but also conscious and proud of their own traditions and ways, which they maintained and passed on to those around them.

Thus, as different levels of slave importing (from the West Indies and from Africa) and different systems of slavery developed at various times in the separate regions of the North American mainland, and as colonial American culture matured generally, variant forms of African-American culture grew and matured. And within the separate African-American cultures of each region, one could make obvious and subtle distinctions in different localities and at various times.

For the first seventy-five years of settlement in Virginia and Maryland, planters made distinctions more on the basis of class than race. Chesapeake blacks, mostly Atlantic creoles, suffered the same hardships as white servants. Some of each group who lived long enough attained freedom and ownership of land. Blacks interacted with whites of their class in work, play, and sex. But a more open racial society did not last. The importation of large

beginning: class distinctions instead of race

numbers of Africans after 1680 altered any rapid acculturation. By 1710 three-quarters of Chesapeake blacks were Africans, mostly men. The sexual imbalance made opportunities for black family life difficult and cut birth rates. Furthermore, Virginia planters often sent new arrivals to the piedmont frontier, where they lived isolated from the tidewater area and most creoles. The smaller number of creoles remained closer to their masters, working as domestic servants and skilled artisans, freer to travel and more comfortable in an Anglo-American culture. Thus, through the 1740s Virginia and Maryland had distinct African and creole slave societies.

But whatever potential there was in the Chesapeake for a long-term African-creole split did not last. Allan Kulikoff explains why in *Tobacco and Slaves: The Development of Southern Culture in the Chesapeake, 1680–1800* (1986). In response to the growing number of blacks, planters in the region forged a unity with lower-class whites. They lumped all blacks together, stifling creole opportunities. Then, beginning in the 1740s, the slave trade from Africa declined and a long period of black natural increase ensued. The population grew with a more balanced sex ratio and African-American creoles—blacks born in America—soon predominated. At the same time, planters brought more slaves together on larger plantations and turned over some areas to wheat production, giving African-American men and women seasonal variety in their work and opportunities to learn new skills and make broader social contacts. This, and the development of a network of roads and markets, enabled slaves from different plantations to interact. Eventually, black families with links going back through generations and reaching broader slave communities existed.

Thus, in some parts of the Chesapeake by the time of the American Revolution, there existed an African-American community with its own ways of life and the time and space to practice them. Race remained a primary determinant of the behaviors of the members of that community; most individuals still did not have great latitude in their personal actions. Many blacks lived near their masters and under the watchful eyes of the white majority. In language, formal religion, and family structure they were more like Anglo Americans than were most slaves to their south. However, by this time many African Americans had close, broad kinship relations, had incorporated many African ways to their religious practice, and enjoyed their own forms of music and dance, diet and dress, and work and play—all of which made their culture identifiable and distinct.

If the African-American population of the Chesapeake drew together and became increasingly acculturated through the middle of the eighteenth century, its counterpart in the Carolina and Georgia Low Country separated into distinct parts. For the first thirty years of coastal settlement, the mostly seasoned, imported slaves worked closely with their white owners and a seemingly mutual cultural exchange transpired. This cultural exchange in early South Carolina may have been more reciprocal and symbiotic than any other in the English colonies.

But such a large-scale blending of cultures as took place in northeastern Brazil or on certain islands of the Caribbean was not long lived in the Low Country. The massive African imports that gave the Low Country its black majority after 1720 changed the direction of the evolution of African-American culture there. In Charleston a creole slave community emerged. These largely mulatto men and women lived close to whites and were more privileged and more thoroughly acculturated than their rural counterparts. Yet, in rural areas the slave trade was continually renewing a growing black community—not with Atlantic creoles or "seasoned" slaves of any sort, but with men and women straight from Africa. Individual segments of this group centered on the rice plantations; its members were independent and self-reliant. Working on the task system gave these slaves more time to socialize with fellow blacks, away from white authority. Their relative isolation and independence enabled them to hold onto more African speech patterns (thus developed a mixture of English and certain West-African languages that made up the distinctive form of English known as Gullah), religious practices, and social customs than could any other African Americans on the English mainland.

By 1770 the two groups of Low-Country blacks, urban creoles and plantation slaves, lived a more separate and different existence than many whites and blacks in the Chesapeake. A handful of recent publications—those by Kimberly Hanger and Gwendolyn Hall, Thomas Ingersoll and Daniel Usner—collectively make the argument that it was in the lower Mississippi, rather than the Chesapeake or Low Country, that the greatest cultural mingling took place over the longest time on the colonial North American mainland. Europeans had difficulty bringing order to the large region, and around the periphery of the narrow colonial control, whites, blacks, and Indians worked and played and fought with one another as they hunted, trapped, herded, and farmed in a frontier setting. Even where administrative controls were tighter, as in New Orleans, an openness existed that provided slaves greater opportunity than elsewhere and led, in Ingersoll's words, to an "interweaving of white and black lives" that produced "two communities, one creole society." It is not clear whether Indians played a greater role in the cultural mixing in the region than elsewhere, or whether French and Spanish keepers of records in the lower Mississippi were simply more aware of the indigenous presence than were the English along the eastern seaboard. But, in any event, powerful Indians and weak indigenous slaves; European soldiers and sailors, planters and peddlers; and African slaves and *libres*, traders, and maroons melded their farming, herding, and hunting techniques; shared their notions of how to build dwellings and cook foods and make music and bring others harm; blended their ways of speaking into a regional patois; and to a considerable extent mixed their DNA. The result by the end of the colonial period was a creole culture shared by many that had an easily identifiable African element at its heart.

North of Maryland, a century of importing small numbers of seasoned slaves brought about, by 1740, a stable society of African Americans largely attuned to Yankee ways. Unlike early black arrivals in other areas, northern slaves increased their numbers naturally, lived in families, often slept and ate in the house of the master, and more than anywhere else existed in a world dominated by white society. Those who worked on farms did not do so in gangs with other Africans and had considerable freedom of movement. Also, a far larger proportion of black men and women in the northern colonies lived and worked in urban areas—with all the freedoms that situation afforded.

However, between 1730 and 1770, increased importing of Africans reoriented northern blacks' tendencies away from complete Anglo assimilation. Standing apart from northern creoles, the "raw" imports reacquainted their fellow African Americans with aspects of their forgotten African heritage. As a result, northern blacks consciously included African elements in their communities and incorporated African social customs and practices—especially in ceremonies, folklore, singing, dancing, and leisure activities. The greater autonomy of northern blacks enabled them to maintain, even readopt, certain African customs even as they conformed more than any others to the white culture surrounding them. And their smaller numbers relative to the regional population made it possible for them to do so without threatening their owners in particular and white society in general.

Within each of the broad regions of colonial America's African-American society, variety existed in individual communities and in local customs and practices. Work routines, family practices, religious thought and modes of worship, circumstances of daily lives, personal interactions, and modes of resistance to bondage differed depending on a host of local circumstances. Examination of these manifestations of African-American culture provides a sense of the variety within a culture group that for most of a century historians so easily lumped together and considered as static and virtually homogenous.

The Daily Toil

If one thing dominated the daily lives of African Americans in colonial America, it was work. English traders brought persons from Africa and colonial landowners and businesspeople purchased these men and women to constitute the colonial labor force, so work they must. It was the rare master who did not want to get as much labor from his slave as he or she possibly could. But Africans received none of the rewards of their labors, so they naturally lacked incentive to work. What had to result was a form of accommodation between master and slave that got neither what he or she wanted, but turned out to be a livable situation.

Complicating accommodation was this: although colonial English master and African in bondage shared preindustrial concepts of time, relying on the sun's position, phases of the moon, crop cycles, and the seasons to measure time's passage, the two brought different ideas about the proper pace of work and the amount of daily or weekly toil one human being could expect another to perform. By the seventeenth century, English landowners and shopkeepers were becoming increasingly aware of the need to use time efficiently and to make a strict accounting of time spent at work. They expected their servants to work from dawn to dusk with breaks only for meals. Before coming to America, upper-class English had difficulty getting what they considered a decent amount of labor out of their "lazy" workers, whose more popular, traditional, quasi-medieval notions of the length of a day's work and its pace differed considerably—and probably naturally—from those of their employers. West Africans' ideas of work were more like those of English servants than those of the gentry. And Africans' approaches to work were practical for the heat of the tropics, based on patience and slow movement, and purposely allowing time to relax and be social. Where possible work was communal and involved singing and talking. It also involved resting. In many West-African societies, women did the heavier agricultural labor and worked more steadily than men throughout the year. While men did some such field work, they protected their villages and served in positions that required them to manage family and village affairs. A general and widely accepted goal for African men—especially for those of the higher classes—was not having to do great amounts of physical toil. It is not surprising, then, that English planters agreed generally with Virginia slave owner Landon Carter's assessment of it being "almost impossible to make a negro do his work well. No orders can engage it, no encouragement persuade it, nor no Punishment oblige it."

As it turned out, the appropriate amount of work for an enslaved man or woman varied with the situation and was subject to almost constant, if often tacit, negotiation. White slave owners went to great lengths to exact work from their bondspeople. Instructions to overseers were explicit on how to do so. It required vigilance and punishment. But sometimes masters or overseers could push too hard, and when they did slaves had valuable chips for the bargaining. Too much coercion often resulted in sick workers, broken tools, and purposely sloppy (thus costly) work. Sometimes the consequences were more serious. One group of South Carolina slaves, in retaliation for being worked far into the night, set fire to their master's barn, burning it and its contents to the ground.

Compromises over work took into account the varying, and seasonally determined, labor requirements of the regional staple. Some crops simply required longer and harder work than others and had different "down times." Masters and slaves came to know and live by these crop cycles, the former altering their work requirements and the latter the amount of work they would do accordingly.

"Rice was a roller coaster," writes Morgan in *Slave Counterpoint*, "tobacco a slow-moving train." By all accounts, rice was the staple grown on the English mainland that required the hardest work in the most unhealthy settings. (While sugar cane truly holds that dubious distinction, only in a few, isolated spots did black slaves grow sugar on the North American mainland during the colonial period.) The rice cycle had peaks of intense work and valleys of less-strenuous toil, however. Continual weeding with heavy hoes in the hottest and most humid summer months made June, July, and August the months during which most slaves chose to run away in the rice-growing regions. Late summer and fall brought a respite as women and men cut, dried, stacked, and threshed the grain, only to be followed by the most exacting work of all: pounding the rice in tall mortars to remove husk and film. From mid-November to mid-January and beyond, writes Edward Ball of his ancestors' South Carolina rice plantations, "a constant sound of *thrup, thrup, thrup* came from the rice barns." That *thrup-thrupping* was physically exhausting and, according to one observer in 1760, "costs every planter the lives of several slaves annually." Slaves then separated rice grains from the hulls with winnowing baskets or fans and bagged or barreled the rice for shipping. Over the latter half of the eighteenth century, such mechanical inventions as horse- and water-powered pounding mills, and such technological innovations as using tidal flows to irrigate rice, alleviated the worst of the pounding and hoeing, making the lot of Low-Country slaves somewhat easier.

Tobacco had a shorter annual cycle than rice and required less heavy work at given times, but the work on tobacco was steadier, lacking the peaks and valleys of rice growing. Tobacco is "a very tender plant," in the words of one eighteenth-century Virginian, and its workers had to pamper it with regular attention, even if the individual tasks—transplanting, debugging, "topping," "suckering," curing, and packing—were not so arduous. Further, tobacco growing lent itself to plowing and the use of carts for hauling. All of this meant, in Morgan's comparison of slaves in the Chesapeake and Low Country, that the former "were more favored" in their basic working conditions.

Indigo had a shorter growing season than either rice or tobacco, but it required nearly constant attention between April and August, hoeing and removing insects from the plants. Then, indigo had to be processed hastily in the early fall, with fairly constant stirring and beating as it fermented in vats—the stench of the fermenting plant matter attracting a great many flies. Wheat growing, which expanded greatly in the Chesapeake in the late colonial period, required less labor than the other staples, two weeks at harvest being the most intense work involved.

Of course, none of this should suggest that the cultivation and processing of those crops was all that slaves did during any given season. A list of the myriad of tasks that enslaved black men and women had to perform during the colonial period, regardless of staple grown or time of year, would fill pages. Fields needed clearing. Fences, ditches, roads, and buildings needed maintaining. Food crops needed to be grown and cattle needed tending. But through it all, a day's work was longer and harder at peak times, and those peak times did vary. If owners accepted "sunup-to-sundown" as the normal work routine in principle, the rigor of its application varied with the crop cycle.

The differences in crop requirements and growing techniques led masters and slaves to work out different ways to organize the slaves' labor. Basically, African-American men and women worked at specific, individual tasks on Low-Country plantations and in supervised gangs nearly everywhere else where they applied themselves to staple production. Rice production lent itself to the task system—men and women working in rice did not need constant supervision and their duties were simple to measure— and the task system spilled over to other forms of work. This meant that individuals were given specific daily or weekly tasks to complete, and once that they had done so, their time was their own. Of course, there was constant negotiation over what were deemed reasonable tasks for a day's or a week's work, but by late in the colonial period most accepted some common standards—a quarter acre of rice weeded (extended to a half acre once planters began using the tidal method of growing) or seven mortars full of rice pounded daily. Once they accomplished their task, slaves were free to hunt or fish or rest. Many used such time to work in their own gardens, growing corn, pumpkins, potatoes, or melons for their own consumption or sale. Masters were happy to turn over land for such use. It was cheap incentive and, along with fish and game, the vegetables added to the slaves' diet.

Tobacco was such a touchy crop, needing constant, careful attention to produce the high-quality leaves packed for export, that it lent itself to gangs of workers under close supervision. Once employed in the Virginia and Maryland tobacco fields, the supervised-gang system spread much more widely. Gang laboring was more of a sunup-to-sundown system and held little incentive for individuals to work quickly. Thus, it is more Chesapeake tobacco planters than South Carolina rice growers who complained of their slaves' penchant for inactivity. If ganged slaves worked less briskly than did tasked slaves, persons working in gangs had less free time and, therefore, much smaller garden plots for themselves. Often, it was only on Sundays when Chesapeake slaves had time to grow things of their own or to hunt, fish, or play.

Slaves seem to have worked more steadily on small farms, where they toiled alongside the master. On large plantations where overseers were involved, slaves became particularly adept at manipulating the rate at which they completed their work. If allowed to work at their own pace they appeared satisfied, but they troubled overseers who drove them hard and complained to their masters of misuse.

But no matter where they lived, a good bit of the Africans' inherent sense of time and pace persisted. No less famous a Virginia planter than George Washington knew of the dangers to plantation efficiency and production of allowing blacks to set the pace and ways of work. He instructed a new manager to be wary of

an error which I have felt no small inconvenience from; and that is, that rather than persevere in doing things right themselves, and being at the trouble of making others do the like, they will fall into the slovenly mode of executing work which is practiced by those, among whom they are. I have experienced this not only from European tradesmen, but from farmers also, who have come from England and none in a greater degree than Mr. Whiting, and one Bloxham, who preceeded him; and who, tho' perfectly acquainted with every part of a farmer's business; and peculiarly so . . . in the management and use of Oxen for the Cart . . . , finding it a little troublesome to instruct the Negros and to compel them to practice of *his* modes, he slided into theirs. . . ."

It was rare when slaves did not get evenings and Sundays to themselves. On this day they could practice their religion, rest, tend their garden plots, and go visiting. Holidays worked into the compromise, too. The biggest holiday that blacks and whites celebrated together was "Harvest Home." Traditionally both West Africans and English always had their biggest feasts once the crops were in, and the two peoples had coinciding celebrations that involved eating, drinking, and general merriment.

A common misconception is that rural slave women, in serving as house servants, had an easier time of it than their male counterparts. The opposite is closer to the truth. Many West African men and women came to the New World with entrenched ideas about women's place: it was in constant, fairly heavy labor. And African Americans seem to have joined masters in perpetuating this idea in the colonial world of work. In the plantation colonies nearly all black women worked in the fields, plowing, hoeing, and harvesting. By 1750 perhaps one slave woman in twenty from Maryland to South Carolina was strictly a house servant. The proportion was greater on larger plantations and practically nil on small farms. As more enslaved men gained opportunity to perform skilled work away from the fields, enslaved women filled in the difference.

As one might suppose, a slave woman's productive functions regularly took precedence over her reproductive ones. Pregnancy did not significantly remove a woman from her tasks in the fields and thus made the condition especially difficult to endure. A study from Antebellum plantations shows pregnant women, as late as between one and four weeks prior to giving birth, picking three-quarters the amount of cotton picked by nonpregnant women, and studies from colonial times tend to bear out the same pattern.

For that matter, colonial slave women bore children under particularly difficult circumstances as well. Many black midwives coated the umbilical stump with mud, a practice sometimes transmitting tetanus, and stood the woman erect and shook her violently immediately after giving birth to deliver the placenta. It is not surprising that the death of the mother in childbirth was common. Women cooked for their families (in an age, lest we forget, when "cooking" meals included building fires after hauling wood to do so, in addition to hauling in water, and took considerable time and effort in preparation with rudimentary utensils) and cared for the young. Not surprisingly, few slaves made it to what today we would consider "old age," but those women who did so earned no respite. Elderly male slaves might "retire" to the homestead when their field-working days were over, but old slave women more often simply got moved to domestic work, child caring, weaving, spinning, or dairying, to free younger women up for work in the fields.

Many similarities existed among the regions in the evolution of the black workforce and in the tasks that slaves performed. With the exception of Africans who brought with them such usable skills as rice-growing, livestock-tending, weaving, or fishing and boating, unseasoned Africans knew the least about their labors. Masters had to teach them to perform simple tasks and then keep close watch on them. Creoles were more aware of how to perform jobs and they knew more about the harsh treatment that awaited those who resisted. Masters gave creoles more autonomy and sometimes more authority over their work, so that physically and emotionally their working lives were better than were those of most Africans.

Slaves practiced skilled trades at different times throughout the colonies, but two generalizations apply to consideration of black Americans and skilled work. One is that opportunities for nonfield labor expanded steadily throughout the eighteenth century as mainland economies matured and required a greater diversity of goods and services. The other is that work outside the field, skilled or not, was not available equally: men had the only real shot at practicing the growing range of skilled tasks; women had only domestic work to remove them from the fields. Thus agricultural work became even more the work of women as slavery grew in America. In that regard, and ironically, slavery from the Chesapeake southward took on an African cast, since women dominated crop production in many West African societies.

Slave men on small farms or urban areas in the North always did a variety of tasks; some were the original jacks-of-all-trades. The more diversified economies of northern colonies or urban areas required a broader range of skills, and whites in these places often felt less threatened if the African Americans among them performed skilled work. Lists of skilled roles slaves played are long and range from barber, blacksmith, and bookbinder to watchmaker, weaver, and whitesmith. Around the docks and boatyards of northern port cities, shipbuilders, ship chandlers, merchants, bakers, brewers, and tavern keepers needed workers with a variety of skills and found them in enslaved African Americans.

Farther south, because plantation size was related to the division of tasks, opportunities for skilled slaves existed earlier, and on a greater scale, in the Low Country than in the Chesapeake. In 1733, when one of every six Low-Country male slaves worked at something other than crop production, nine of every ten slave men and probably all slave women in one Maryland county were field hands. Eventually, as larger proportions of the slave populations became native born and as the growing plantations demanded craftsmen of all sorts, black men began practicing a wide range of skilled work. Even in the Virginia tidewater, but especially on the

Low-Country rice and indigo plantations, by the middle of the eighteenth century large plantations were becoming self-contained production units with slaves doing the necessary artisanal work as well as producing the crop. In 1768 James Grant of South Carolina could write, "In established Plantations, the Planter has Tradesmen of all kinds in his Gang of Slaves, and 'tis a Rule with them, never to pay Money for what can be made upon their Estates, not a Lock, a Hing, or a Nail if they can avoid it." Woodworking was the first and most widely held plantation skill. In addition to the need for dwellings, there were barrels and hogsheads to be made, cart bodies to be constructed, and boats to be fashioned. Blacksmithing, butchering, leatherworking, and sewing eventually became skills essential to most farms and plantations, and over time slaves on the larger units began weaving, cobbling, brickmaking and bricklaying, and distilling. Some of the products of these skills—pots and baskets made on Low-Country plantations, for instance—evinced African styles and motifs. By the time of the American Revolution, African Americans were performing some of all of the above types of skilled labor in all of the English colonies.

The rise of urban areas brought increased opportunities for more diversified slave craftsmen—even for craftswomen. In Charleston slaves dominated stalls in the public markets. One particular group of skills, those related to the water, was one that many Atlantic West Africans brought with them to the mainland and used all along the coastal settlements from the earliest times. In New England blacks worked as sailors. Carolina plantations had "fishing Negroes," and throughout the southern lowlands African Americans manning skiffs and lighters were the heart of a transportation system that carried plantation goods to market, brought imported wares back from ports, and ferried whites across the maze of coastal waterways and landings.

It was as houseservants that male and female slaves served in nearly equal numbers, though still largely without equal status. African-American men around the house—manservants and grooms—had the greater chance of gaining whites' attention and appreciation. Women did the routine, and less-noticed, household work, including cooking, cleaning, dairying, marketing, and repairing clothing. Late in the eighteenth century, partly out of necessity caused by the cutoff of imports during the Revolution, slave women began doing much more carding, spinning, and weaving of "homespun" cloth. Yet, most planters continued to believe that women were best employed in crop production, so that even as specialization rose toward the end of the eighteenth century, no more than 5 percent of slave women served in and around the house. Throughout the colonial period, the African-American woman's place remained in the field.

As the eighteenth century wore on and the colonial economy grew, slaves played increasingly diversified roles in it. W. Jeffrey Bolster in *Black Jacks* shows how growing numbers of blacks took to the sea after 1740, some skippering small coasting vessels, some serving as cooks or stewards, and more hoisting and trimming the sails of Atlantic vessels as common jack tars. These men met racial discrimination and difficult working conditions on the one hand, but found much greater possibilities for freedom and, at least for a time, enhanced their status in the black community on the other. African Americans in general also assumed more tasks as colonial industries grew. In New England, blacks worked in shipbuilding and such related industries as rope and sail making. They were involved in much of the building construction in towns or rural areas. Also, they mined coal and iron and worked many of the iron forges and furnaces in the colonies. By the 1770s slaves were performing most of the skilled and manual labor in Chesapeake iron industries. Larger than most tobacco farms, these industries employed 1 percent of all adult slaves (women as well as men) in the Chesapeake. If the ironworks were representative, industrial slaves were the most privileged black laborers in the colonial period. They worked five-day weeks on average, were paid for work they did on the other two days, had access to goods in company stores, and had more freedom of movement than typical persons in bondage.

And by the eve of the nineteenth century, slaves simply did a lot more. Where there was work to do, unskilled or skilled, simple or complex, requiring a few minutes or half a year, slaves did it. There was such a variety of slave work that it defies easy generalization. Any individual, any group, any civic body in any British mainland colony that had work to accomplish could purchase slaves to perform it. The military was intricately involved with slave labor. Ranking officers normally had slave valets; Charleston's (South Carolina) artillery department owned forty-two slave women and their children in 1782, using them to cook, wash, and tend to horses; and British troops occupying Philadelphia during the Revolution had a "Company of Black Pioneers," a group of fifteen slave women made to "assist in Cleaning the Streets and Removing all Newsiances being thrown into the Streets."

As everywhere, technology was a factor in the working lives of slaves. Early technology in most places was simple and seemed to be of mixed English and African origin. English had ways of doing agricultural work they thought best, but so did Africans. It was difficult for masters and overseers to dictate the kinds of tools the workforce used, and for a long time they did not do so. Africans devised many of the tools for rice production based on their African experience, and they clung, sometimes proudly and tenaciously, to their ways of threshing with hooped poles instead of "proper flails" until overseers stopped trying to coerce them out of it. African workers had "perseverance" and "Greatness of Soul," overseers noted, referring to their adherence to their own farming methods. Slaves on some Chesapeake lands did not use carts and plows, as English farmers had done for centuries, until after 1750. Once carts and plows became commonplace, though, slaves were better able still to regulate the pace of work, working slowly for periods and then catching up quickly through use of the new implements.

Still, no matter how or how much slaves were able to manipulate the pace of work in their favor, no matter how good the enslaved black men and women became at their work, no matter what personal skills he or she acquired, the crux of slavery was that the fruits of the labor belonged to the master. If a slave reached a level of proficiency in a skill in great demand, or if field labor came to be in oversupply, as it did on some plantations after 1750, the master might "hire out" a slave to another party to provide additional income. Hiring out was especially prevalent in northern colonies or in grain-producing areas where landowners had seasonal labor requirements and could not afford to keep large numbers of slaves yearlong. In some areas, masters hired out women slaves more frequently than men. After the 1750s in the Chesapeake, a small but growing number of slave artisans hired their own time—that is, they were allowed to live by and fend for themselves, finding their own work and paying their masters a weekly or monthly fee. Blacks normally received lower wages than whites for the same work, but it seems clear they liked hiring out their own time. In doing so they worked and mingled with a wider range of people, and they appreciated the relative freedom the situation afforded them.

Although masters controlled slaves and held almost boundless legal authority to exact labor from them, no statutes or pressures could bring humans to perform endless toil. What developed were patterns of labor that did not fully satisfy either master or slave, but evolved, through fairly constant negotiation, to accommodate both. If the African-American men, women, and children had to work, the master alone could not define the quantity and quality of that labor. Colonial America was largely a black world of work, so African Americans had something to say about the setting of the standards in that world.

Family

As mentioned, African-American culture hardly could perpetuate itself in identifiable form in colonial America until black families came into existence. The family was the place where community began. It was also the unit for educating and socializing the young. If adults were to create and adhere to common values and customs, it was the family that transferred these to subsequent generations.

Of course, it was not in America that the family first became central to blacks' existence. In West Africa kinship was the basis for all social organization. The extended family on the village level and kinship links across broader areas gave Africans their individual and collective identities. These institutions united people separated by space and provided material and psychological support essential for daily living. Loss of the kinship network was probably the most disruptive force in the Africans' enslavement and movement from the homelands. It follows, then, that for Africans, recreating the family in America was especially important.

Yet, African-American families were destined to be different from the families that had been such a key part of the slaves' African heritage. West-African families tended to follow single lines of descent, through males or females, but not both. This enabled brothers and half-brothers, sisters and half-sisters, aunts, uncles, and more distant relatives—all who shared a common ancestor— to identify with an enormous group of kin. Marriage united two such kin networks in relationships of obligation and responsibility, so Africans arranged marriages carefully and bound them together with family pressures and payments of bridewealth. Thus across West Africa, bridging whatever linguistic or ethnic divides that may have existed, was a grid of related kin groups that held society together much more tightly than political authority or national loyalty. Even if slaves in colonial America could have practiced African-style unilineal kinship, it would have taken generations, and complete freedom in marriage and residence, to recreate the thread that held together West-African society. In the end it was impossible.

Not that Africans did not try. Even on slave ships they began seeking relatives. Children called friendly adults "uncle" or "aunt," and adults tended to look after younger children whether or not they were related. Where slaves existed in some numbers on the English mainland there developed a broad pattern of slave children addressing all older slaves with kinship titles and regarding them as the equivalent of relatives. Younger slaves respected their elders in the African fashion. And those children who developed bonds to fictive kin had a broader community of support and were better able to cope following the death or sale of their parents or other blood relatives.

Eventually, however, not fictive kin but real family relationships provided the foundation for the African-American community. Although regional differences in the process were consider-

18th C

family matured

able, it was during the eighteenth century that the black family came into existence and matured in English mainland North America. Once demographic circumstances—sufficient numbers of blacks in roughly equal proportions of men and women— made black families possible, what emerged was an English-style nuclear family with monogamous marital relationships that traced descent through both parents. This occurred earliest in the Chesapeake, later—after mid-century—in the Low Country and lower Mississippi Valley. Of course, for the nuclear family to prevail, black Americans had to overcome considerable obstacles, the greatest of which was the regular movement of slaves at the hands of their owners and thus the separation of married adults from one another and parents from children. Kulikoff describes a continuing process of slave household and family development and redevelopment in eighteenth-century Virginia and Maryland, variants of which were probably typical of other areas:

A young [white] man tended to receive slaves from his parents or purchase them on the open market, thereby separating [slave] family members. If economic disaster did not intervene, his slaveholdings grew through natural increase, slave families were reestablished, and extended family networks developed. When the master died, the family's slaves were divided among heirs, and the process began again. Only during the second stage [of family building in a new location] were slave families even relatively secure. At the same time, as generation followed generation, households, or adjacent huts, became increasingly complex and sometimes included grandparents, uncles, aunts, or cousins as well as the immediate family. Since other kin lived on nearby plantations, geographically dispersed kinship networks that connected numbers of quarters emerged during the pre-Revolutionary era.

families commonly lived apart

But because of the obstacles in the way of smooth family development for blacks, and because of remnants of African family patterns, black families in America only partially resembled the nuclear families of English colonists. It was common for African-American families in the Chesapeake to live apart, for instance. Men often lived in separate households—out of necessity in areas of small black population or few concentrations of slaves on the same plantations. In Virginia there even was a term for this sort of arrangement, "marrying abroad," which meant marrying someone off the home farm or plantation. In these cases, women frequently played the most important role in child rearing. Men tended to be older than their wives and to be domineering in marital relationships, a possible throwback to African customs that fit well into colonial America. Some blacks did not have attitudes toward sex and monogamy in accord with the wishes of their Christian masters. Premarital sex in limited practice was the norm in some West-African societies, and so were freer sexual connections in polygynous marriages. Some African Americans seem to have clung to African sexual customs in their largely monogamous relationships, often to the consternation of their masters, white church officials, and others who believed promiscuity a flawed part of the black's natural makeup.

sexual relations

Few masters thought it necessary to bother with legality in slave marriages, but many of the African-American men and women involved regarded the ceremonies as important and binding. Marriage rites varied and seemed to mean as much as the couples desired. Christian marriages occasionally took place for blacks, especially in New England, but common-law marriages, called "Negro marriages," were the norm. Farther south, slaves conducted their own wedding ceremonies, often at night, sometimes with good-sized crowds in attendance and much merriment. Though there is no evidence of it having taken place anywhere in colonial America, the practice of "jumping the broomstick," thought of as a popular, symbolic way of uniting slaves in marriage in the nineteenth century, may have had its roots in unrecorded practices of eighteenth-century African Americans.

marriage rites

Better than anyone at the time or since, slaves knew how tenuous was their family stability and security. Such seemingly unrelated matters as the death of a master or a sharp economic downturn could mean sale of loved ones and separation from them. As the master-slave relationship moved in the direction of paternalism over the course of the eighteenth century, more masters professed greater concern for slave families and greater reluctance to separate family members through sale. But evidence shows that neither the professed concern for the mother-father-child relationship nor plaintive appeals from those involved mattered much when the breakup of a family was deemed "plantation necessity," or even

sep of families → 18th c owners becoming more sensitive

when it merely promised greater profits. Masters sometimes would regard the African-American mother and her young children as a unit, separating them from their husband and father with little concern, but at other times a callous, even casual attitude about separating mothers and children seems to have existed. Contemporary newspapers carried evidence for some of this in advertisements of slaves for sale: "likely Negro wench, about 22 years old and a child about four years old . . ."; "likely Negro wench with a likely male child, ten months old . . ."; "A Negro woman age about 24 years, and her child, a girl about five years." The *Boston News Letter* of May 1, 1732, listed for sale a nineteen-year-old African-American woman and her infant son, to be sold "together or apart." Masters were even known to ponder what to do with the "future increase" of women they owned.

Yet in spite of the difficulties they faced, it is probably inaccurate to describe slave marriages or slave families as "unstable" with the implication that contemporary white marriages and families were necessarily more "stable." Granted, not as many black husbands as white husbands lived with their wives and children, especially on small farms, and black families were always liable to forced separation, a master's sexual incursions, and more, but the older and more established colonial African-American society became, the more black husbands lived with their families. However, simply because a man, black or white, resided with his wife and children did not mean necessarily that he cared greatly for any of his coresidents, nor did cohabitation automatically make for a "stable" or "secure" family. It is also not fair or safe to assume that a man living apart was one who cared little for his family or failed to nurture a loving group. White husbands of the time were not ones to involve themselves in child rearing. Many white men who resided "at home" spent hours or days away from it. William Byrd of Westover, Virginia, spent more waking time with those he called "his people," his black workforce, than with his white family. Conversely, some black husbands who lived in quarters removed from their families found ways to visit at nights and on Sundays and holidays, giving them, perhaps, as much intimate contact as some whites who resided with their families. In addition, some African-American women seem to have had especially *diff* close ties with their children that were rewarding for both. One *in* should not suppose that white women did not have such close ties, *mother* but tendencies of upper-class whites to hire nurses and nannies for *roles* their young children imply that some white women did not experi- *for white* ence as close and fulfilling relationships with their children as did *vs* some black women—the specter of forced separation notwith- *black* standing.

Ties between black marriage partners, parents and children, brothers and sisters, and even distant kin a generation or more apart tended to be strong. The best evidence is in advertisements for runaway slaves. One-third of the slaves mentioned in 589 Virginia advertisements before 1775 ran off to rejoin members of *Runaways* their families who lived in the vicinity, and the proportion of *looking* Maryland slaves who stole away for the same reason between *for ext.* 1745 and 1779 may have been higher still. "His parents are free *family* and live in Port-Royal," read one Virginia advertisement; "he is about Mr. Samuel Thomae's in Warwick County, where he has a father and grandmother," read another; and a third read, "supposed to be harboured by Colonel John Snelson's Negroes . . . among whom he has a wife, or by his Brother, John Kenny, a Mulatto Slave belonging to Mr. Thomas Johnson of Louisa." According to Gerald W. Mullin in *Flight and Rebellion: Slave Resistance in Eighteenth-Century Virginia* (1972), "owners' understatements [in advertisements] indicate a depth to slave family life—and the whites' tacit recognition of that life—that up till now has not been dealt with in interpretations of American Negro slavery."

Religion

Religion was the heart of African-American culture in colonial America, but through much of the period the form of religion most blacks practiced was minimally Christian. African slaves came to the New World with strong religious beliefs and thoughts of the afterlife. In the American colonies they encountered masters and Christian ministers, Puritans and Anglicans, Methodists and Baptists, Quakers and Moravians, some of whom were intent (in varying degrees, at different times, and mostly where they perceived it useful to their own ends or to white society) on turning slaves into Christians. But religious belief is personal, often developed individually, and the private world of religion was a sanctuary to which slaves could turn during the periods of anxiety and stress that were such a large part of their lives. Religions that could not accommodate their preferred cosmologies and customs, based in part on their African heritage, were of little interest. Thus, slaves kept their distance from Christianity for much of the colonial period, and when they did take more notice of it, they did so by blending Christian tenets into African religious practices and beliefs. But regardless of the form it took, religion was a source of individual strength and collective security for African Americans as their culture matured.

African religions, of course, were not at all alike, but West and West-Central Africans held some patterns of belief in common. (It is probably important to note that in some manifestations of this belief—spirits, magic, taboos, use of amulets, and more—Africans shared ideas with common English people of their day.) The living bodies of many Africans held their spirits, which, upon death, returned to a greater spiritual world where they joined those of their ancestors. They believed spirits were also about in inanimate objects—trees, rocks, hills, rivers—and that these forces controlled much of the workings of their everyday world. The spirits of ancestors also intervened in the world of the living. Acts of placation, magic, and taboos were important in controlling all of these spirits. So workers of magic, diviners, and healers were manipulators of spirits, often through the manufacturing of amulets and charms, and as such were powerful people in the African world. Beyond this, many West Africans had a sense of there being one or more hegemonic deities involved with creation and events of the world beyond the local realm. These powers, naturally, were less personal, less intimate, and more difficult to manipulate. It was to these sorts of religious beliefs and practices that Africans and African Americans clung through the first half of the eighteenth century and beyond.

In the New World, blacks received Christian teaching in more or less strenuous doses at different times and in various locales.

Some owners opposed attempts to make slaves Christians, masking fear of loss of control of their property with arguments of insufficient black intellect for an appreciation of religion or the inappropriateness of the doctrine. Following the lead of New Englanders, however, many whites came to believe that slavery was part of God's plan for bringing "heathens" out of Africa and giving them "knowledge of the True God." In this spirit, Protestant evangelicals began filtering through colonial America after the first quarter of the eighteenth century, attempting to instruct slaves in the "proper faith." To slave owners amenable to such activity, this was a selection of Christian teachings that stressed meekness, humility, obedience, discipline, and work. Brotherhood of man *exclusions* and the escape of the Hebrews from bondage were noticeably ab- *from Chris* sent from the Gospel according to the master. *teachings*

An ironic but instructive axiom is that, generally speaking, the more closely blacks worshipped with whites, the less they wanted to become Christians. Those who did worship with whites and still converted, however, practiced a form of Christianity that paralleled closely that of their Anglo-American fellow Christians. The opposite was also true. Where there was greater distance between master and slave in religious practice, blacks were more eager to *their* become Christian, but their Christianity was different, much more *Chris-* a blending of African and European religious practices and beliefs. *was diff.*

In New England, for example, where social interaction was greatest and Christian proselytizing strongest, the majority of African Americans remained outside the white church. Only 3 percent of Newport, Rhode Island, blacks were Christians in good standing in 1775, and only a quarter of them attended church at all. This was so because, in spite of proselytical intentions that seemed noble, New England whites segregated blacks in church and treated them as second-class Christians in worship. Requirements *bapt* for the baptism of a black person were especially rigorous. They *req.* included demonstrable theological knowledge on the part of the would-be convert as well as a Christian demeanor. Sermons to African-American congregations justified the proper relationship between master and servant. Most important, slave owners refused to allow their bondspeople to worship by themselves for fear of the "mongrelization" of Christian practices, meaning the infusion of

African-based religious practices they thought bound to occur. The failure to make good Christians of more than a tiny minority of African Americans "was not so much that Yankee masters did not tell their servants about Christianity," observes William D. Piersen in *Black Yankees: The Development of an Afro-American Sub-culture in Eighteenth-Century New England* (1988), "but that the Christianity they offered was self-serving and neither emotionally nor intellectually satisfying to most Africans and Afro-Americans." Those who did not convert continued to practice their own folk religion or a blending thereof.

The situation was not significantly different in the Middle Colonies. The Society for the Propagation of the Gospel in Foreign Parts had been busy working to bring Anglican Christianity to blacks in the Middle Colonies since 1701, and in southern New York the society baptized on average some twenty African Americans per year into Revolutionary times. But as the century progressed, blacks followed their New England counterparts in keeping to themselves in religious matters, and they began to manifest a renewed respect for traditional African ways. A Philadelphia minister complained that the city's blacks "gathered on Sundays and holidays and were seen dancing after the manner of their several nations in Africa, and speaking and singing in their native dialects." African Americans continued to congregate for funerals at their own, separate burial grounds and prepare the dead for eternity in ways that reflected African customs.

Farther south, African Americans learned of Christianity from their fellow slaves most frequently, but also from their masters, evangelical missionaries, and regular clergy. Worship often was with lower-class whites. An important difference from their northern counterparts, however, was that southern whites either allowed their slaves more freedom to worship alone in ways they chose, or, as in the Chesapeake, accepted enough African religious practice themselves to help form a blend of Christian worship satisfactory to both. In Maryland and Virginia especially, but also in the Carolinas and Georgia, the middle decades of the eighteenth century, the time of the so-called Great Awakening, an evangelical movement that swept out of England and quickly reached the lands of southern slaveholders, was a special time for slave conversions and the blending of African and English modes of worship. During this period poor blacks and whites joined in worship and song in small prayer houses throughout rural Virginia. Together they "proclaimed" and "witnessed" and had emotional religious experiences. And a burst of African-American conversion occurred around the Chesapeake between 1785 and 1790. Still, the increasing black acceptance of Christian doctrine did not result in rising church membership among slaves. By the last decade of the eighteenth century not one in twenty blacks was a member of the Methodist or Baptist church, the two denominations with the largest African-American membership. In the Low Country, the number of black church members was much smaller still. Only in towns did evangelicals have any real success among blacks. But wherever southern slaves became Christians, they practiced a blended religion like the African-American folk variety extant in New England.

African Americans everywhere tended to hold onto the idea that upon death one's soul went to one's homeland, almost always in the ground rather than in the sky. Funerals prepared the deceased's spirit for entry into the spirit world of the ancestors. The services this practice of folk religion entailed were not at all the somber functions of most whites, but loud, raucous, joyous affairs with music, singing, dancing, laughing, and drinking. African Americans' practice of worship might also involve soft singing or frenzied behavior. Presbyterian minister Samuel Davies, who was important in bringing the Great Awakening to blacks in Hanover County, Virginia, at the middle of the eighteenth century, recorded how African Americans' religious singing affected him spiritually:

March 2, 1756. Sundry of them [the Negroes] have lodged all night in my kitchen; and, sometimes, when I have awakened about two or three a-clock in the morning, a torrent of sacred harmony poured into my chamber, and carried my mind away to Heaven. In this seraphic exercise, some of them spend almost the whole night.

But such religious ecstasy was more characteristic of organized services. Leaders of African-American congregations exhorted their listeners and sought emotional response. Singing and dancing, standing and shouting were important parts of the services. In these assemblages, blacks (and whites) frequently had spiritual experiences—visions of ancestors, journeys to other times and places, encounters with God or the devil, views of heaven or hell. A common experience was spiritual death and re-birth, bringing about heightened religious feeling. Efforts to control spirits were manifested in various magical practices, many involving the wearing of amulets and charms for protection. Black mediums who made the charms became powerful persons in the black community—sometimes in the white community. Through frenzied worship and spiritual experiences, African Americans were able to select from Christian worship the stories from the Old Testament that made them, too, feel a chosen people and allowed them to love their fellow humans in situations where being loving was not a natural tendency.

Folk Culture

The idea that most slaves lived in "Negro quarters," clusters of small, individual dwellings set off by themselves and resembling tiny villages, is out of time and place for most regions of mainland North America through a good part of the colonial period. Permanent groupings of slave quarters existed only on the largest plantations and individual dwellings or duplexes were a development signaling the maturing of slave societies—by the mid-eighteenth century in most places—when masters saw the utility of separating Africans from creoles or allowing families to live by themselves, or recognized that diseases spread more quickly among persons living in the same quarters. Slaves not long in the colonies more often lived in quartering houses, which were dormitory or barracks-like structures that held the most people for the least expense—and offered the least privacy and comfort. In tobacco-growing Maryland of 1720, slaves tended to live scattered about the countryside in relatively isolated groups of half a dozen adults and their children. Even on large Chesapeake plantations prior to

1750, masters divided their lands into separate units and housed groups of slaves on each to allow easy access to the fields they tended and to spread grazing livestock around their holdings. Small planters' field hands slept in barn lofts, tobacco houses, or other outbuildings.

Some slaves relied on African building styles as much as English forms in constructing their dwellings. This seems to have been the case especially in South Carolina and Georgia. Houses tended to be small and square, twelve by twelve feet on average, and seldom were they permanent structures, allowing for movement with seasonal crops, fallowing, or removal from waste pits. In the Chesapeake, they built houses of wood mostly—clapboard structures early on and then log constructions. In the Low Country more dwellings had mud walls or walls of a cement-like mixture of lime, crushed oyster shells, sand, and water called "tabby." Archaeologist Theresa A. Singleton (in "Breaking New Ground," *Southern Exposure*, 15, 1988) reveals "striking evidence" from excavations at eighteenth-century sites in South Carolina of African-style dwellings with mud walls and thatched roofs. Slaves typically slept on straw bedding set on earthen floors and cooked by open fires or under wooden chimneys. They fetched water from springs, which were sufficient for most locations. Dwellings tended to grow in size and improve in construction—with such amenities as brick fireplaces—during Revolutionary times, but slave families were larger then, too. Thus, the amount of room per individual seems to have changed little through the eighteenth century, and that amount was almost always small.

With cramped, dark, and often smoky quarters, it is not surprising that much activity went on outside, in yards surrounding the houses. "Gathering around a fire, pipes in hand," writes Philip D. Morgan in *Slave Counterpoint*, "singing, dancing, and telling stories in communal yards; congregating in front of a cooking pot—these images probably convey much of the domestic life in the slave settlements." Many of the yards seem to have been grassless, in the fashion of a West-African compound. Fires were aburn outside most evenings and tended to be the focal point of group interaction. Chickens and dogs were part of the assemblage; garden plots surrounded the yards; and garbage heaps were nearby, sometimes close enough to smell them.

In northern colonies, many slaves lived with their masters, sometimes in back rooms or attics of the same houses but most often in small outbuildings. Late in the eighteenth century, as Boston, New York, and Philadelphia grew, blacks moved into the cheaply constructed tenements that appeared. At the end of the colonial period one could see the beginning of the movement of blacks into the southern part of Philadelphia, presaging a larger movement of subsequent decades that would plant the seeds for the city's nineteenth- and twentieth-century black neighborhoods.

Slaves' material standard of living was lean, but not static. Enslaved men and women were not allowed to own property in most places, but many of them did. When they stayed in the same place for considerable lengths of time they made furniture or acquired utensils. The longer they remained in one place, the more material goods they acquired. Masters intended slave clothing to be fairly standard. They supplied the men and women with imported clothing or plain cloth, perhaps five to ten yards annually of coarse linen or heavy, durable, often imported, and sometimes unbearably warm wool. Planters often hired tailors to make the slaves' clothing. In Revolutionary times, when imports were restricted, more slaves wore homespun and made their own clothes.

If course, drab, tough, and functional clothing was the master's intention, it was not the slave's, and the latter found ways— sometimes theft, more often cajoling masters out of their castoff items or buying garments in a quasi-licit market—to acquire additional items more to their liking. Thus, as Shane White and Graham White write in Stylin: African American Expressive Culture from Its Beginnings to the Zoot Suit (1998), there turned out to be a "bewildering variety in slave apparel." Men wore shirts and trousers, women shifts tied at the waist, and nearly everyone had a coat for colder times. The color of these garments varied widely, but all of them tended to turn drab with wear, even if they had not started out that way. Nonetheless, black men and women often did their best to remedy the situation. Responsible for keeping their own clothes in adequate repair, slaves tended to patch them with bright colors and express themselves by adorning their shirts with distinctive cuffs and collars. Men wore hats while working in the field, women handkerchiefs. Both worked barefoot in the summer, but all had shoes for cooler times. No one considered undergarments a necessity, and socks were a luxury. Perhaps because of their tropical-African ancestry, slaves tended toward being cold rather than hot. They complained of the cold and damp a good bit, and their earliest personal acquisitions often were coats, blankets, and additional items of warm clothing. Of course, in the hot and humid Low Country and elsewhere when scorching hot made clothing a burden, much of it was shed. Slave children went naked much of the time, anyway.

Wealthy masters dressed personal servants better, in waistcoats and petticoat breeches, and rewarded some slaves with clothing for exceptional work or behavior. Artisans often earned enough to buy finer cloth and generally to dress better. Those who could afford to do so brought an African eye for color to their garments. Piersen notes in *Black Yankees* that the African Americans' style of dress in New England "celebrated life in bright colors, demonstrating joy in physical attractiveness." Plantation slaves demonstrated that joy, too, but they had to concern themselves more with basic warmth. White and White believe that, in either case, "through the ways they fashioned their appearance, African and African American slaves discovered an often surprising degree of social and cultural space."

Slave cabins were sparse in their furnishings. An inventory of one in Henrico County, Virginia, in 1697 shows "several chairs and a bed, an iron kettle weighing fifteen pounds, a brass kettle, an iron pot, a pair of pot racks, a pot hook, a frying-pan, and a beer barrel." Slaves probably had been in the cabin for some time. It was common for slaves to start or move with little more than a single iron pot and one frying pan. Enslaved men and women were not resourcelesss, however. They could purchase or barter for household items, and as the eighteenth century progressed, more cabins contained tables, linens, chamber pots, and a means of interior lighting. Raised beds were a luxury that few slaves enjoyed.

Food

What slaves ate varied greatly from one farm or plantation to another, depending on the regional produce and the ideas of the master. That they ate out of bowls rather than plates suggests that most of their meals were of the slow-cooked, stew variety. Most colonial slaves seem to have existed on a basic core of meat and meal with some supplements. This was sufficient in quantity but lacking in quality. Advertisements for runaway slaves are full of references to physical problems associated with nutritional deficiencies: bad teeth, crooked legs, knocked knees, eye problems, poor posture, jaundiced or splotchy skin. Morgan points out that slaves in the Chesapeake were better fed than those in the Low Country, masters in the latter region giving their bondspeople less grain and meat than their Chesapeake counterparts, expecting them to make up the deficit through gardening or hunting. This resulted in Chesapeake slaves being generally taller and experiencing a lower rate of infant and child mortality than Low-Country slaves.

The idea that slaves existed on a "hog and hominy" routine is fairly sound, though one must remain aware of the local variations and the adaptations free blacks and slaves made when they provided their own food. Most masters allowed a weekly ration of cornmeal—a peck for each slave was standard, or about a pound a day—and pork, usually the least desirable parts in small amounts. There were regional additions. African Americans in the southern Low Country ate the rice that was broken in the cleaning process, and thus unsaleable, but they still consumed more corn than rice; those in the Chesapeake in later years had greater access to wheat flour, from which they baked biscuits, but they preferred corn and cornbread and their masters preferred giving it to them. Adult African Americans did not drink milk because of their genetic intolerance for lactose, and they ate little beef because it did not preserve well. Few slaves in colonial times supplemented their diets with peas, beans, sweet potatoes, or greens, as they may have done in the Cotton South of later times. Most masters allowed slaves to raise produce, poultry, and pigs, but many did so to barter for tobacco, alcohol, or better clothes for Sundays and holidays rather than to improve their diets with fruits, vegetables, and more meat.

The most popular (and dietarily useful) supplements were fish and game, the former important especially for persons in the Low Country and around New England ports. Blacks in Gracia Real de Santa Teresa de Mose ate good amounts of fish (croaker, sea catfish, sea trout, drum, silver perch, spots, mullet, sheepshead, shark, and ray), shellfish, deer, rabbit, raccoon, and turtle.

Kenneth F. Kiple and Virginia Himmelsteib King in *Another Dimension of the Black Diaspora: Diet, Disease, and Racism* (1981) show that blacks had two major difficulties relating to diet and nutrition. Over centuries they had become adapted for survival in the African tropics, so once removed from that specialized environment they faced particular nutritional requirements that could not easily be satisfied in the British mainland colonies of North America. But regardless of their special needs, the diet they received in America, if sufficient in bulk, was not entirely sufficient in balance. Under such circumstances blacks in colonial America lived a kind of nutritional nightmare. The majority of slaves received insufficient protein of good quality and insufficient amounts of the vitamin B complex, vitamins C and D, and calcium and iron. The results included a rate of African-American child mortality much higher than that of whites, development of personality disorders now recognized as associated with malnutrition, and a host of ailments and diseases in the slave population—what masters called the "Negro diseases"—that were largely foreign to whites. Among the debilitating and often fatal diseases particular to African Americans were rickets, pica (often referred to as "dirt-eating"), hookworm, and pellagra ("black tongue"). Of course, malnutrition often made slaves more susceptible to common diseases and made them vulnerable to secondary infections once they had been wounded or had acquired a common ailment.

Diet was one of the factors that led to African-American children faring as poorly as they did. In fact, the old image of throngs of thinly-clad children playing gayly about the slave quarter needs to be laid to rest. The more one learns about slaves' diet, the disease environment in which they lived, and work patterns of slave mothers and children—the elements most directly affecting infant and child mortality—the more one must agree with Richard H.

Steckel that the African-American experience in childhood during slavery times was "dreadful." In his most recent work, "Women, Work, and Health under Plantation Slavery in the United States" in *More than Chattel: Black Women and Slavery in the Americas*, edited by David Barry Gaspar and Darlene Clark Hine (1996), Steckel summarizes data from just after colonial times that show the effects of diet, work demands, and disease on infant and child health as manifested in height. In a word, slave children were tiny. At age five the average height of enslaved blacks did not make it into the first percentile of modern height distribution. Steckel writes, "The slums of Lagos, Nigeria, and urban areas of Bangladesh provided environments for growth superior to those faced by slave children." Life's harshness showed in rates of mortality as well. Over half of all children born to slave parents died in their first four years—a mortality rate almost exactly twice as high as that of the entire United States population at the same time.

Given the nature of medical treatment in colonial times, which included the letting of blood, application of leeches, administration of harsh purgatives, and lancing with unsterilized instruments, slaves who were unwell frequently were better off when masters did not summon professional medical advice. Blacks maintained their own medical system in the form of plantation or neighborhood "root doctors," men and women who combined knowledge of herbal remedies and ritual skills with a holistic approach to devise therapeutics for many ills. Actually, practitioners of folk medicine in Africa long had been adept at matching the medicinal properties of certain plants to the symptoms of certain diseases. Also, the psychological benefit of believing in the healer, as African Americans seemed to do in their "root doctors," may have been as important as the medication in this early form of holistic treatment.

Closely tied to black medical practice was another group of activities important to black folk culture that included magic, sorcery, and witchcraft. Belief in individuals with special powers to manipulate the spiritual realm to effect good and evil was widespread in West Africa, where it moved beyond the religious and into the secular world. Africans brought such traditions to colonial America and melded them into a body of beliefs and practices sometimes called "voodoo" or slave magic. Most sizable groups of African Americans comprised one or more individuals, often called "conjurers" by whites, who worked their magic to help or harm people as requested. One of the most frequently used magical practices was the wearing of amulets or talismans to ward off illness or misfortune. Blacks visited conjurers to ascertain ways to get even with evil overseers or cruel masters, or to "give the mis'ries" to fellow slaves who had done misdeeds. Individuals in the African-American community practiced divining, which included discovering lost property and predicting the future. Belief in ghosts was common. It is important to note that in colonial America such African-American folk beliefs were close to those of whites of the time and place. New England slaves feared witches nearly as much as whites did, and many were the white Yankees who visited noted black mediums for protection against ghosts or witches or to be healed of some affliction.

Speaking to spirits was one thing; speaking to humans was another. To do this, African Americans learned and developed forms of English comprising, to varying degrees, elements of African languages. Colonial masters deemed arriving Africans particularly slow learners of a usable language (which had to have a basis in English, since whites were not at all willing learners themselves). Africans "brought hither from their own Country," wrote a white South Carolina minister in 1712, "seldom or never speak good English." This varied with age, of course—younger immigrants having an easier time of language acquisition than older ones— and with the amount of contact the newcomers had with English speakers. Still, it was practically axiomatic in the colonial Low Country that almost no adult Africans having resided there for less than a year spoke any recognizable English, and that some of those who had "been above twenty years in this Province," lamented another South Carolinian, "can hardly speak even common things, so as to be understood." The situation was slightly different farther north, where saltwater slaves had more contact with creoles and whites.

The linguistic challenge was about as difficult as any the newest arrivals faced. Because West Africans spoke hundreds of mutually unintelligible languages and because most slaves in mainland

North America were sufficiently dispersed to rarely be in close contact with same-language speakers, it was almost never possible for the newcomers to talk easily with others. Thus, over several generations African Americans developed their own ways to communicate. Across most of the mainland colonies, blacks held onto certain common elements of African languages—certain grammar, words, sounds, tones, and more—as they fashioned their own variants of English. This resulted in sharp local differences in earlier periods, followed by regional variation—with a language closer to standard English being spoken farther north and more of a creole tongue, lingering longer, farther south in the mainland colonies. In places where African slaves were relatively isolated for a long time, they spoke what are often regarded as wholly different languages—"Gullah" in the Sea Islands off the Low Country and an African-French-Portuguese creole along the lower Mississippi.

Voice was a factor in music, too. West Africans surrounded themselves with a music that had a deep heritage, and music was always an important element in the lives of African Americans. Considerable African influence was evident in black forms of music and dance. African technology went into the making and playing of a host of stringed instruments, most notably the banjo, certain fiddles (though this style melded quickly with that of the European violin), tambourines, flutes, xylophones, and drums. Blacks played these instruments in times of joy and sorrow; they sang together while hoeing crops, grinding corn, or rowing boats; they sang relatives to the afterlife in funerals; and they joined together on moonlit nights to sing "sweet chants." Disgruntled slaves in the 1770s met among themselves to play African gourd-guitars and sing about what John Lovell, Jr., in *Black Song: The Forge and the Flame* (1972) describes as "the usage they have received from their Masters and Mistresses in a very satirical style and manner." African-based call-and-response forms of song served this and other purposes. Finally, folk narratives merged with song to provide instruction to children while entertaining them. Storytelling ranged from the amusing to the raunchy, depending on the audience.

Though there is little evidence of the forms of African-American dance in the colonial period, it was clearly a major part of celebrating. On African-American holidays, recalled New Englander Jane Shelton, groups of women "shuffled and tripped to the sound of the fiddle." African-style ring dances were popular, and some dances were raucous, noisy affairs that whites neither understood nor appreciated. Thomas Hazard seemed not to care for the dancing style of the Rhode Island slave Sam, "who had a way of his own of fetching a terrific screech like a catamount, and then dashing forward to the middle of the floor." Likewise, Pierre de Laussat wrote that slaves in South Carolina celebrated the Christmas holiday in dance by "distorting their frame in the most unnatural figures and emitting the most hideous noises." Not all neighbors of blacks appreciated these dances a great deal more. When a considerable number of African Americans persisted in gathering at William Grimes's "upper room" in New Bedford, Connecticut, dancing late into the night, Grimes's neighbors complained until his landlord revoked his lease.

African Americans knew how to enjoy a holiday or an evening away from work. Alcohol regularly had a place in relaxing and merriment. Low-Country slaves enjoyed boat races; blacks in port towns from Charleston to Boston liked to drink and play dice, especially "paw paw," an African gambling game. A black/Indian/lower-class-white tavern culture existed in cities of any size. White authorities did not approve of much of what went on in and around the taverns—they were places where the poorer folk could fence stolen goods and, with boldness enhanced by spirits, plan acts of resistance—and neighbors seemed especially to dislike the noises that accompanied tavern revelry. As early as 1692 New York's Common Council ordered the sheriff to give twenty lashes to any slaves "making any hooting or disorderly noise in the Street on the Lords Day." Such efforts tended to be in vain, however. Among the biggest single celebrations in colonial African-American culture was Election Day in New England, when slaves took a holiday to elect their own "kings" and "governors" in a satire of white society. Free of normal restraints, slaves dressed elaborately for the day and celebrated it with parades and "inaugural" parties. The officers elected even became important personages in the black community. In coastal slave communities, mainly in the Low Country, Christmas-time extravaganzas called John Canoe festivals (seemingly named after a mythical or historical figure from the West-African coast) served the same purpose. In attendance of these mixtures of African and Anglo-Saxon celebrations, some slaves dressed in animal masks, others might adorn themselves with headdresses shaped like houses or ships, and music and dance prevailed everywhere.

Whites and Blacks, Men and Women, Humanity and Inhumanity

Of a work so grand in scope and stature as Morgan's *Slave Counterpoint,* it is probably inappropriate to highlight any one particular element. But among the things that set the book apart from many others is Morgan's illumination of the relationships between and among different groups of whites and blacks in colonial America. Morgan not only describes these relationships, but he shows how they changed over time and how such changes affected African Americans throughout the period. After all, blacks in a subordinate position in society had to relate constantly with white people considered above them in the social order, and how they did so affected much about their existence. So too, of course, did the fact that some of those white people owned them, making them at once pieces of property, like farm implements, and human beings with souls and feelings and minds of their own.

Into the early eighteenth century, a social model of patriarchalism was dominant among persons of power in British mainland North America. In a perceived, distinct social hierarchy, male father figures existed at the top. From their positions of power, these patriarchs protected the weak, from whom they demanded obedience and loyalty. Colonial planters, the patriarchs, regarded slaves as property, made decisions about them with profit in mind, and applied discipline impersonally and severely to exact work from these physically close but socially distant subordinates. Yet many of these same masters could not overcome the notion that it was their duty to look after the well-being—in the lights of that time and place—of their dependent underlings, who were part of the planter's household in its broadest sense.

enlightened Patriarchalism

After the middle of the eighteenth century, the more austere and less emotional patriarchal relationships slowly began to change and become, on the surface, at least, softer and gentler, less authoritarian. Morgan cites the rise of evangelicalism, romanticism, and humanitarianism, among other things, as reasons for this shift to a more "enlightened patriarchalism." Eventually, masters who had dealt with members of the same slave families for several generations developed closer relations with them, perhaps cared more for them as individuals and treated them more humanely. Masters also grew increasingly concerned with their reputations for benevolence: some made efforts to ameliorate slave codes and to provide their bondspeople better food, clothing, and housing. Through all of this, whites expected loyalty from their slaves and grew to develop a false sense that the men and women they owned and worked were generally grateful to them and happy with their lot. It was as if persons of African descent, who previously were unfortunate (and perhaps dangerous) beings of a lower order, became perpetual children. The change was not equal across colonial America. It came more slowly and to a lesser degree in the Low Country than in the Chesapeake, and in such venues as North Carolina, where the slave system matured late and African imports rose after 1750, it hardly appeared at all. But by the end of the colonial period master-slave relations were moving toward the out-and-out paternalism that would characterize black-white dealings through much of the nineteenth century.

whites began to expect loyalty, gratefulness

Lower-class whites generally did not share these views, and in earlier stages blacks and whites tended to work together and interact considerably. The evidence of white servants running away with enslaved blacks in the seventeenth century is extensive, and on the fringes of plantation country and in the growing urban settings of eighteenth-century colonial America, blacks and whites worked together, drank together, and produced offspring together outside the law. In time, however, forces worked to separate African Americans and lower-class whites. The economic condition and general status of plain whites rose, if haltingly, and poorer whites began to see blacks more clearly as potential competitors in the economic sphere. At the same time, members of the white gen-

lower class whites

try, for a multitude of reasons that included the need for greater control in societies that contained a great many slaves, courted poorer whites to identify and align themselves with their wealthier and more powerful neighbors. The result was a steadily growing antipathy between black slaves and white laborers of all sorts. "The eighteenth century was a crucible in which the deep and increasingly reciprocal contempt felt between lower-class whites and blacks was forged," writes Morgan. "The contempt had not emerged in fully polished form by 1800, but the essentials were in place."

There was never enough antipathy to keep blacks and whites entirely apart in sexual relations, however, and the considerable number of persons of mixed black and white parentage is mute evidence of such activity. Sex between white men and black women, and black men and white women, was bound to occur in societies that had such thorough contact. Inter-racial sexual relations probably took place more—at least per capita—in earlier colonial times than later, because strictures against such activity—public condemnation and ridicule often the most effective—grew stronger with the heightened religiosity of the later eighteenth century and the movement toward creation of a common white identity. They also took place more frequently in some places—along the lower Mississippi or around the Chesapeake, for instance, than in the Low Country. But colonial America was a place where men and women of both races were together frequently and alone sufficiently for sex to take place. And it did.

Black-white sexual relationships in the colonial period could indeed be caring and affectionate. Edward Ball in *Slaves in the Family* found evidence that his eighteenth-century Low-Country ancestor, the planter Elias Ball, had a long and seemingly caring relationship with his slave Dolly, thirty-six years his junior, which produced two children, Edward and Catherine, the only of his slaves to bear English forenames and the only ones to be granted their freedom. The elder Ball summoned a physician for a house call when Dolly took ill—a momentous occurrence indeed—and he hired a cobbler to make her expensive shoes that were a far cry from the "Negro shoes" allotted to the rest of his slaves. Other evidence from various places shows white and black men and women living together as man and wife; a Virginia record from 1738 calls attention to a white woman in Northampton County, Virginia, who paid a fine and served a six-month prison term so she could marry a mulatto man.

Of course, a good portion of the inter-racial sexual activity must have been less caring. Sex for money was certainly known in colonial times, and as cities grew larger, toward the late eighteenth century, blacks and whites met in "disorderly houses" and did as they would, in spite of the law. Out on plantations, some masters and their male offspring could be downright predatory in nature toward their own, and others', women slaves. It is not clear how frequently these liaisons constituted violent rape, since such incidents did not come before the law.

But that some of the sexual unions between white men and black women were even violent in nature should hardly be surprising, given that slave societies were based on violence. Wherever one turned and regardless with whom the slaves were dealing, the world of master and slave was a world of violence. It was corporal punishment that coerced the African-American men and women to work for another's gain, and such punishment and its threat maintained order in the larger slave societies. Plantation justice, meted out on the spot by a master or his agent to an offending slave, was the most common form of "correction." Often, this involved whipping, a punishment done in public for the deterrent effects of the display and one that brought the danger of infection with the slicing action and pain of the cowhide. Greater crimes invoked a greater number of lashes or escalated beyond whipping to dismembering. Perhaps it was only economic practicality—the wariness of losing a working hand—that kept plantation justice from resulting in larger numbers of deaths from punishment. This occurred in the more formal court systems. Marvin L. Michael Kay and Lorin Lee Cary analyze criminal justice in North Carolina in *Slavery in North Carolina, 1748–1775* (1995) and leave no doubts about the barbarity of the system. All whites executed by order of North Carolina courts were hanged, but slaves, whose rate of execution exceeded that of whites by thirteen times, faced sadistic treatment before meeting a savage death. Half the slaves whose mode of execution is known in North Carolina between the mid-seventeenth century and the outbreak of the Revolution suffered clear brutality. "One was chained alive in a gibbet to die slowly and horribly," write Kay and Cary as they describe some of the executions:

BRUTALITY

Six were burned, two were castrated and then hanged, five were hanged and decapitated with their heads displayed on poles, one was hanged and burned . . . , two died as a result of castration, seven slaves . . . were shot or beaten to death when captured, and five outlawed runaways drowned themselves to avoid capture and sadistic treatment.

In populated areas from New York City to New Orleans, such executions often were prolonged and public. African-American men and women accused of plotting a rebellion might be burned alive or killed "at the wheel," a torturous medieval device that broke the person's limbs and left him or her out in the elements to linger in pain before dying. For the purpose of teaching appropriate lessons, white authorities sometimes left bodies hanging in gibbets or severed heads atop poles, about town or at busy crossroads, until they decomposed.

Such brutality had to affect all elements of slave societies. One need not wonder where the men who wrote the United States Constitution in the 1780s came up with the idea for strictures against cruel and inhuman punishments.

Resistance, Escape, and Rebellion

A spirit of resistance and the potential for escape or rebellion ran deep in the colonial slave population. Masters who were honest with themselves never harbored any notion that the men and women they held in bondage were truly a contented lot. They lived in a world where African Americans were daily expressing rebellious disgust for their situations in dozens of little ways, and one where the potential for uprising was always present. Proof is in the body of laws that existed to prevent such action. As slave populations grew, suspicion, distrust, and fear filled the minds of white colonists and became manifest in colonial statutes. Eighteenth-century slave codes limited the number of blacks who could meet in groups, forbade their carrying anything resembling weapons, kept blacks on the farm or plantation and off streets after dark, and even outlawed their possession of drums or horns, "which may give notice to one another of their wicked designs." Capital offenses included arson, poisoning, repeated theft, inciting insurrection, and resisting interrogation. Police kept a close eye on urban blacks, slave patrols guarded rural areas, and white colonists remained vigilant. Local justices could resort to the equivalent of medieval torture to keep the slave population docile, but it was masters and overseers who most frequently corrected slave misbehavior in ways the law allowed. Colonial statutes permitted branding, flogging, burning, amputation of limbs, hamstringing, and execution. Records of administration of these punishments are wondrously matter-of-fact. Middlesex County, Virginia, in the first twenty-five years of the eighteenth century was probably typical. During that period the government saw to the sale of eight blacks to the West Indies (with compensation for their owners) for "frequent disorderly meetings." A minister and two accomplices beat to death the clergyman's slave for running away. A vengeful slave owner castrated one slave for "running away, lying out and distroying peoples Stocks"; cut off the toes of another for "lying out and doing Severall Misdemeanors"; and pilloried and cut off the ears of a third for a second offense of stealing. Another Middlesex court executed a slave for treason, dismembering him and hanging one of his quarters in a public place.

In the face of such punishments, slaves were imminently practical. Forms of resistance ranged along a continuum from small acts of forgetfulness (failure to remember critical parts of a message, for instance) or carelessness (which might result in breaking a tool, ruining a plant, harming a pig or cow, or burning a stack of hay); to feigning illness or malingering; to mocking whites (and masters in particular) in clever words, songs, and actions; to stealing; to running away; and ultimately to organized, mass, armed rebellion. The particular form resisting slaves selected at any time or place depended on its chances for success, but the extent of slaves' acculturation and the kind of work they did also had a strong bearing on the ways they resisted.

"Saltwater" slaves had a tendency on arrival to run away with others who spoke the same language—or even, sometimes, with shipmates. However, it did not take them long to grasp the reality of their situations. Africans not long in the colonies, still without much command of English and living an isolated existence with few other slaves, resisted in subtle ways. They ruined crops, broke tools, malingered and balked, feigned sickness or stupidity, or stole goods or animals for sale on the black market. Household slaves under closer supervision simply worked slowly, acted surly, or got drunk regularly. Alcohol consumption among certain groups of slaves was considerable. Most blacks not fully acculturated who did run away were more truant than long absent. Their limited ability to exist unnoticed in white society made them "outliers" upon escape. They hid in the woods and stuck close to the people they knew.

More often than people at the time wished to admit, African men and women headed for the near or more distant frontier and attempted to form settlements of runaways—called "maroon" settlements (from the Portuguese *cimarrón*, for runaway). It was harder to do this in the Chesapeake, given the African minority and a topography that did not lend itself to hiding, but the Low Country, with its black majority and a terrain difficult to cross, with more places to remove oneself and go unnoticed, was the scene of more runaways and maroon camps. Once Spanish authorities established the aforementioned town of freed Carolina slaves at Gracia Real de Santa Teresa de Mose, some two miles outside of St. Augustine in 1738, more Low-Country slaves lit out southward to gain their freedom. Some, who chose not to attempt the difficult passage all the way to Florida, built their own settlements. A 1765 expedition against a maroon group up the Savanna River found the escapees inhabiting a small "town" surrounded by a swamp. Running off the residents (including "two Negroes on a Scaffold one Beating a Drum and the other hoisting Colours"), the members of the force found "a square consisting of four Houses 17 feet long and 14 feet wide, that the kettles were upon the fire boiling rice and about 15 bushels of rough rice." White colonists were especially intent on rooting out these settlements and then taking steps to prevent their further establishment. At the Savanna River town, they gathered up "Blanketts, Potts, Shoes, Axes, and many other tools all of which together with the Town they set fire to."

The more assimilated slaves became, the more wise they were to the ways of whites and thus the more capable of finding more subtle, but still satisfying intellectual responses to their condition in bondage or, in more extreme cases, fleeing it. Runaway advertisements provide unintended evidence of African-American expressions of resistance and contempt for whites through such normal manifestations of feelings as body movements. Colonial masters described fugitives who, "when speaking looks you full in the face," or who possessed "a sneaking down look," a "sour countenance," or "a Swaggering Air with him in his Walk." Piersen in *Black Legacy* calls attention to "a resistance too civilized to notice"—blacks' reliance on aggressive humor, satire, and pointed song and verse, all with bases in African methods for defusing hostility and checking antisocial behavior, to mock white figures of authority generally and their masters particularly. During celebrations of the annual black Election Day in colonial New England, the pomposity of black officials were characterizations of whites that the latter regarded with humor, "good naturedly submitting," wrote one observer, "to the hard hits leveled against themselves." Outside of Charleston, South Carolina, in 1772, a white man who sneaked up to view African Americans at a Saturday night country dance failed to find it so funny. "The entertainment was opened by the men copying (or taking off) the manners of their masters," he reported in the *South Carolina Gazette*, "and the women those of their mistresses, and relating some highly curious anecdotes, to the inexpressible diversion of that company." Songs of colonial Louisiana slaves could be more biting still, relating white thoughts and actions that were far beyond blacks' normal mention or ability to control:

> Negro cannot walk, without corn in his pocket,
>   It is to steal chickens.
> Mulatto cannot walk without rope in his pocket,
>   It is to steal horses.
> White man cannot walk without money in his pockets,
>   It is to steal girls.

Piersen believes that Americans have failed to recognize such forms of "intellectual resistance" because of a "national predilection for physical violence." We therefore have tended to focus on "the brute force of isolated rebellions," he believes, while overlooking "more civilized and more common forms of social pressure based on the African predisposition for wry humor and verbal cleverness."

Perhaps it was those less clever with words and better with their hands who took to flight. Skilled artisans who were fully acculturated and moved freely between rural and urban environments were the ones most likely to try to escape from slavery altogether. Carpenters, "fishing Negroes," and boatmen were especially apt to run away for good. In the colonial era there was no northern bastion of freedom to run to, of course, but these runaways often headed for towns where they could get lost among the handful of free blacks and lower-class whites that made up the substratum of society. The North Carolina piedmont, populated by nonslaveholding whites, was another haven for fugitives. So was Spanish Florida. Fugitive blacks ran away alone, many to rejoin relatives, and they relied on their skills and savvy to get jobs and carry on new lives.

Outright rebellion occupied the extreme end of the resistance-rebellion spectrum. Herbert Aptheker in *American Negro Slave Revolts* (1943, rev. ed. 1969) notes that periods of widespread slave rebelliousness came in waves every generation or so, "as though anger accumulated and vented itself and then a period of rest and recuperation was needed before the next upsurge." There seem to have been waves of general slave unrest, which may have corresponded with slave rebelliousness in the Caribbean and the greater Atlantic world, between 1710 and 1722, 1730 and 1740, 1765 and 1780, and 1790 and 1802. If full-scale rebellions did not occur regularly every few years, when they did they surely gained notice in colonial society, sometimes out of proportion to their significance. Here, again, chance of success was a guiding principle. African Americans greatly outnumbered by whites thought better of joining insurrections. Because this was frequently the case in the mainland colonies—different from most other New World slave societies, where slave rebellions were more common—incidents of open rebellion were relatively rare. Still, since colonial publications did not spread word of conspiracies and insurrections, there is a sense that more were planned than most white colonists (and, subsequently, most historians) perceived. Evidence from such widely separated locations as New York City, Charleston, and New Orleans suggests that Africans, or blacks who were able to create some real or artificial African identity with other slaves in this country, were involved in some of the largest conspiracies and rebellions. The urban setting, where slave men and women had greater freedom of movement and broader choice of their contacts—and where blacks met with all sorts of people in back-alley taverns where rum flowed freely, was particularly conducive to organized rebellion. Benjamin Franklin seems to have captured the general tone of some urban slaves when he described Philadelphia blacks as being of a "plotting Disposition."

And plotting that occurred in New York City and its environs bore fruit that was deadly for some whites and painful for many more. Only recently have historians given the general black unrest and slave conspiracies of eighteenth-century New York their due. During the century's first decade, slaves in New York and New Jersey grew increasingly angry over new, harsher laws restricting their activities. In rural areas the result was an occasional murder of a slave owner, followed by the horrors of a slave execution; in the city, slave unrest involved group activities. On April 1, 1712, a group of some two dozen slaves led by a core of Gold-Coast Africans (to whom contemporary whites gave an ethnic or national identity as Coromantee) set fire to the home of a prominent New Yorker and then shot and stabbed whites who were coming to extinguish the flames. Altogether the group killed eight whites and wounded about a dozen others. New York authorities eventually captured twenty-one of the conspirators and, after a quick trial, publicly executed eighteen of them in a variety of inhumane ways for their participation.

Other plots and conspiracies turned up in New York City in 1721 and 1734, but the grandest one of all took place in 1741. Over the winter of 1740–41 a group of blacks, with support from poorer Irish, English, Dutch, and Spanish men and women, who frequented some of New York's waterside taverns, joined together to plan a rebellion with mighty potential. Graham Russel Hodges in *Root and Branch: African Americans in New York and East Jersey, 1613–1863* (1999) detects "a powerful proletarian republicanism" in the plot, the conspirators being held together by the fact that (as one of the slaves involved was reported saying) "a great many people had too much, and others too little." Evidence turned up also of some of the conspirators being aware of a general black rebelliousness around the western Atlantic and many slaves being displeased that their Christianity held out little prospect for freedom. As before, arson was the favored tool of the conspirators. Fire destroyed New York's Fort George and several white homes before whites in power uncovered the plot. "Only the discovery of loose talk," Hodges writes, "kept the 1741 plot from becoming the worst racial uprising in colonial North America." Trials of the conspirators lasted through the summer of 1741 and the resultant executions were an almost daily occurrence for several weeks. Yet, it seems that no matter how many accused black conspirators were gibbeted about the city, no matter how many black bodies were broken at the wheel in the most public of places, African Americans continued to chafe at their bonds and join others in plots of rebellion along and around the lower Hudson.

But slave uprisings were not limited to northern cities. In fact, most historians consider the slave uprising that began near the Stono River, within twenty miles of Charleston, South Carolina, on September 9, 1739, to have been the most serious of the colonial period—in part because it triggered other rebellions and acts of resistance over several years. A core of perhaps twenty newly arrived "Angolan" slaves—more likely men who once were part of the Kingdom of Kongo just north of the Congo River—apparently planned the Stono Rebellion. Since many of these people were Portuguese-speaking Catholics, and since Spanish East Florida offered freedom in a setting friendly to Catholicism, some at the time speculated that Spanish propaganda played a role in instigating the uprising. Under the leadership of a slave named Jemmy, twenty blacks broke into a store, where they stole small arms and powder, killing the storekeepers and leaving their severed heads on the front steps. By daybreak, as they moved southward along the road toward Georgia, they had killed eight whites. Through the early afternoon they killed most of the whites they encountered— they spared the life of a white tavern keeper who was known for his kindness to his slaves—and burned houses. Around midday the group, whose ranks had swollen to fifty or sixty, met up with South Carolina's Lieutenant Governor, William Bull, returning to Charleston for the commencement of a new legislative session. Bull apparently had to ride hard to escape with his life.

After halting in an open field in midafternoon, the rebels, according to a contemporary "Account of the Negroe Insurrection," "set to dancing, Singing and beating Drums to draw more Negroes to them." Although before evening a force of mounted planters attacked and dispersed the gathering that at one time may have approached one hundred persons, it took nearly a week for a white militia company to catch and overcome the largest remnant of the group. John Thornton in "African Dimensions of the Stono Rebellion," *American Historical Review*, 96 (1991), suggests that the remaining core of fighters may have been individuals who had been soldiers in Africa, knew how to use firearms effectively, and relied on proven tactics of engagement, withdrawal, relocation, and reengagement to hold off their pursuers. Certain of the rebels were not apprehended for several months after the uprising began, and one leader remained at large for three years. Altogether, thirty whites and forty-four blacks died in the slaughter associated with the insurrection, and the spirit of rebellion remained in the Low-Country air for several years afterward. This uprising prompted South Carolina to lump together all blacks as dangerous to white society, whether "of a rebellious nature" or not, and systematically tighten restrictions (on free blacks as well as slaves) with the harshest penalties of any mainland colony.

Through the middle of the eighteenth century, newcomers from Africa seem to have been the ones most likely to join in rebellion. Thereafter, open rebellion was something plotted by the most highly assimilated slaves in the colonies. Mullin in *Flight and Rebellion* explains the irony of slave rebellions being tied to the acculturation process. As slaves acculturated according to their masters' designs, they learned their roles on the farm or plantation or in the house or factory, but they also learned strategies that would help them rise against their owners. Late in the colonial period the liberal influence of the American Revolution and the increased need for skilled slaves around cities led to a relaxing of restraints upon African Americans in urban areas. Freer to meet and more able to plan, it was these slaves who in 1800 organized "Gabriel's Rebellion," which Mullin considers "the most sophisticated and ambitious slave conspiracy" in American history. Acculturation, he concludes, "ultimately created slaves who were able to challenge the security of the society itself."

Yet, one final form of rebellion in which African Americans participated turned out to be more ambitious than any other. James Oliver Horton and Lois E. Horton in *In Hope of Liberty: Culture, Community and Protest Among Northern Free Blacks, 1700–1860* (1997) place northern blacks in a class grouping with Indians and poorer whites, who increasingly resisted what they perceived as gross injustice of their social and economic position. "Interracial ceremony and celebration, social interaction, and familial connection became the building blocks of their alliance," write the Hortons. "Arson, riot, and even armed insurrection became their political tools." As the century wore on and notions of liberty spread among persons living around the colonial Atlantic, groupings of the so-called "lower sorts," which included blacks, became more willing to take action on such ideals in the ways that worked best for them. After the middle of the eighteenth century, the British government became a target for such rebellious action.

After 1763, African Americans in northern cities joined others in feeling the pinch that came with the economic downturn following the end of the Seven Years War, and they were in the mobs that took to the streets in protest of the tightening British regulations that were only making things worse. Interracial gathering spots—taverns and back-alley gaming spots—again became centers for this rebellious activity in northern colonial cities. It must have been with mixed feelings that white colonial elites and middle-class elements looked on, disliking England's tightening controls on the colonies more than they feared the public expression of the "lower elements." Many in Boston approved of the activities of the "saucy boys, negroes and mulattoes, Irish teagues and outlandish jack-tarrs," led by runaway slave Crispus Attucks, who on March 5, 1770, following an incident with a British soldier in a dockside tavern, taunted and harassed the guards at the Custom House until the Redcoats opened fire. The Boston Massacre was a spark for the fire of liberty that swept across the colonies soon afterward. African Americans in and out of slavery played no small part in the work of kindling that flame.

CHAPTER FOUR

The Revolutionary Era

= contradictions

For African Americans the American Revolution was full of contradictions, the clearest of which involved slavery and the ideology the Founding Fathers used to justify breaking with England. A third of the men who signed the document declaring their right to independent nationhood on the self-evident truth that all men are created equal owned other humans. In addition, the nation these men would create—one that would secure the blessings of liberty to themselves and their posterity—was one whose social and economic fabric was woven with the thread of black slavery, whose population included half a million African-American slaves, and whose wealthiest southerners would not consider joining a union of states without a clear recognition of their right to own black men, women, and children.

But the contradictions involved more than slavery and Revolutionary ideology. Among the results of the Revolution were paradoxical changes in African-American society and culture. The Revolution helped make it possible for some blacks to gain their freedom. It played an important role in the ending of slavery in the states north of Maryland and in considerable manumission in the

good changes

Upper South, and it gave even more African Americans the idea that freedom was not merely something good to obtain, but something one had a right to expect. Yet, when one considers numbers, it becomes clear that the Revolutionary era did little to reduce the country's reliance on slaves. Not 500,000 slaves lived on the British North American mainland in 1776; nearly 700,000 were counted in the first census of the new United States in 1790. Where emancipation did occur, in the North and Upper South, in almost every instance it came grudgingly, and in all areas white sons of the Revolution began circumscribing that freedom soon after more than a few blacks had gained it. North and South, white men in positions of authority cut away at African-American rights, privileges, and opportunities, so that the black men and women who no longer were slaves remained separated and ostracized from the rest of American society.

BUT country still reliant on slaves

separate

Also, for those thousands of Americans who remained in bondage and for the many thousands of Americans who would be slaves over the next four-score years, the Revolution made freedom more difficult to obtain. Following the break with England, slavery in the states south of Maryland grew in size and strength. Southern slave-holders became all the more convinced that the institution was necessary for their economic survival. And American independence entrenched slavery into the laws of the new land. Without mentioning slavery, the Constitution made the institution legitimate and gave slaveholders greater means to protect and defend their human property. In legitimizing slavery and strengthening the hold of slave owners, founders of the new nation set the stage for the enormous expansion of slavery into what would become the Cotton South—the open and newly acquired lands to the south and west early in the nineteenth century.

Yet most important for blacks in the United States over the long term, and probably most ironic, the Revolution brought a broadening and strengthening of the hierarchical order to American race relations. Although most English colonists held strong feelings about race before the Revolution, they did not need to use race so centrally to justify enslaving other human beings. Once Revolutionary theory made all persons free and equal with God-

English used race but not to enslave

given inalienable rights, many who spoke the new ideals had cause to further entrench their racist feelings. Now they could rationalize slavery only by recognizing African Americans as a lower order of persons, short on morals, long on muscle, quick to pilfer, slow to move, and hard to work. And they could remain above the new and rapidly growing body of free blacks they despised only by using the same rationale. This affected all Americans and laid the foundation for a stronger and more pervasive racist ideology that would plague the country from the time the Revolution had run its course until the present day.

Slavery and Ideology

Westerners had long been in conflict over the existence of slavery in their society. Within the eighteenth-century body of thought we know as the Enlightenment, strong intellectual forces emerged that worked against chattel slavery. Based initially on religious principles, and then bolstered by philanthropic tendencies accompanying the early growth of capitalism, antislavery sentiment arose in continental Europe and spread to England. By the time of the American Revolution, regardless of what else was going on, Western intellectuals and philosophers were reading and thinking and acting in a world that was debating slavery.

It was not as if there had been no opposition to slavery among British colonists on the North American mainland before 1750. To a few seventeenth-century Americans, human bondage had always been immoral and unChristian, and the number of opponents to slavery grew with the size of the slave population. A handful of New England Puritans and a few Scots and Salzburgers in Georgia spoke out against slavery in the eighteenth century, but those who took the lead in expressing antislavery sentiment were members of the Society of Friends—the Quakers. But the Quakers were an anomaly because many of them made profits from the slave trade, owned slaves themselves, and harbored doubts about black peoples' abilities. Not until the 1760s, when the supply of indentured servants increased and the supply of slaves decreased, did significant numbers of Philadelphia Quakers, for instance, begin following the antislavery principles they expressed formally in their yearly meetings. Nevertheless, as David Brion Davis writes in *The Problem of Slavery in Western Culture* (1966), "It would be difficult to exaggerate the central role Quakers played in initiating and sustaining the first antislavery movements." Some of them spoke out early. At a Friends meeting in Germantown, Pennsylvania, in 1688, a group of Quakers drafted a formal protest against slavery and "the traffic of men-body." In 1711 the Society of Friends in Rhode Island rid itself of a member who was mistreating a slave, and a year later a prosperous Philadelphia Quaker vainly petitioned the Pennsylvania Assembly to emancipate all slaves in the colony. By the middle of the eighteenth century the English-speaking world was becoming increasingly aware of the official Quaker antipathy for slavery. Under the leadership of such persons as Benjamin Lay, John Woolman, and Anthony Benezet, uncompromising Quakers were pressing for disowning members of the Society who continued to hold slaves. If, as Donald L. Robinson argues in *Slavery and the Struggle for American Politics, 1765–1820* (1971), the Quaker efforts were "like fireflies in the night," at least by the time of the Seven Years' War the nighttime horizon that framed the hills and valleys and village greens of the American colonies was aglow. By then, Quakers had launched a frontal attack on the slave trade and had brought the broader ideas of antislavery thinking before the educated public, where they were ripe for debate. The tensions that grew between England and its mainland colonies after the Seven Years' War thus raised arguments against and flushed out a rationalization for slavery, even as they prompted colonists to question existing mercantile practices and to dwell on ways in which their political and economic lives could be better.

Many of the men who provided the ideology of the American Revolution considered themselves scions of the Enlightenment. Their faith in Man's limitless creative intelligence and rational, benevolent behavior brought them to apply their minds to creating a new order. No more oppression from religious zealots or tyrannous monarchs, no more misery or deprivation for the people in their society. The new order would provide persons of all classes the freedom to seek happiness and unleash their talents on their natural circumstances to the benefit of all. The result would be what the rational, benevolent Creator intended.

Of course, this was an ideology into which slavery did not fit, and the American patriots knew it. Like despotism, slavery was a vestige of the Old World, a violation of human rights. By being born human, people had inherent rights to freedom, to gain from their work, and to improve their lives as they wished. Skin color was not supposed to matter.

Much of this kind of thinking was in the mind of young Thomas Jefferson when he wrote the document that would justify the colonists' political break with England. Jefferson even blamed the English monarch for the slave trade in the first draft of the Declaration of Independence. Members of the Continental Congress excised those portions because of the absurdity of blaming George III for what Rhode Island merchants and Virginia planters had been getting rich from for scores of years. However, slavery seemed to be doomed with the Declaration's first paragraph. All men were created equal; their God-given, unalienable rights included life, liberty, and the pursuit of happiness; governments were created to secure these rights. Nowhere did it limit application of this heady language.

But the new republic did not end slavery. It perpetuated the institution for the better part of another century. Why this happened and how the signers of the Declaration and framers of the Constitution (which put ideals into policy) could justify slavery even as they asserted the inalienable right of freedom for all are questions with which historians still grapple.

Jefferson easily becomes a symbol of the Revolutionary paradox and thus the focus of much of the questioning. Because he penned the words of the Declaration of Independence and espoused most eloquently its ideals, he stands out among those "enlightened" men who waged the rebellion and put together the new nation. Jefferson spoke often of wanting to end slavery in the spirit of the French *philosophes* he admired. Many have asked why the framer of the Declaration, the future president, and the slave owner never put into action his libertarian ideals, even with his own slaves.[1] Answers have varied. One turns on the practical argument. In addition to being one of the most respected men in colonial America, Jefferson owned over two hundred slaves. They built his beloved Monticello and made it run. Jefferson also was one of Virginia's wealthiest citizens. He recognized that his economic position and political status were tied to a slave system. And he knew that system was growing; demand for slaves was increasing steadily, values of human property were rising. Ending slavery would have meant political, social, and economic suicide for Jefferson and wealthy slave owners like him.

Another answer is based on Jefferson's deep-seated feelings of dislike for blacks. Today we would speak of his racism. It is difficult not to be startled by the strength and character of his racist feelings. In his *Notes on the State of Virginia* (1785), which he intended for European intellectuals, Jefferson described blacks as "inferior to the whites in the endowments of body and mind." From "scientific observation" he wrote of blacks' laziness and slowness, their inability to reason, their lack of imagination, their "disagreeable odour," and their unsightly appearance compounded by "wooly hair" and an "ungainly" physique.[2] If Jefferson truly joined others of the Enlightenment in wanting to end chattel slavery, as he often wrote, his commitment to do so was only theoretical. He expressed strong dislike for African Americans and did not want to live with them as his equals in a free society. Racial prejudice joined with economic necessity, as he saw it, to keep him from putting theory into practice.

Jeff. was racist

---

1 Paul Finkelman in *Slavery and the Founders: Race and Liberty in the Age of Jefferson* (1976) argues that questions about Jefferson and slavery arise primarily because historians and biographers who treat Jefferson as "the most popular saint of American civil religion," have regularly "tried to fudge the evidence, or simply ignored it, to make Jefferson into something he was not. . . . Admirers of Jefferson would like him to be one of us—an opponent of slavery," Finkelman writes. "But he was not."

2 The recent DNA-based affirmation of Jefferson's long-standing sexual relationship with one of his slaves, Sally Hemings, brings out the sharp contrast between his beliefs and prejudices on the one hand and his actions on the other. And that he enslaved—and kept in slavery—individuals who were his offspring and other close relatives only heightens the paradox relating to the man and his views on blacks and slavery.

A third answer goes beyond Jefferson and has to do with proslavery sentiment among whites in at least part of the British North American mainland. White Virginians seemed to have shared Jefferson's dislike for blacks, but not so many held his expressed concern for slaves as humans. After all, Jefferson was one of the most enlightened members of American society—schooled at William and Mary, thoroughly read in history and philosophy, and by the age of thirty well versed in current libertarian ideas. Most of the rest of American society was different. In 1784 and 1785 over twelve hundred people signed petitions to the Virginia General Assembly opposing a 1782 Virginia law that simply allowed masters to free their slaves without legislative approval. The signers based their proslavery arguments on scripture and the right to private property that the Revolution had affirmed, and they felt less of a necessity to rationalize their stance on slavery than did the man who wrote so eloquently about the "rights of man" in the Declaration of Independence.

Important to remember, too, is that the fragile coalition of diverse economic and social groups that joined forces against England did so to wage a political revolution. What held the coalition together was agreement on wanting to rid themselves of tight English control. It was necessarily to justify independence that they agreed on the application of Enlightenment theory. But the small farmers and urban artisans, the northern capitalists and southern planters agreed on little else—indeed, the coalition broke apart before the newborn United States of America was past toddling— and they clearly did not agree on whether the new nation should proceed with or without slavery.

So, in spite of the lofty ideals held up to effect it, the Revolution failed to eradicate slavery from the nation that replaced British rule over the North American mainland. But in raising the issues of freedom and human dignity the Revolution did bring significant change to all parts of American society. For blacks in the northern states and for growing numbers of them in the Upper South, this change meant becoming free persons. For many in the Lower South it meant greater personal independence, albeit within a slave system that was growing and becoming more deeply entrenched. Finally, the arguments for freedom and the growing presence of free blacks in certain segments of society led toward a hardening of racial lines and movement toward a system in which all African Americans, slave or free, would be regarded as members of a despised lower caste.

Freedom for Some

The history of African Americans in the English North American mainland colonies for the century between 1670 and the outbreak of the American Revolution is a story of persons in bondage. In most places in North America there simply were no blacks who were not enslaved. Good population figures do not exist for the colonies, but it seems that before 1770 free blacks made up only about 5 percent of the colonial African-American population. Nearly all of these people resided in the northern colonies, where they lived largely without influence in white society. Many of the free blacks in pre-Revolutionary America were children of black-white marriages. A few had physical disabilities or were simply too old to be useful slaves.

But the situation with free blacks changed considerably during the time of the American Revolution. The 1770s and 1780s saw the beginning of the slow but steady eradication of slavery in the North and the startling growth of a free-black population in the Upper South. From the situation, it is natural to assume considerable cause and effect: that the moral, intellectual, political, and military ferment of Revolutionary times prompted the colonies' white population to take action that resulted in slavery's demise in one section and its decline in another. But recent scholarship has shown that other factors besides the moral arguments of the rising libertarian ideology were important in the turn away from dependence on slavery in some locales. In particular, it has shown that no end of resolute African Americans, mostly (though not entirely) those enslaved, forced the issue on a white public not altogether eager to end their advantaged and exploitative position with those in bondage and, as it turned out, not at all ready to provide opportunity for, or witness the social or economic advancement of, persons of African descent.

From the time of the codification of slavery a century earlier, whites steadily had been reducing the liberties of those few free African Americans in their midst. In various places blacks' political rights did not exist, and African Americans were ostracized socially. Through most of the eighteenth century individual Virginians could manumit their slaves only with permission of the state assembly. Whites in southern colonies were especially blunt in expressing their views on free blacks. The governor of Virginia in 1723 asserted whites should place "a perpetual Brand upon Free-Negroes & Mulattos by excluding them from the great Priviledge of a Freeman," in order to "make the free Negroes sensible that a distinction ought to be made between their offspring and the Descendants of an Englishman, with whom they never were to be Accounted Equal."

Neither Virginia's governor nor other southern whites—nor northern whites, for that matter—had cause to worry about free blacks before 1770, but the Revolution altered the situation for all. The slave system of the nonplantation North did not last in the milieu of Revolutionary America. By the middle of the eighteenth century it was already a weak institution in the rural areas. Landholders were busy dividing large estates that slaves had worked into small farms. And those who owned more than a few slaves were having difficulty finding employment for their bondspeople through winter months. Persons not fond of African Americans in the first place began questioning the necessity of slavery and, thus, of a black presence in the colonies. And after 1763, with large numbers of German and Scots-Irish eager to come to America and work off indentures or for low wages, the notion of getting along without forced black labor gained support.

Then came war. A few owners manumitted slaves on condition they enlist in colonial militia units, and some northern blacks participated in the earliest skirmishes of the war. Benjamin Quarles in *The Negro in the American Revolution* (1961) names a dozen African Americans who fought with the other "minutemen" at Lexington and Concord, and he cites a December 1775 petition of fourteen Massachusetts officers to the General Court, stating "that a negro called Salem Poor, of Col. Frye's regiment, Capt.

Ames' company, in the late battle at Charlestown [Bunker Hill], behaved like an experienced officer, as well as an excellent soldier."

Not so many slaves simply waited around for their masters to act, however. Once fighting began in earnest and armies were afoot in the land—foraging, stealing, occupying and then evacuating cities, and bringing general chaos to broad areas of the eastern seaboard—African-American men, and eventually women and children as well, took advantage of the situation and set out for the combat zones. Soon fugitive slaves were doing everything from scouting, foraging, and cooking for armies of both sides. Some served as camp prostitutes. Regardless of their personal skills, escaped slaves chose to ally themsevles with the side offering them the easiest route to freedom.

escaped slaves choosing sides

Fears that southern whites harbored at the prospect of arming blacks led to prohibitions on black recruitment, but not for long. By 1777, when Congress fixed troop quotas for each state and legislatures began offering bounties for enlistment, free blacks and slaves sent to serve for their masters began filtering into recruitment stations. By 1781 several states were ready to grant freedom to the slave and a bounty to the master for the slaves' three-year enlistment.

A good number of northern slaves ended their bondage by siding with the British. When British regulars and Hessians swept across Long Island and moved into New Jersey over the summer and fall of 1776, slaves from all about the region fled their masters, and when the patriots pushed the British back into New York City, the fugitive blacks went along with the Redcoats. In all of the coastal cities to which British forces clung tenaciously, blacks served as auxiliaries on the promise of freedom. They worked as teamsters, carried messages, prepared food, and collected rubbish in New York and Philadelphia. In the latter city, following its evacuation in 1778, a local newspaper admitted that a "great part of the slaves hereabouts, were enticed away by the British army." And rarely did those who joined the British ever return to their masters. At war's end British officers refused to turn over the former slaves who had joined them prior to 1782. When they evacuated New York in 1783 the British took with them three

working w/ the Redcoats

thousand African Americans, many of whom ended up as residents of Canada or England.

The Revolution was a fertile medium for a growing moral opposition to slavery in some of the northern colonies. Antislavery forces had been active on the local level in New England since the 1750s. The Quaker campaign was strongest in Pennsylvania, and in Massachusetts and New Hampshire blacks' petitions for freedom and land of their own did not always appear before blind eyes. And by the late 1770s these efforts paid off, as states began drafting constitutions that contained the Revolution's humanitarian ideals. Vermont was first to spell these out: "No male person ought to be holden by law to serve any person as a servant, slave, or apprentice after he arrives to the age of twenty-one years, nor female in like manner after she arrives to the age of eighteen years."

Meanwhile, in Massachusetts, in an atmosphere of rising religous moralism and growing debate about English oppression, the executions of two slaves, one for murder and one for rape, focused public questioning on the morality of slavery. Test cases began pecking away at the institution's constitutionality. As they did, slaves began leaving their masters, feeling certain that courts would not support their forced return. One such fugitive was Quock Walker, who, during the Revolutionary War, left his master, Nathaniel Jennison, and took a job for wages with a neighbor about a mile down the road in Barre, Massachusetts. In 1781 Jennison approached Walker at work in the neighbor's field, beat him soundly, and took him home. Whites in Barre reacted strongly and Walker sued. In 1783, Massachusetts's Supreme Judicial Court, in *Commonwealth* v. *Jennison*, found that the clause of the state's 1780 constitution declaring "all men are born free and equal" applied to Walker and indeed to all. According to T. H. Breen in "Making History: The Force of Public Opinion and the Last Years of Slavery in Revolutionary Massachusetts," in *Through a Glass Darkly: Reflections on Personal Identity in Early America,* edited by Ronald Hoffman, Mechal Sobel, and Fredrika J. Teute (1997), stories of the executions and of Walker's exploits "briefly influenced the course of public opinion, shaping it, driving it forward, exposing tensions, crystallizing doubts, so eroding the institution of slavery that, at some critical moment in the history of Massachusetts, emancipation became common sense."

Elsewhere in the North abolition moved more slowly. In *Many Thousands Gone,* Berlin writes that slavery's waning there "was propelled more by atrophy of the slave population—owing to high mortality, low fertility, the close of the transatlantic slave trade, and the southward exportation of slaves for profit—than by the growth of liberty among blacks," and Nash and Soderlund in *Freedom by Degrees* write of post-Revolutionary, non-Quaker slaveholders as having been "overwhelmingly oblivious to the antislavery message." Policies of gradual abolition that northern state legislatures drew up ensured the Revolutionary generation its labor supply and enabled whites to keep African Americans in service until they could replace them with inexpensive white workers. The Pennsylvania General Assembly passed a gradual abolition law in 1780, long regarded favorably because it was the first of its kind, enacted before the British defeat at Yorktown. But Nash and Soderlund argue that the Pennsylvania act was most remarkable for what it did not do: free a single slave. The act consigned to twenty-eight years of labor (at a time when the average life expectancy of African Americans was thirty-four years) every child born to a slave woman after March 1, 1780, meaning that Pennsylvanians would continue—legally—to have black slaves in their midst for another seventy years. Connecticut and Rhode Island passed similar, though less-restrictive, acts in 1784. New York and New Jersey, where Hudson River farmers dug in their heels on the issue, were slow to follow. Each passed its own gradual abolition bill, New York in 1799 and New Jersey in 1804, so slavery lingered in the two states for several decades. New York remained the last northern bastion of the institution—its slave population grew by 25 percent in the 1790s and there were nearly twenty thousand slaves in the state in 1800. These numbers declined through the next two decades, however, and for all practical purposes slavery ceased to exist in the northern states by the end of the first quarter of the nineteenth century.

In the end, two factors helped abolition spread in the North. One simply was African Americans' unstoppable propensity to run away. As many as three-quarters of all young slave men in Philadelphia escaped in the 1780s; those who were caught ran again. In time, some slave owners recognized the impossibility of continuing to own human beings who had a will for freedom and an element of assistance in society to escape. The other factor had to do with the economic conditions of the North. Basic to the issue was that the northern economy did not have to rely on slavery, especially with the increasing number of inexpensive white laborers entering the country. Those who did not own slaves began to resent the advantages of those who did, and white workers resented having to compete with slave labor. Both groups soon favored abolition. So it turned out to be easier to apply the humanitarian ideology of the Revolution to all people in places where universal freedom did not ravage the economy and even seemed to open the marketplace to fairer competition.

Freedom did not bloom in the same fashion in the states of the Deep South, however. South Carolina and Georgia masters prohibited enlistment of blacks in the militia and freed only a tiny number of slaves during Revolutionary times. In fact, fears of any hint of a conspiracy that would lead to emancipation caused southern whites to react, sometimes with little respect for the law or humanity. In the summer of 1775, Jeremiah, a fisherman and valuable free-black harbor pilot in Charleston, was accused, on thin and questionable evidence, of collecting guns and urging other blacks to ready themselves to fight against the patriots in South Carolina. The court retained him in the workhouse for two months as they sought further evidence and hoped for his confession. As neither came and fears heightened, the court brought him to trial ("if such a process deserves the name," admitted South Carolina Governor Lord William Campbell), convicted him, and sentenced him to be "hanged and afterwards burned." After reviewing the trial transcripts, Campbell wrote, "my blood ran cold when I read on what grounds they have doomed a fellow creature to death."

Not even public dealing with episodes of such dubious disloyalty could keep slaves in the Lower South from seeking their freedom. The British-occupied islands off Charleston and Savannah became havens for runaways; patriot militias mounted raids on the islands to discourage their growth. But over time it became clear to Low-Country slaves that British forces had no more inclination to serve as their liberators than did the patriots. "While the war for the low country raged," writes Robert Olwell in *Masters, Slaves, and Subjects: The Culture of Power in the South Carolina Low Country, 1740–1790* (1998), "neither the royalist nor the republican combatants expressed much interest in slaves' hearts and minds. Rather, they fought for control of slaves' bodies to use as labourers, soldiers, or merely as confiscated property." To have an honest shot at achieving freedom, Low-Country slaves had to escape the bounds of what would become the new nation—heading west or south, toward Spanish Florida. In 1790, South Carolina had fewer than two thousand free blacks, mostly around Charleston. Georgia had four hundred. At the beginning of the nineteenth century the two states held only 7 percent of the free African-American population of the South.

Many of the forces that affected African Americans in other areas of the land during Revolutionary times seemed to have been magnified for blacks in the Chesapeake. Perhaps this was because the region was the heart of the mainland slave society, just as it was the seedbed of rebellion and revolutionary ideology. Talk of abolition and acts of manumission had greater implications for whites who were so dependent on a system of human bondage. For Chesapeake blacks, the lure of freedom, which seemed closer and more real than to their counterparts in the Lower South, prompted men and women to take bolder action for their cause.

Virginia planters were quick to recognize their vulnerable position. Late in 1774, not long before British naval officers in Norfolk Harbor began taking aboard runaway slaves, a young James Madison wrote to a friend in Philadelphia:

If America and Britain should come to a hostile rupture I am afraid an Insurrection among the slaves may and will be promoted. In one of our Counties lately a few of those unhappy wretches met together and chose a leader who was to conduct them when the English troops should arrive—which they foolishly thought would be very soon and that by revolting to them they should be rewarded with their freedom. Their intentions were soon discovered and the proper precautions taken to prevent the Infection. It is prudent such attempts should be concealed as well as suppressed.

Through the summer of 1775, slaves weighed their options and made whites fear their armed revolt in every southern colony. Then, as Madison feared, in November Virginia's British governor, John Murray, fourth Earl of Dunmore, who was fighting the provisional government for control of the colony, offered freedom to slaves and servants who would join the British and bear arms against the rebellious colonists. In less than a year a thousand slaves made off to Dunmore's vessels in Chesapeake Bay. He would likely have gotten more had not a smallpox epidemic among the refugees discouraged others who thought of following. The governor was able to use some fugitives in the December 1775 British defeat at Great Bridge; then over part of the next year he sent small bands of armed blacks on boats and barges to forage and plunder tidewater plantations, luring or forcing away more slaves.

After Dunmore's expulsion from a land base, British armies and privateers struck from the water at the plantation district between the James and York rivers, stealing livestock, tobacco, and slaves. When heavier fighting came to the region, royal armies in Virginia and North Carolina took in runaways. Members of the Virginia Convention reacted by instituting measures to keep their labor force intact. They authorized summary punishment of runaways, sanctioned transportation and sale of recaptives to the West Indies, and sentenced others to incarceration with the hardest labor. Still, the African Americans fled. Over the course of the fighting five thousand Chesapeake men and women in bondage found their way to the British forces. Many more learned of the promise of freedom, and their lives would never again be the same.

Unfortunately for the runaways, once cast with the British their lot seldom improved. Neither Dunmore, who never freed his own slaves, nor British army officers in Charleston or Savannah, nor privateers were advocates of emancipation. The British army was interested in undermining the patriots' economic base and getting military laborers for its campaigns in North America or recruits for service in the West Indies. Black "spoils of war" ended up victims of army priorities. The poorly fed, clothed, and quartered African Americans worked long hours in hot weather constructing earthworks, digging and filling latrines, burying garbage, and generally doing labor no one else cared to perform (to save British soldiers for battle, officers argued). Bouts of dysentery swept through their ranks, and because officers ordered the inoculation of white troops only, smallpox epidemics hit blacks frequently, and they died at alarming rates. Those who survived faced transport to East Florida, the British West Indies, or Nova Scotia, where life in slavery or freedom would be hard.

smallpox & dysentery amongst blacks

But fleeing to join the British was not the only way African Americans in the Upper South gained freedom. In the years immediately following the fighting, the existence of a new group of free blacks became apparent to residents of Maryland and Virginia. These free African Americans were darker skinned than the small handful of prewar free blacks in the two colonies, and soon their numbers were substantial. Fighting on the side of the patriots, especially as substitutes for their masters, brought freedom to some slaves in the Upper South. Wartime chaos helped slaves run away too, and some fugitives found their way to Maryland or Virginia cities and worked hard at blending into the lowest urban class. Then, throughout the 1770s and 1780s abolition sentiment, abetted by a sense of egalitarianism from the evangelical revival movement that continued to sweep the South, grew teeth. As Methodist and Baptist ministers chastised their congregations over the evils of slaveholding, some guilt-ridden masters began freeing slaves or letting them accumulate enough personal property to purchase their freedom. Around Baltimore, masters with less religious motivation acted out of awareness that the promise of freedom was the best incentive to get unmotivated slaves to work, knowing they could always buy replacements for those they eventually freed. In this milieu, some of the laws barring manumission fell to repeal.

egalitarianism through churches

With public acts of manumission occurring and talk of freedom in the air at war's end, more African Americans began taking individual action to join the ranks of the free. Black fugitives began heading north toward freedom, sometimes with assistance but largely unaided, beginning a trend that would continue and grow over the next seventy-five years. Although slave patrols increased, flight from slavery was easier now. With more free blacks in circulation and with light skin no longer a determinant of free status, runaways of all shades of skin could avoid detection once in the free African-American society. This was especially true in urban areas of the Upper South.

And once secure in their freedom, blacks worked to free their relatives. Some with good jobs saved for years to purchase kinsmen. In New Bern, North Carolina, black farmer and barber John C. Stanley had extraordinary success following his freedom in 1798. Between 1805 and 1818 Stanley purchased and freed his wife and two children, his wife's brother, and nineteen other African Americans in slavery. Some free blacks, unable to buy their loved ones, took other action. Enough free blacks assisted kinsmen in running away that wise masters kept tabs on their slaves' free relatives and thus knew where to look first for their fugitives.

Thus, it was in northern Virginia and Maryland where the ranks of free blacks swelled most steadily and dramatically. By 1790 there were thirty thousand African Americans living in freedom in the Upper South—more than in the northern states—and over the next decade that number would double. The presence of such a sizeable body of African Americans outside the controls of the slave system would cause white society considerable anxiety and would consequently be a factor in bringing change to the Chesapeake's black society.

Changing African-American Society

Up and down the Atlantic Coast and inland toward the newly opening backcountry, the Revolution altered the lives of African Americans. North of Maryland, blacks naturally experienced greater personal freedom as slavery there died its slow death. In South Carolina and Georgia, slaves achieved greater independence, but it was an independence within a slave system that was growing rapidly and becoming even more entrenched in white society. Blacks in the Chesapeake enjoyed greater freedom, too, with the rapid appearance and growth of the free-black population and with more liberties for those within slavery, but this occurred against a backdrop of growing commitment to slavery through the southern parts of the region. And the geographical parameters of black life in bondage were spreading through the period, for out on the Virginia and Carolina frontiers a new slave society was forming, with implications for further expansion of the institution.

So through the last decades of the eighteenth century, black society continued to evolve differently in various sections of the country. There was even growing diversity within regions. But, as the group of essays in *Slavery and Freedom in the Age of the American Revolution,* edited by Ronald Hoffman and Ira Berlin (1983), shows, across the growing diversity of black living conditions and lifestyles one could detect the beginnings of a single, broad, distinctly African-American society.

[margin note: diff experiences being free diff'n places]

The transition from servitude to freedom in the North was surprisingly difficult. The timing of his or her manumission, which varied by decades among the northern states, affected how the individual made the transition. So did regional demographic patterns, economic conditions, and white attitudes.

The popular image of African Americans learning of their freedom, usually through a statement from a sad master, and immediately casting off toward new and better lives appeals to romantic notions, but probably is inaccurate. Ties to "home," however connected with bondage "home" may have been, were strong, and there were practical considerations before one could hie for the city or even the farm down the road. First was livelihood. Freed slaves had to care for themselves, which usually meant they had to enter into arrangements of wage labor. Many went to work right away where they lived, and extrication from the master's household turned out to be a slow process. Between one-half and two-thirds of the men and women freed in the North were able to leave their masters' estates within a few years of abolition, but for a third or more ties were firm, the security was real, and leaving for good took longer.

[margin note: now free ↓ need to care for selves]

Still, even those African Americans who remained in or around the master's residence with the end of slavery quickly gained a clear sense of being different people, no longer bound by the personalities or rules of their masters. Studies of slave naming patterns in northern states show how slaves broke with their past almost immediately upon becoming free by ceasing to use the old, derisive first names their masters had given them—the classical Pompey or Caesar, the African day names of Cuffee or Quash, or such place names as York or Jamaica. They moved away also from the surnames of their masters. The names they chose, however, with many biblical first names and more English first and last names, suggest how far acculturation had come for African Americans in the North.

Blacks in northern rural districts, with little chance to obtain land and the wherewithal to gain true economic independence, quickly experienced the bite of rural poverty. Their lot resembled that of the sharecropping families of the Deep South a century later, with every family member working from youth to old adult, with children often bound out to apprenticeship, with men frequently hitting the road or seeking better times at sea, and with women left to hold the family together as the heads of house, often as they worked in white people's homes for next to nothing. In such circumstances, it is hardly surprising that many newly freed blacks tended to move toward the greater opportunities offered in the northern coastal cities. African-American populations of Boston, New York, and Philadelphia fairly soared with the ending of the war. New York's population of free blacks lagged behind that of the other two cities because of the continuing existence of a large slave population in the area. Philadelphia attracted newly freed blacks and runaways from Maryland and Virginia to the extent that between 1780 and 1800, while the city's white population doubled, its African-American population increased sixfold.

If the urban setting offered little room for true economic advancement, it still held the possibility of sustaining oneself on a low level. More African-American women moved to the city than men because jobs there as domestics were always plentiful, if not lucrative. Meanwhile skilled urban black men began losing their positions, finding discrimination in apprenticeships once open to them as slaves and realizing that whites would now hire free blacks for only the most menial labor. Some free men took to the sea, figuring that work on vessels provided the greatest economic opportunity, but most free African-American men remained in the city and worked as day laborers or servants. So even in their new status, it was black men and women who ended up doing much of a city's dirty work.

What the city did offer free blacks was the advantage of living with others of their culture. Blacks living in small numbers in the northern countryside were isolated and thus targets for white hostility, which rose with the ending of slavery locally. But in the city, African Americans in good numbers lived near one another and soon black community institutions existed that provided them security. It was in the city that men and women could more easily find marriage partners and begin families; it was there they could join in worship, combine resources to educate their young, and come together for camaraderie and mutual support.

Cities: Could live w/ others of their culture

All of this movement associated with freedom, however, was hard on African-American families. By 1770 the family was the cornerstone of most of black society in America. Becoming free and moving away from the master's household disturbed family stability. In addition to normal problems associated with poverty, especially husbands and wives being too poor to live together, many black families experienced the unsettling circumstances of wholesale relocation. It would take time to recreate a stable family life in a new setting. Once extricated from white residences but not yet able to form their own nuclear households, poor blacks often combined with relatives or friends to establish separate residences. Having two or more nuclear families in a single household or taking in boarders helped pay expenses. Transition to a pattern of two-parent households took time following abolition. Yet far from being the unstable, matrilocal institution that social scientists long portrayed, the post-abolition African-American family in the North became stable and autonomous about a generation after it appeared. Both parents lived at home and played important roles in the maintenance of the household. What is more, the black family broadened its boundaries and tended to include everyone who was part of the household, from boarders to members of other families. Thus it quickly resembled the extended family of the African village more than it did any similar American institution.

FAMILY

In rural areas black residence patterns remained separate and varied, but in northern cities one could see by the 1780s the beginnings of a pattern of residential clustering and the formation of small but integral neighborhoods. Separate black churches appeared, initially as refuges from discrimination in white churches and as places where blacks could worship in the emotional fashion they preferred. Churches provided burial grounds, centers for common activities, and seedbeds for benevolent and fraternal organizations. Congregations pooled their resources and started "African" schools for training their young. Pulpits of the early black churches in the North were the springboards of the leaders of the new free-black community. From unimpressive beginnings, usually in small church buildings with minimal facilities, came recognition of blacks as individuals with a common culture as well as common problems. Along with this recognition came some of the earliest efforts to improve the lot of those persons in America who began thinking of themselves as "free Africans."

Gary B. Nash in "Forging Freedom: The Emancipation Experience in the Northern Seaport Cities, 1775–1820" in *Slavery and Freedom in the Age of the American Revolution* shows how the continued existence of slavery delayed development of community institutions in northern cities. Obtaining freedom required the resources of those who were free. Then, once free, a generation passed before African Americans were able to relocate and become part of a neighborhood where people had a community of interests. But by the end of the Revolutionary era, the basis would be there for the growth of black social and community institutions that, by the early nineteenth century, would be the envy of poor whites in similar situations.

If the Revolution prompted questioning, and then the demise, of slavery in the North, it generally failed to cause whites in the country's southern extreme to reflect seriously on the rectitude of slave society. In fact, slavery in South Carolina and Georgia began a period of entrenchment and expansion just as the institution began to die in the northern states. The result by the time of the new country's beginning would be the existence of a more powerful and viable southern institution, with prominent whites sure of slavery's necessity and, therefore, adamant about their right to own and forcibly work other humans. For the slaves, ironically, the same period brought still greater autonomy on the plantation and, with the start of a new wave of importation of Africans, a re-invigoration of a subculture that became more "African" than any other on the mainland.

Philip D. Morgan in "Black Society in the Low Country, 1760–1810" in *Slavery and Freedom in the Age of the American Revolution* argues that demographic and economic changes of the last half of the eighteenth century had considerable effect on the lives of African Americans and on the institution of slavery in South Carolina and Georgia. The natural increase of the slave population from about 1750; the growing size of Low-Country plantations, with increasing specialization of slave duties; the movement of rice cultivation to tidewater lands, which changed the kinds and amount of work black people performed; and the gradual opening of the backcountry to slavery, with overland im-portation of slaves, brought greater change to the lives of blacks in the Lower South than did the Revolution.

For the half-century Morgan covers this may be so, but for about a decade following 1775, when South Carolina and Georgia either were prime theaters of the Revolutionary conflict or recov-ering from the effects of the conflict, one can hardly imagine any-thing more disruptive. The British military presence was stronger, for a longer period, in South Carolina and Georgia than anywhere else, and loyalists knew well which issues were most likely to set off patriot alarms. Before beginning the critical South Carolina campaign in the summer of 1779, General Henry Clinton, British commander in chief, issued his "Phillipsburg Proclamation" (from his headquarters in Phillipsburg, New York), similar to Dunmore's earlier edict, promising sale into slavery of every black serving the patriot forces but "to every Negro who shall desert the Rebel Stan-dard, full security to follow within these lines, any Occupation which he shall think proper." Some African Americans heeded the call, but more hunkered down in their plantation existence, waiting to see where their best options might lie. Alarmed white patriots reacted in a variety of ways. Sylvia Frey in *Water from the Rock: Black Resistance in a Revolutionary Age* (1991) argues that the Phillipsburg Proclamation was critical to the southern theatre of the war because it galvanized Low-Country planters, ever fearful of a slave uprising as well as the loss of their laboring force, "and turned a potentially loyal area [to the British] into a hostile countryside." At least part of what made South Carolina the site of "the most savage civil war fought in America during the Revolution," she contends, was Clinton's raising "the specter of emancipation" and the planters' decision to fight ferociously to keep intact the heart of their social and economic system.

Nowhere was the revolutionary warfare more fierce and pervasive than in South Carolina and Georgia. British armies occupied Charleston and Savannah; marauding groups of soldiers from both sides marched back and forth across Low-Country lands, foraging, plundering, and killing. Some planters hustled their human property off, ahead of one or another army. Others just took care of themselves. Out of the disturbance came real hardship for many blacks on the one hand, but the opportunity to flee on the other. As in Virginia, African Americans in South Carolina were the victims of kidnapping and plundering, and epidemics swept off many more than usual. A good number, of course, and more women than usually was the case, simply made off and sought their fortunes wherever promise might lead them—to the backlands to join bandit or maroon groups, to Indian settlements, or off toward Florida. Eventually, a throng of slave refugees were moving around the Low Country in the wake of the royal army, looting whatever grand estates they came upon. Royalist William Bull had to watch as his "plantation at Ashley Hall . . . [was] plundered and greatly damaged by the irregular and great swarm of Negroes that followed . . . [the British] Army." That the refugees did not distinguish between rebel and loyalist plantation owners, writes Olwell in *Masters, Slaves, and Subjects,* indicates "that their war was against slavery itself."

Boston King, a slave of patriot Richard Waring living near Charleston through the late 1770s, tells in his memoirs of the difficulties the Revolution brought and the kind of opportunities for a new life it provided. When the British captured Charleston in May 1780, King "determined to go to Charles-Town, and throw myself into the hands of the English." So many others did so at the same time that the British troops were nearly overwhelmed. King recalled feeling "the happiness of liberty, of which I knew nothing before, altho' I was much grieved at first, to be obliged to leave my friends, and reside among strangers."

King's happiness soon was tempered, however, as he fell victim to the smallpox epidemic that was sweeping through the ranks of the African Americans in the city. He spent miserable days at a camp where the British army attempted to quarantine the sick fugitives. "We lay sometimes a whole day without any thing to eat or drink," he remembered, "but Providence sent a man, who belonged to the York volunteers whom I was acquainted with, to my relief. He brought me such things as I stood in need of; and by the blessing of the Lord I began to recover." Eventually, soldiers hauled him in a cart with twenty-five other invalids to a cottage, near a British hospital, where slowly he regained his health.

King then marched off with the army of General Cornwallis, serving as an orderly to a succession of British and loyalist officers. Somehow, he found himself with a unit of 250 British soldiers who were surrounded by a force of 1,600 patriots. On promise of a reward, King stole through the patriot lines and traveled twenty-four miles to a larger British force, taking word of his unit's plight. His reward turned out to be a few shillings. Soon back in Charleston, King joined the crew of a British man-of-war and sailed to New York. He was one of the three thousand blacks evacuated from New York in 1783 and taken to Nova Scotia.

By war's end, countless African Americans in South Carolina had died, disappeared, or gained their freedom. The colony's black population had been reduced by about one-quarter—twenty-five thousand men and women. More Georgia slaves actually escaped through the period, two-thirds by some accounts, as many as 7,000 to a haven behind British lines and untold numbers to Spanish lands or Indian territory to the south and west.

For the blacks who remained, the war had long-term effects. British occupation and the unsettled conditions in the countryside left a void in control. South Carolina slaves did not run away in the enormous numbers owners feared because of continual, more careful patrolling and because both sides in the war discouraged runaways. South Carolina's white leaders "received with horror" a

Continental Congress proposal in 1779 to recruit slave soldiers, and British forces in this area were hardly armies of liberation, the Phillipsburg Proclamation notwithstanding. Without resources to handle large numbers of dependents, and never having much desire to liberate enslaved African Americans anyway (since many loyalists were slave owners), the British army rationalized that the slaves were "ungovernable" and saw to it that they stayed put. British officers published names of runaways picked up in Charleston so their loyalist masters might reclaim them, and sometimes they even gave captured runaways to soldiers as bounties for their enlistment.

Out in the countryside, those slaves who stuck it out on the plantation often found themselves entirely on their own. With masters off fighting or seeking their own safety away from possible military action, these African Americans were in a position to carve out new, more liberal bounds for their activities. Black slave drivers, already powerful with the frequent absence of owners, became more involved in plantation planning and management. Their authority reached new levels, and as the war made it nearly impossible to export rice or indigo, some blacks took it upon themselves to begin growing crops they could eat or make into clothing. Other slaves shouldered greater responsibilities, accumulated more property, and participated more in inter-plantation commerce and regional trade. Black women in particular became fixtures at urban and crossroads markets, hawking vegetables, poultry, and clothing. Once the English left and the planters returned, it was practically impossible to return to the old, more restrictive ways of Low-Country plantation life, and some whites were not convinced they should, since women and men active in the black underground economy purchased imports from whites without offering them any competition in the regular marketplace.

Urban slaves expanded their parameters in the Lower South, too. By 1770 many Charleston slaves had grown up in the open urban environment and were typical of city populations everywhere—more autonomous, more highly skilled, more ready to take advantage of opportunities, especially in trade. Between periods of loyalist and patriot control, African Americans assumed larger roles in supplying each side with provisions. And they marketed their skills to the highest bidders. Slaves worked for both armies as spies, informants, and couriers. One Savannah slave, Quamino Dolley, guided British forces through a maze of swamps to surprise colonial forces from the rear, helping ensure British capture of the city. Blacks from the region were especially adept at foraging, as they knew the plantations with the best livestock and other provisions.

When the British evacuated Charleston and Savannah in 1782, they took with them more than fifteen thousand African Americans, and they removed six thousand from St. Augustine. Unfortunately, freedom for those readying to leave the plantation South was anything but assured. The British allowed masters to reclaim some of the African Americans to whom they had promised freedom, and some others they sold into slavery in the British West Indies, Louisiana, or West Florida. Others had to try to scratch out an existence in the rocky soils of Nova Scotia.

The greater independence of the blacks who remained in South Carolina and Georgia allowed them to strengthen family ties and broaden their already strong, hybrid subculture. After the Revolution, more African-American men and women on plantations were able to live with their families, which now extended over several generations, and owners showed more respect for the family units of their slaves. African-American culture remained divided as before the Revolution, with urban slaves more acculturated and rural blacks clinging to African customs. The small but growing number of free blacks in Charleston and Savannah, many of them children of white-black relationships, remained close in identity and proximity to the white master class. Taking advantage of their positions in the skilled trades and marketing, and perhaps recognizing that they were better off economically than most other blacks in the country, these men and women of the southernmost cities looked down all the more on the Lower South's black majority. Some even became slave owners themselves, and though unable to associate socially with whites, they formed institutions—

like the Brown Fellowship Society of 1790 Charleston—to advance and protect their own, unique place in the social and economic hierarchy.

But out on the plantations, things would soon move in the opposite direction. The reinstitution of the Atlantic slave trade after
the war's end brought a final influx of Africans into the rural Low
Country and ensured that its society would continue to have strong
African influences and be, as Morgan puts it, "in many ways dis-
engaged from the white world." On the other side, the end of the
Revolutionary years saw Low-Country landowners believing more
strongly than ever in the efficacy of the slave system and more
willing and able to perpetuate that system. The idea that acquiring
slaves was the way to prosperity flourished; nowhere in the new
country was it more current than in South Carolina and Georgia.
Soon after the end of hostilities, the economy of the these states
boomed as rice exporting made a steady comeback, helped along
by the final rush among planters to incorporate the labor-saving
tidal techniques into rice production. Georgia first and then South
Carolina reopened the Atlantic trade and rapidly imported enough
Africans to replace losses from the war. They kept their ports open
to Atlantic slaving so that whites moving into the opening backcountry could take laborers with them. The power and wealth of
southern landowners began to increase as the system of slave labor
expanded to include the growing of new crops. With the loss of the
English market in the war years and competition from Louisiana,
the market for Low-Country indigo disappeared, but planters began growing a new crop, cotton, which started spreading slowly
inland after 1790. By 1800 slavery in South Carolina and Georgia
had new life. Planters would be in good positions to take advantage of opportunities the expanding economy would offer.

As had happened in the Lower South, fighting associated with
the Revolution loosened planter controls in the lower Mississippi.
Patriot forces were involved in only one major British foray into
the region in 1778, but Spanish authorities in Louisiana, seeing
Britain preoccupied with the Revolution, decided the time was
right to enlarge their holdings. For four years, from 1779 to 1783,
troops from Spanish Louisiana that included elements of the free-
black militia waged war east of the Mississippi until they suc-

ceeded in winning all of British West Florida. When the fighting was nearby, slaves on British and Spanish plantations ran for their freedom, many ending up in already established maroon settlements along the lower Mississippi's bayous and backwaters. Some of these settlements south of New Orleans grew to the size of small towns. Maroons traded with, and sometimes protected, slaves from nearby plantations, and their very existence served as a symbol of the freedom that Louisiana planters were denying their slaves.

Revolutionary times provided enhanced opportunities for freedom in lower Mississippi towns as well. In control of Louisiana since the 1760s, Spanish authorities had established relatively liberal policies for slaves' self-purchase and Spanish masters had frequently seen fit to manumit favored men and women from the plantation labor force. When manumission declined in the Revolutionary years and afterward, self-purchase increased, bringing significant growth to the existing free-black populations of New Orleans, Mobile, and Pensacola. Instrumental in this were members of the expanded free-black militia, who used government rewards for their vital services in fighting the British and maintaining order at home to purchase kinsmen. Also involved were urban artisans and market women, who used money made in a postwar building and commercial boom for similar purposes. New Orleans's free-black population nearly doubled over the decade following 1777; it numbered 850 in 1791 and stood as the nucleus of what would become one of the largest and most significant, independent, and successful groups of free African Americans in the United States. By 1810 free blacks made up nearly one-third of the New Orleans population and nearly the same proportions of the urban populations of Mobile and Pensacola. For a variety of reasons, which included tendencies of masters to manumit their slave wives, mistresses, and mulatto children, and of black family members to purchase from slavery their women kinsmen and thus ensure the freedom of their offspring, the free-black population of the lower Mississippi was disproportionately female and light-skinned.

As with free blacks in Charleston and Savannah, many of those in the gulf port cities lived, worked, and identified closely with whites. Many kept and bore proudly the family names of their former masters; nearly all performed the sacraments of the Catholic Church. As their economic situation continued to improve, their desire for status as well as wealth increased, bringing some to own and work slaves just as did white associates.

But if prospects for free blacks looked reasonably bright through the time of the writing of the United States Constitution and the beginning of the new country, they appeared considerably less so, at least in hindsight, for those remaining as slaves on lower Mississippi plantations. Spain had wanted an economic boom for Louisiana and thus had taken measures to ensure a stable labor force for its planters, tightening the laws regulating slavery and opening ports to African slaves. During the Revolution, some planters had moved their slaves out along the mainland's eastern seaboard to the lower Mississippi, where they found an open market for tobacco or indigo. Following the war, a few slave owners in northern states, where slavery's end was in sight, sold bondspeople into the region. Then, as the Chesapeake economy continued to evolve and the slave population appeared to some to be larger than needed, masters began selling off "surplus" slaves whose destination, perhaps after many months, would be Louisiana or West Florida.

Given the enormity of postwar activity in the slave societies of the new country's eastern seaboard, including the reopening of the Atlantic trade, the reinvigorating of the slave-based economy of the southernmost states, and the movement of planters with their slaves into the South Carolina and Virginia backcountry, few had cause to pay attention to this virtual trickle of slaves. Yet, this movement—this domestic trading of slaves off to areas of expanding potential to the south and west in the 1780s—held ominous portent. During the next decade, Spanish planters would introduce sugar production in the region around New Orleans and their American counterparts in Natchez, with newly invented "engines" to speed the previously slow seeding operation, would begin growing cotton for export. The plantation revolution that would follow, made possible primarily by importation of Africans at first, but then by an enormous expansion of the domestic slave trade, would turn the lower Mississippi into one of the country's harshest slave societies and significantly alter the lives of slaves and free blacks through the first half of the nineteenth century.

In Virginia and Maryland the Revolution brought even greater dislocation and change. Blacks and whites appeared on the move everywhere through the years of war and beyond, and to some the movement seemed to be turning society about. In Virginia there was westward movement toward the Blue Ridge—and eventually beyond. Some slave owners took their bondspeople out of reach of the fighting; others merely saw advantage in establishing upland farms on fertile new lands. Those who stayed recognized that the heavily creole slave population would grow rapidly through natural increase. Already there were plenty of slaves—George Washington believed he had "more working Negros by a full moiety, than can be employed to any advantage in the farming system"— and land was available. As the market for tobacco fell with the war, Chesapeake planters turned still more to mixed farming and livestock raising. Although the tidewater soils had lost fertility over the generations of tobacco growing, planters relied on manure from the growing herds and increasing numbers of black workers to squeeze profits from the land.

Farmers in the Upper Chesapeake did not have the same outlet of a western frontier. Planters in Maryland already had turned to producing cereals, which thrived on small farms with free labor, so slavery did not grow and expand as it did in the central and southern parts of Virginia. Now slave prices fell in Maryland. So while the numbers of persons in bondage grew in the Upper Chesapeake for two decades after the war, the Revolution marked the beginning of the splitting of Chesapeake slave society. In Maryland and northernmost Virginia slavery would be less important for the economy and there would be a movement toward greater freedom. In the central and southern Virginia tidewater and piedmont the trend would be in the opposite direction. Slavery there became more entrenched, the number of white slaveholders increased, and the African-American population grew rapidly by natural increase as the nineteenth century approached.

As in the North, the number of free African Americans and their proportion to slaves skyrocketed during the Revolutionary era. Free blacks in the Chesapeake went through changes similar to those in the North. They found jobs, took new residences, changed names, reconstructed families or made new ones, and slowly developed the community institutions—schools, churches, benevolent societies—that helped ease the social transition, prepared people for life's problems, and provided individuals a communal identity.

It was common for some blacks in the Upper South to experience a decline in occupational status with freedom. Because white artisans feared competition from free blacks, they were hostile to African Americans trying to practice trades. Furthermore, free blacks seldom had resources to purchase or even rent land, and even when they did, whites were reluctant to sell or rent to them. Small numbers of free blacks overcame these obstacles and became successful farmers, professionals, shopkeepers, artisans, and showmen. They formed the seedbed of the southern African-American elite that would appear in the first decades of the nineteenth century.

Those who were not so fortunate still found benefits in the southern economy, which was changing in America's early years. With tobacco declining and cereal production increasing, whites were leaving the tidewater for opportunities in the newly opened lands to the west. Landowners needed to replace white tenants, and poor blacks saw farm tenancy as a step toward accumulating resources to buy land. Thus, with the exception of those in Baltimore or Fredericksburg, free African Americans in late-eighteenth-century Maryland and northern Virginia tended to live a rather isolated existence in the country, renting land or working as hired laborers at grain farming.

Slavery may have remained the dominant institution in southern Virginia, with all its tight controls over the activities of black men and women, but the area was one of several in the country that had new, rapidly growing cities where free blacks and slaves could find heightened opportunity. (Richmond was one such place—it had only 500 residents in 1775, but in 1779 it became Virginia's capital and by 1790 its population was 3,700.) African Americans did some of the building in the urban boom, worked in the tobacco factories and grain mills, and performed a share of the skilled and unskilled work that was ancillary to all the new economic activity. Black women gained their first opportunities in the region to participate in urban marketing; seamstresses, cooks, and washerwomen by weekday could be sellers of vegetables, breads, and fish at weekend markets. All of this infused an element of freedom of movement in the Upper-South urban scene that saw free blacks mixing formally and informally with slaves and both groups rubbing elbows at work and in backstreet taverns with white laborers in what James Sidbury in *Ploughshares into Swords* terms "intricate webs of alliance and contention." The increased autonomy urban blacks experienced and their broadening social contacts would bring some of them to form a culture that Sidbury calls "oppositional" to the slave society and lead to widespread unrest and in some places rebellions.

Unrest among blacks and whites that related to liberty was not limited to Virginia cities over the quarter century following the ending of the Revolutionary War. The libertarian rhetoric of the Revolution and the temporary weakening of planter authority made it difficult for many blacks to accept their servile status. Even before ideas of Revolutionary France began spreading among blacks and whites in the new American nation, even before black rebels in Saint Domingue fought successfully for the notion that those ideas of liberty, equality, and fraternity applied to them as well, African Americans still in slavery were seething, plotting, rebelling. Lesser-known organized black uprisings occurred in such widely separated places as Boston; Ulster County, New York; Perth Amboy, New Jersey; the Tar River valley of North Carolina; and St. Andrews Parish, South Carolina. And it was the atmosphere in and around Richmond in the 1780s and 1790s, where talk of natural rights and liberty ran high, that nurtured Gabriel and his fellow conspirators for what may have been the most elaborately planned slave uprising in United States history, foiled the night before it began in the summer of 1800.

In addition to the culture of opposition, Sidbury shows how complex were black society and identity by late-Revolutionary times. The split between whites and blacks that one assumes always existed was not evident everywhere in the new republic. Outside of the urban centers and sometimes within them, the Revolutionary generation of free blacks in the Upper South did not try immediately to separate themselves from whites and their institutions. This is evident in black participation in white-dominated evangelical churches and, less commonly, in their joining with whites to establish integrated schools. Some evangelical ministers welcomed all who accepted the Gospel, and their emotional, participatory services appealed to many blacks, who flocked to the revivals, if not so fast to church membership. By the 1790s congregations of black and white Methodists and Baptists, although normally segregated, on occasion listened together to exhortations of African-American preachers.

By late in the century, however, a tendency of Chesapeake blacks to identify more broadly with other African Americans, regardless of their status as slave or free, and a related movement to separate institutions was underway. Barred from some white churches and never full members of others, free blacks began taking control of their religious lives by forming "African" churches. These black churches spawned fraternal organizations and benevolent societies, and often developed auxiliary institutions for educating their young.

The most widely known example of this process was in the city that beckoned so many former slaves and fugitives from the Chesapeake, Philadelphia. It involved the work of Richard Allen in forming the Bethel African Methodist Episcopal Church. Allen had been a slave in Delaware until 1777, when he purchased his freedom and, almost simultaneously, was converted to Methodism. He was already a successful preacher when he moved to Philadelphia in 1786 and became a leader of prayer meetings for fellow African Americans. He attended and sometimes preached at the integrated St. George Methodist Church until white officials spoke of segregating blacks who came to hear Allen's exhortations. When a church trustee interrupted Allen and several companions in prayer, pulling one from his knees and sending the group to the rear of the gallery to assume their "proper" place to pray, Allen led his flock elsewhere. Within a few years he would establish what would become the Bethel AME Church, and by 1799 Allen would be the church's first deacon.

Ministers like Allen were the focus of activity in the free African-American community. They preached on Sundays, led social and religious gatherings on weeknights, and during the day served as schoolmasters. Their churches grew rapidly to become the heart of the free-black society. The ministers became the community's leaders, and from their institutional bases they guided the long evolution of independent African-American culture through the nineteenth century.

Neither the growing independence on the plantation nor the development of the free black community held the greatest implications for southern African Americans in 1790, however. It was the opening of new lands, the westward movement of slaves, and the early formation of expanded slave societies in new areas that would most effectively change their lives over the long run.

Once the fighting of the Revolution had ended, Americans quickly pushed Indians out of lands on the western frontier. Availability of these lands to white settlers brought adventuresome men in the 1780s and 1790s to migrate into Kentucky, Tennessee, and western parts of Georgia and South Carolina. To perform the difficult process of clearing land for farms, they brought along slaves. There were surplus slaves enough in the Chesapeake to meet the demands of the western migrants, but not nearly so in South Carolina and Georgia, where slave agriculture was booming and where many African Americans had run away or died during the war. Once Spain ceded much of modern Mississippi and Alabama to the United States in the Pinckney Treaty of 1795 and thus opened new lands to settlement, the southern states needed still more enslaved workers. As a consequence, South Carolina and Georgia insisted on keeping the Atlantic slave trade open for another two decades. Between 1788 and 1808 these two states imported Africans at a greater rate than ever before. Nearly one hundred thousand Africans entered Charleston, Savannah, and smaller ports along the Low-Country coast before Congress ended the traffic in human beings on January 1, 1808.

Western migration disrupted the already settled African-American communities and slowed acculturation. In many cases such movement forcibly separated slaves from their families, relocating them permanently to different parts of the country to perform new and more grueling kinds of work. The proportion of southern slaves who had to face this separation grew steadily. In the Chesapeake it was one in twelve in the 1790s, one in ten in the 1800s, and as cotton production became increasingly important and Chesapeake slaves moved south and west, one in five in the 1810s. Africans arriving in the Low Country around the turn of the century, fresh from the middle passage, faced rapid sale and movement westward, where they mixed with native-born slaves and began to acculturate out on the frontier. Here, black communities would have to form all over again, and this would take time. In Kentucky and Tennessee slaves had difficulty finding new marriage partners in spite of a balanced sex ratio. Living in groups of fewer than four slaves on small farms, these workers did not enjoy the contact with large numbers of fellow blacks that made the formation of community possible. Farther south, slaves lived on larger units, but the creole-African split kept them separated for a generation. Back in the Chesapeake, African-American families had to weather the disruption. Those who remained rebuilt networks of kinship and camaraderie. Now, however, they were keenly aware of the enhanced threat of forced removal and of what would be a continuing struggle to maintain family and community ties.

By the end of the Revolution, ironic circumstances appeared in African-American society. On the one hand there was the new, clear division between free blacks and those enslaved that was similar in many ways to the old split between Africans and creoles. But on the other was the first indication of broad unity across the breadth of all African-American society. As always, regional variants of black society continued to evolve in their own fashion, and there remained obvious differences in black ways of life. No doubt it was difficult to recognize social commonalities between African Americans living in Philadelphia, for example, and Gullah slaves on Low-Country plantations. Also, the waning social and cultural split between Africans and slaves born in America lingered in the South Carolina and Georgia backcountry.

But beyond these divisions was a hint of the emergence of the broad-based African-American cultural unity that would eventually prevail. Hardening racial attitudes of whites and their growing inclinations to separate and treat in discriminating fashion everyone of African descent, regardless of servile status, brought African Americans to recognize what they all had in common. In addition to their African heritage and such unifying manifestations of culture as religious practice, close kinship ties, and general folkways, free blacks were not so long out of slavery and not welcome enough in white society to lose contact and identity with their cultural counterparts in bondage. Thus, as African-American society continued to evolve—indeed, as free blacks in the North and Upper South proceeded to grasp what advantages they could find while southern blacks were becoming involved in a slave system of expanding scope and importance—it soon would become increasingly evident that their lots were cast together. By 1800, African Americans were part of a single American society. Over the long run of the nineteenth century, what befell one group would come to affect the other.

The Foundations of Caste

The debate over the origin of racism in America comes alive again with examination of the Revolutionary era. Before coming to America, the English had strong feelings about Africans; racism was important in the establishment of black slavery in the British mainland colonies; and the existence of slavery in colonial times, with the required brutal punishments to make black men and women work as hard as their masters demanded, reinforced and even strengthened the racist sentiments and beliefs of white colonists. But race was not of overriding importance in the day-to-day workings of colonial society—perhaps only because it did not need to be. The bodies of laws that governed slavery reflected the racial prejudices of the lawmakers, but few questioned society's right to design laws to regulate its lowest class of laborers. One did not have to justify slave codes with arguments of black inferiority. And through the middle of the eighteenth century, African Americans and white Americans continued to mix and share their values, their customs, and many aspects of their lives.

Developments that occurred through the time of the American Revolution changed all this. The debate over slavery on moral and religious grounds took on new meaning when colonists began discussing the position of slavery in their new, democratic society. If the country's existence rested on the doctrine of people having individual freedom, where did slavery fit? More convinced than ever of the necessity of slavery for their economic well-being and their elevated social status, southerners were on the spot. How could they simultaneously subscribe to American principles and defend slave society? In devising answers to this question they fell back on old racist assumptions that focused on the "nature and character" of blacks.

Southern white racism thus descended into the depths of the evil and absurd. Blacks were different, white southerners argued. They could not live in a free society as equals of white men because of their *racial* inferiority. They were *naturally* of lower intelligence and lazy, making it impossible for them to compete in a free society; they were inclined toward crime, excessive drink, and boisterous behavior; and they had no compunction against lying. Most serious, southerners insisted, blacks were sexually depraved, the women promiscuous and the men rapists at heart. They argued that such people were dangerous in a free state lest society watch them closely and provide careful control. Keeping them in slavery, they reasoned, was the best way to do so.

As so often happens in such instances, southern whites took note of certain evidence that sustained them in their beliefs and ignored things that did not support their racist notions. Some of what was happening in urban centers, where a free African-American society was getting on its feet, seemed to support their thinking. Blacks in American cities were having expected difficulties. They were in jail or were wards of the community out of proportion to their numbers. But few considered the lingering effects of slavery or of life's struggles in poverty when pointing out these social ills. (Of course, southern whites had to ignore the highly skilled slaves all around them if they were to believe the problem was African Americans' base nature and general inability, but such were the workings of the racist mind.)

Compounding the problem was some of the crude social-scientific inquiry of Western intellectuals of the time. A common belief was that humans were at the top end of a long "chain of being" with whites higher up on the chain than blacks. Linnaeus's *Systema Naturae,* tenth edition (1758–59), a standard reference for educated persons of the late eighteenth century, identified variants of *homo sapiens* in physical and cultural terms. *Europaeus* was white, sanguine, and muscular with long, flowing hair and blue eyes; was gentle, acute, and inventive; was covered with close vestments and governed by laws. *Afer,* located below *Europaeus* on Linnaeus's vertical chart, was black, phlegmatic, and relaxed, with black and frizzled hair, silky skin, flat nose, and "tumid" lips. Black women were, in Linnaeus's view, "without shame"; their "Mammae lactate profusely." *Afer* was also crafty, indolent, and negligent; self-anointed with grease; and governed "by caprice." Those believing in human brotherhood had only Christian doctrine or Revolutionary principles on which to base their beliefs. It was difficult for anyone to disagree with the vehement southern slaveholders when they held up "scientific evidence" to support their argument.

It was in this context of a growing racist rationale for enslaving blacks that the states sent representatives to Philadelphia to agree on a Constitution setting up a stronger union. Northern states were beginning to dismantle slavery, and some of their delegates thought abolition should be a natural, if gradually instituted result of the Revolution. But delegates from the Lower South blocked the road. Increasingly as convinced of their racist beliefs as they were of the necessity of slavery for their survival, southern statesmen simply refused to join a union that would not guarantee slave interests. The greatest split among state delegates at the Constitutional Convention was between those from North and South.

The Constitution that resulted rested on compromises between slaveholders and nonslaveholders, and was remarkable for the words it left out. Delegates from South Carolina and Georgia made known their opposition to any government that might immediately restrict their ability to import slaves or ignore human property in counting population for representation. They found northern delegates willing to compromise on these issues for the sake of union—and for southern concessions to federal authority in regulation of interstate and foreign trade. So the final draft of the Constitution showed agreement on prohibiting Congress from interfering with the importing of slaves before 1808 and on counting three-fifths of all slaves for apportioning taxes and representatives. Delegates came to terms more easily on a clause requiring states to return fugitive slaves.

The Constitution neither authorized specifically the holding of humans in bondage nor mentioned the words *slave* or *slavery* in its entirety. It forbade Congress to prohibit importation of "such persons as the several states shall think proper to admit"; it added to the whole number of free persons "three-fifths of all other persons" for representation and taxation; and it required a state to deliver up on claim a "person held to service or labour" in another state. But the document did not have to sanction slavery or even refer to it by name to solidify the institution in southern society. The Constitution was a document that guaranteed individual rights to property above all else; as such it accommodated slavery, for slaves were the property that, next to land, was most important to white southerners. Providing a tacit recognition of slavery, the Constitution left to the individual states the authority to determine the institution's fate, and it provided the power of the federal government to enforce the law generally and keep order. In so doing, it strengthened the hold slaveholders had on their bondspeople, and it made possible the steady extension of slavery across newly opened southern and western lands as the nineteenth century unfolded.

With antislavery agitation spreading and with increasing numbers of free blacks in their presence, southern whites began, as Winthrop Jordan asserts in *White Over Black* "hardening and polishing the structure of slavery." In parts of Virginia, proslavery petitions abounded. One, signed by 161 freeholders of the state's southside Lunenburg County, showed the animosity that fear wrought, as it predicted that general emancipation would result in

Want, Poverty, Distress & Ruin to the free Citizens; the Horrors of all the Rapes, Robberies, Murders, and Outrages, which an innumerable Host of unprincipled, unpropertied, vindictive, and remorseless Banditti are capable of perpetrating; Neglect, Famine and Death to the abandoned black infant and superannuated Parent; inevitable Bankruptcy to the Revenue; Desperation and revolt to the disappointed, oppressed Citizen; and sure and final ruin to this happy, free and flourishing Country.

Now the Southern states began to curb the practice of hiring out slaves, according to a Maryland act, "to prevent the inconvenience arising from slaves being permitted to act as free." Steadily, they made private manumission more difficult to accomplish, and they moved even more in the direction of establishing slavery as the tightly guarded and restricted institution it would become in the Antebellum South.

The early manifestations of hardening racist ideas fell most directly not on slaves but on free blacks. For a short time after the war, when their numbers were small, free African Americans basked in the limelight of the Revolution. Even southern states wrote constitutions guaranteeing basic rights to all, and there was little thought of barring some free citizens from these rights. But as the group of free blacks in the Upper South grew, and as it included many who were not easily identified by their skin tones, southern whites began a fear and loathing of African Americans not in bondage. Free blacks were dangerous to the institution of slavery, southern whites asserted. They could promote unrest and aid runaways and rebels. Even more threatening, by their very existence (heightened by any success they might attain) they undermined the racist justification for black slavery that was the crux of slaveholders' arguments for the perpetuation of the institution in the era of the "rights of man." No longer could whites allow free blacks a hint of equal treatment. Controlling the size of the free African-American community became a priority for state legislatures. In the 1790s states began limiting and then banning African American immigration. Southern states encouraged free blacks to emigrate to middle and northern states, prompting some of the latter to enact laws prohibiting blacks entering for purposes of residence.

When states could not purge themselves of free blacks, they set about expropriating the new liberties their Revolutionary constitutions provided them. African Americans had to register with state governments and in some cases provide security for good behavior. Authorities presumed blacks to be slaves until they proved otherwise, and requirements for free blacks waxed stringent the farther south one went. In North Carolina, for instance, all free blacks in urban areas had to register with the city government and wear a shoulder patch inscribed "FREE." States restricted intercounty mobility and made possible the binding over to white guardianship of young, free African Americans. Some free blacks soon found themselves required to pay special taxes, refused enlistment in militias, and deprived of their rights to vote and bear arms.

Before the eighteenth century was over a clear tendency to separate the races was becoming evident. This was neither necessary nor possible on plantations and smaller farms, but in cities throughout the country whites moved to exclude all African Americans, free or slave, from social activities where whites were involved. In public facilities African Americans received separate, and inferior, accommodations. White churches either proscribed blacks or treated them as second-class members. Restaurants and taverns removed blacks to separate sections; clubs, fraternal organizations, and trade unions simply refused to admit blacks to membership. African Americans were not welcome in white schools or, in many cases, in white cemeteries. The issue was no longer slavery. It was race.

Such patterns of segregation seldom needed to be written into law. They entered into custom and became society's norms. These customs spread out of the South and across the free states through the first half of the nineteenth century. By the end of the colonial era, racist ideas and practices of separation were part of the American scene—patterns of thought and modes of behavior that would persist for two more centuries.

EPILOGUE

For African Americans there was nothing magic about the ending
of the Revolution and the beginning of the new country. In most of
the states that ratified the Constitution, slavery proceeded un-
checked. Its death in the North would be slow, and in the South the
institution would not be many years away from gaining new vital-
ity. As the first Congress was working on constitutional guarantees
of what Representative James Madison called the "great rights of
mankind," which included the Fifth Amendment assurance that no
person was to "be deprived of life, liberty, or property without due
process of law," New England merchants were beginning again to
bring captive Africans into southern ports. Also at that very time,
southern planters were experimenting with varieties of cotton they
could produce to meet the demand of the expanding English textile industry. It would be only a few years before invention of a device to separate cotton seeds from the lint would make feasible the
widespread growing of a short-staple variety of the plant. Cotton
production was then quick to spread in the new country's fertile
soils. Once it began doing so, even such momentous events as the

successful slave revolutions on Saint Domingue in the Caribbean
or the prohibition on the importation of slaves into the United
States, after January 1, 1808, could not check slavery's expansion
in those southern states where cotton might grow.

What was important for African Americans about the ending
of the colonial period, however, was that by then the major institutions and forces that would affect their lives and those of their descendants over the next two centuries were established or well in
motion. By 1790 the South's economy and society were so thoroughly bound up in slavery that its most prominent citizens opposed entering a union that threatened their right to own human
beings. Adventuresome southern whites, who knew the way to get
ahead was to obtain land and make it produce with slave labor, already were beginning to move westward with the African-American men, women, and children they held in bondage, anticipating
the movement of the cotton boom a generation later. To help recover from the Revolution and to service the expanding economy,
southerners imported nearly one hundred thousand more African
slaves between 1790 and 1808.

Yet by 1790, the sectional split among states that would lead
to the Civil War and then to slavery's demise was evident. The libertarian ideals of the Revolution and the egalitarian spirit of the
Great Awakening had served as catalysts for antislavery sentiment,
and a movement toward abolition, although weak, was alive in the
country. The Northwest Ordinance of 1787 already marked lands
north of the Ohio River as free states for the union's future. Most
of the arguments for and against slavery (and its extension into
new territories) that statesmen would debate so vigorously in the
1840s and 1850s had been aired by the time the Founding Fathers
signed the Constitution.

By the end of the eighteenth century, black individuals had
established their own modes of resistance to the institution that
bound their lives, and they would continue to make fun, malinger,
hide out, steal, escape, or rebel as their situation made possible until slavery ended. Even afterward, when free blacks in the South
found themselves bound to tenant farms on the same land their ancestors tilled as slaves, they would use some of the same means to

resist their oppressors. On into the twentieth century, running away—after 1910 it occurred so frequently that it was thought of as "migration" out of the South, to northern and western cities— remained a popular black reaction to onerous conditions.

Moreover, the long period of black Americans' social and cultural evolution brought into existence by 1790 a stable, identifiable African-American culture that encompassed the societies of free blacks as well as slaves. This black culture was anchored in the expanded family and a community that had found the means to survive under difficult circumstances. Variants of the culture existed in different parts of the new country, to be sure, but the church was a focal point for African Americans, who shared religious beliefs as well as unique folkways and traditions. After 1790, when African Americans moved, their culture moved with them. Thus, a variation would constitute the culture of slaves in the Antebellum South. As Genovese shows in *Roll, Jordan, Roll,* this culture, which continued to grow and change and move with American blacks from its earlier foundation, formed the basis for African-American identity in a hostile world.

Late colonial demographic trends among African Americans even show the beginnings of population movements and settlement patterns characteristic of free blacks before the Civil War and of all persons of African descent for the century thereafter. A vague and gradual, but still noticeable, northward movement of black people began in the Revolutionary era, at least out of the Upper South toward the Middle states. As the body of free blacks increased in size, individuals and groups began moving toward urban areas, where jobs were more numerous and existing African-American communities offered more comfortable settings and group support. In the largest northern cities, Philadelphia and New York in particular, the seeds that would grow much later into African American neighborhoods, then black ghettos, were already in the soil by the close of the colonial period.

Finally, one does not have to look deeply into the American society of 1790 to see the roots of the racism that has since plagued the nation. Rigid, unreasonable racial prejudice was evident and spreading, and it was more than a southern phenomenon.

Already by 1786 New Jersey had prohibited free blacks from entering the state. Other states would follow suit. Within two decades northern states began disfranchising blacks—President Jefferson signed a bill in 1802 excluding African Americans from voting in the nation's new capital—and as soon as blacks threatened to take white jobs, whites moved to deny skilled African Americans opportunities to practice their trades. Across the growing country, from bases where whites and blacks lived together, spread customary racial separation and along with it the discrimination, social ostracism, and exploitation that would persist and continue to evolve.

Thus, the truly formative years of the black experience in America were the earliest ones. By the beginning of the nineteenth century major forces already were in motion that would affect the way African Americans would live over the long period to follow.

BIBLIOGRAPHICAL ESSAY

Until recently, study of the experience of African Americans from their African origins through the American Revolution necessitated working in two distinct bodies of historical literature. To examine the African background and the slave trade one had to consult work done largely by specialists in Africa or the South Atlantic zone, but to study the institution of slavery in the British mainland colonies one needed to rely on the work of American historians who considered their study as part of a larger body comprising a history of the United States. To some extent, this remains the case. It is fortunate, however, that over the past decade a growing number of persons have focused more specifically on "Atlantic history" and thereby brought greater awareness of the economic, cultural, and intellectual relationships of peoples on all four continents bordering the Atlantic. One might say that we have begun erasing the artificial lines that separated early American history from its Atlantic context, which has allowed heightened recognition of the importance of Africa, transatlantic slaving, and slave-based production for a foreign market in our (collective) colonial past. Americans historians are increasingly aware that Africa and Africans are an important part of the American heritage. And a number of the new books noted in this essay reflect this awareness. Our understanding of all American history, not simply early African-American history, is better for it.

Useful bibliographies for each topic are *Slavery and Slaving in World History: A Bibliography*, edited by Joseph C. Miller, 2 vols. (1998); and Peter H. Wood's "'I did the Best I Could for My Day': The Study of Early Black History During the Second Reconstruction, 1960 to 1976," *William and Mary Quarterly*, 3rd series, 35 (1978), which was itself a marvelous tool for its day. William D. Piersen's *From Africa to America: African American History from the Colonial Era to the Early Republic, 1526–1790* (1996) and Gary B. Nash's *Red, White, and Black: The Peoples of Early North America*, 4th ed. (2000) have good bibliographical essays, as does Peter Kulchin's *American Slavery, 1619–1877* (1993).

Piersen's *From Africa to America* and Nash's *Red, White, and Black* are the best recent surveys of the topic. The latter examines African Americans in the context of those with whom they interacted. Other useful introductions are the early chapters of John B. Boles's elegantly written *Black Southerners, 1619–1869* (1983) which obviously treats the southern mainland colonies, and the first volume of Philip S. Foner's *History of Black Americans: From Africa to the Emergence of the Cotton Kingdom* (1975).

Atlantic Origins

The most important recent event for students of the Atlantic slave trade is the compilation of a set of raw data concerning some 27,000 slaving voyages, most of which took place between the mid-seventeenth century and 1870. Under sponsorship of the W. E. B. Du Bois Institute of Harvard University, several scholars collaborated to bring together the data set from a number of separate, published and unpublished compilations. They now are available in David Eltis et al., *The Transatlantic Slave Trade, 1567–1867: A Database CD-ROM* (1998). The best new studies of the slave trade rely on data from this set and on studies by others who have used the data.

A thorough and up-to-date exposition of the Atlantic slave trade is Herbert S. Klein's *The Atlantic Slave Trade* (1999). A long-time student of the subject, Klein summarizes the latest findings and points toward the newest directions in old arguments. Separate chapters (some noted below) of *Routes to Slavery: Direction, Ethnicity and Mortality in the Atlantic Slave Trade* (1997), edited by David Eltis and David Richardson, provide in a concise and useful format some recent arguments relating to various issues regarding the trade. Hugh Thomas's *The Slave Trade* (1997) is a popularly written 800-page compendium, that, while not flawless, is grounded in solid scholarship; Joseph C. Miller's "The Slave Trade" in Volume 2 of the *Encyclopedia of the North American Colonies*, edited by Jacob Ernest Cooke et al., 4 vols. (1993) is an excellent short survey; David Northrup, ed., *The Atlantic Slave Trade* (1994) contains excerpts from primary and secondary sources relating to the most important issues concerning the trade. Good, though now dated, studies of the Atlantic slave trade are Edward Reynolds's *Stand the Storm: A History of the Atlantic Slave Trade* (1985) and James A. Rawley's *The Transatlantic Slave Trade: A History* (1981), the latter treating European aspects of the trade in particular detail.

Several books examine the Atlantic trade and focus on its effects on Africans. A work by the British Africanist Basil Davidson, *Black Mother: The Years of the Atlantic Slave Trade* (1961), was the first to draw attention to the destructive nature of the trade for African societies. Two studies by Walter P. Rodney, *A History of the Upper Guinea Coast to 1816* (1968) and *West Africa and the Atlantic Slave Trade* (1967), broaden and advance Davidson's argument. P. E. H. Hair's *The Atlantic Slave Trade and Black Africa* (1978) is a remarkable little book—pamphlet-size, actually—that takes issue with the focus on destructive effects. Hair's work echoes an interpretation expressed more fully by Anthony G. Hopkins in *An Economic History of West Africa* (1973). Patrick Manning's *Slavery and African Life: Occidental, Oriental, and Atlantic Slave Trades* (1990) places the Atlantic trade in its widest perspective and suggests, among many other things, that Atlantic slaving caused serious demographic problems for particular regions of Africa at particular times.

To understand why there was a trade of slaves from Africa to the British mainland colonies, one must examine the context, looking into reasons for the existence of a grand Atlantic economic system. Three exceptionally good and up-to-date studies that place American slavery in that context are Philip D. Curtin's *The Rise and Fall of the Plantation Complex: Essays in Atlantic History*, 2nd ed. (1999), David Eltis's *The Rise of African Slavery in the Americas* (2000), and Robin Blackburn's *The Making of New World Slavery, from the Baroque to the Modern, 1492–1800* (1997), the latter with a focus on the British Caribbean. James Walvin's *Questioning Slavery* (1996) focuses on the broad parameters of slavery in the English-speaking Americas. Various articles in Paul Lovejoy and Nicholas Rogers, eds., *Unfree Labor in the Development of the Atlantic World* (1994) are insightful, as is Seymour Drescher's *From Slavery to Freedom: Comparative Studies in the Rise and Fall of the Atlantic Slave Trade* (1999). William D. Phillips Jr.'s "The Old World Back-ground of Slavery in the Americas" in *Slavery and the Rise of the Atlantic System* (1991), edited by Barbara L. Solow, traces the plantation system nicely to its origins, and Patrick Manning's "Migration of Africans to the Americas: The Impact on Africans, Africa, and the New World," in *Slave Trades, 1500–1800: Globalization of Forced Labor* (1996), edited by Patrick Manning, Vol. 15 of *An Expanding World: The European Impact on World History, 1450–1800*, looks at the Atlantic trade from its broadest perspective. Michael Craton's *Sinews of Empire: A Short History of British Slavery* (1974), James Walvin's *Black Ivory: A History of British Slavery* (1992), Richard S. Dunn's *Sugar and Slaves: The Rise of the Planter Class in the English West Indies, 1624–1715* (1972), and David Hancock's *Citizens of the World: London Merchants and the Integration of the British Atlantic Community, 1735–1785* (1997) are good background for the wider economic realm of the mainland colonies. Johannes Postma's *The Dutch in the Atlantic*

Slave Trade, 1600–1815 (1990) highlights that country's critical contributions to expansion of the plantation system. Curtin's "Epidemiology and the Slave Trade," *Political Science Quarterly*, 83 (1968) is the classic study discussing the importance of disease factors in decisions to import Africans.

It is difficult to understand what African societies were like before the heavy flow of slaves to the Americas. Even if the Atlantic trade had not altered those societies, Africans did not leave many written records and in many places oral history has fallen short of its promise as a tool for reconstructing the pre-colonial African past. In spite of this, John Thornton has done a marvelous job of describing ways of life among societies of West and West Central Africa some time in the past and relating those societies to the Atlantic trade in *Africa and Africans in the Making of the Atlantic World, 1400–1800*, 2nd ed. (1998). Thornton's "The African Background to American Colonization" in *The Cambridge Economic History of the United States, Volume I: The Colonial Era*, edited by Stanley L. Engerman and Robert E. Gallman (1996), is a fine, much briefer survey of the topic. Philip D. Curtin and Paul Bohannon's *Africa and Africans*, 4th ed. (1995) remains a useful overview of African cultures and their histories.

Recent studies of slavery in Africa are valuable for discussion of how the institution differed from American chattel slavery and the role it played in the development of slave trading in Africa. The best single accounts in this regard are Paul E. Lovejoy's *Transformations in Slavery: A History of Slavery in Africa* (1983) and Claude Meillassoux's *The Anthropology of Slavery: The Womb of Iron and Gold*, translated by Alide Dasnois (1986). Essays in *Slavery in Africa: Historical and Anthropological Perspectives* (1977), edited by Suzanne Miers and Igor Kopytoff, add useful insight. Lovejoy's article with Martin A. Klein, "Slavery in West Africa," in *The Uncommon Market: Essays in the Economic History of the Atlantic Slave Trade* (1977), edited by Henry A. Gemery and Jan S. Hogendorn, and his "Indigenous African Slavery," *Historical Reflections/Reflexions historiques*, 4 (1977) provide sharp focus on African slavery as it pertained to the external slave trade, and Herbert S. Klein's "African Women in the Atlantic Slave Trade," in *Women and Slavery in Africa* (1983), edited by Claire Robinson and Martin A. Klein, covers that topic well. Discussion of numbers of slaves traded across the Atlantic begins with Philip D. Curtin's pioneering *The Atlantic Slave Trade: A Census* (1969). Before publication of this book, even careful historians tended to cling to a "rounded off" figure of 15 million for the total of African slave exports, a figure supplied casually in 1861 by an American publicist for Mexican independence, who had no real basis to know. Some of those less careful spoke of much higher numbers. Curtin spent years corralling existing data and arrived at the admittedly tentative estimate of 9,566,100 for slave imports into the Americas between 1451 and 1870. He regarded his book as a "point of departure" and challenged other scholars to produce data revising his figures.

What followed was a forceful attack on Curtin's accuracy and methodology. A persistent leader of this criticism, suggesting Curtin seriously underestimated the volume of slave exports, is J. E. Inikori. His initial argument is found in "Measuring the Atlantic Slave Trade: An Assessment of Curtin and Anstey, *"Journal of African History*, 17 (1976), to which Curtin replies in the same volume, and a summary of Inikori's critique is in the introduction to the book Inikori edited, *Forced Migration: The Impact of the Export Trade on African Societies* (1982). Inikori continues to call attention to estimates he considers low, as is evident in his "The Volume of the British Slave Trade, 1655–1807," *Cahiers d'Études africaines*, 32 (1992). Other scholars, including Roger Anstey in *The Atlantic Slave Trade and British Abolition* (1975), have worked to revise Curtin's figures, and Curtin himself revises some of his original figures upward in "Measuring the Atlantic Slave Trade" in *Race and Slavery in the Western Hemisphere: Quantitative Studies* (1975), edited by Stanley L. Engerman and Eugene D. Genovese. A useful work that sorts through the first decade of the numbers argument is Paul E. Lovejoy's "The Volume of the Atlantic Slave Trade: A Synthesis," *Journal of African History*, 23 (1982). Lovejoy argues that, after much challenge and revision, Curtin's original estimates are low, but remain close to the mark.

In recent years, a small group of scholars has further refined Curtin's figures so that by the mid-1990s a broad, general agreement on numbers seems to exist. The consensus is reflected in David Richardson, "The Eighteenth-Century British Slave Trade: Estimates of Its Volume and Coastal Distribution in Africa," *Research in Economic History*, 12 (1989); David Richardson and Stephen D. Behrendt, "Inikori's Odyssey: Measuring the British Slave Trade, 1655–1807," *Cahiers d'Études africaines*, 35 (1995); David Eltis's, "The Volume and Origins of the British Slave Trade before 1714," *Cahiers d'Études africaines*, 35 (1995); and Stephen D. Behrendt, "The Annual Volume and Regional Distribution of the British Slave Trade, 1780–1807," *Journal of African History*, 38 (1997). Persons wanting a concise summary of the numbers debate with the most recent, reasonable estimates should read David Eltis and David Richardson, "The 'Numbers Game' and Routes to Slavery," in *Routes to Slavery* (1997).

No work on the slave trade to the British colonies on the North American mainland should begin elsewhere than with Elizabeth Donnan's four-volume *Documents Illustrative of the History of the Slave Trade to America* (1930–35). Donnan introduces the documents nicely and supports them with full annotations.

Studies of European aspects of the trade often focus on an individual country or colony. A good overview of English-Atlantic commerce that emphasizes the sophistication and competitiveness of the market in the late-seventeenth and early-eighteenth centuries is David W. Galenson, *Traders, Planters, and Slaves: Market Behavior in Early English America* (1986). Works dealing with more particular aspects of British and colonial American participation include Walter E. Minchinton's *The Trade of Bristol in the Eighteenth Century* (1966); Richard B. Sheridan's "The Commercial and Financial Organization of the British Slave Trade, 1750–1807," *Economic History Review*, 11 (1958); several articles in *Liverpool, The African Slave Trade, and Abolition: Essays to Illustrate Current Knowledge and Research* (1976), edited by Roger Anstey and P. E. H. Hair; and Jay Coughtry's *The Notorious Triangle: Rhode Island and the Atlantic Slave Trade*

(1981). K. G. Davies's *The Royal African Company* (1957) remains the standard for British operations on the African coast in the time of seventeenth-century monopolies. Those interested in the material basis for the European side of the trade can refer to Stanley B. Alpern's "What Africans Got for Their Slaves: A Master List of European Trade Goods," *History in Africa: A Journal of Method*, 22 (1995), which emphasizes the reasonable nature of African demand and includes detail on the various products.

Knowledge of how the slave trade operated along various sections of the African coast has advanced considerably in recent years with a group of specialized, regional studies. Among the best for different parts of the coast and related inland areas are, generally from north to south, James L. A. Webb's *Desert Frontier: Ecological and Economic Change along the Western Sahel, 1600–1850* (1995); Philip D. Curtin's *Economic Change in Precolonial Africa: Senegambia in the Era of the Slave Trade* (1975); James F. Searing's, *West African Slavery and Atlantic Commerce: The Senegal River Valley, 1700–1860* (1993); Donald R. Wright's *The World and a Very Small Place in Africa* (1997), the small place being a slave-trading entity at the mouth of the Gambia River; Boubacar Barry's *Senegambia and the Atlantic Slave Trade* (1998); Kwame Y. Daaku's *Trade and Politics on the Gold Coast, 1600–1720: A Study of the African Reaction to European Trade* (1970); Ray A. Kea's *Settlements, Trade, and Politics in the Seventeenth-Century Gold Coast* (1982); Patrick Manning's *Slavery, Colonialism, and Economic Growth in Dahomey, 1640–1960* (1982); Robin C. Law's *The Slave Coast of West Africa, 1550–1750: The Impact of the Atlantic Slave Trade on an African Society* (1991); K. O. Dike's pioneering *Trade and Politics in the Niger Delta* (1956); David Northrup's *Trade Without Rulers: Pre-Colonial Economic Development in South-Eastern Nigeria* (1978); A. J. H. Latham's *Old Calabar, 1600–1891: The Impact of the International Economy upon a Tra-ditional Society* (1973); Phyllis Martin's *The External Trade of the Loango Coast* (1972); and two works by Joseph C. Miller, "The Slave Trade in Congo and Angola" in *The African Diaspora: Interpretive Essays* (1976), edited by Martin L. Kilson and Robert I. Rotberg, and his truly monumental *Way of Death: Merchant Capitalism and the Angola Slave Trade, 1780–1830* (1988). Although its focus is on Portuguese slaving in Angola and the middle passage to Brazil at a time that touches only the very end of the colonial era, if a person could read but one book to understand the operation of the Atlantic slave trade in order to get a sense of its horrors, *Way of Death* should be it. Paul E. Lovejoy's *Caravans of Kola: The Hausa Kola Trade, 1700–1900* (1980) is good for organization of caravans in the Central Sudan. Philip D. Curtin's *Cross-Cultural Trade in World History* (1984) has useful chapters on trading communities and such topics as landlords, brokers, and caravan leaders in West Africa.

For a number of years, study of the middle passage rested on contemporary accounts, some of which were published. The best examples are John Newton's *The Journal of a Slave Trader, 1750–1754* (1962), edited by Bernard Martin and Mark Spurrell, and Alexander Falconbridge's *An Account of the Slave Trade on the Coast of Africa* (1788). The historical validity of tracts such as these was always open to question, given that some were written by former slave traders who had seen the immorality of their ways through religion—Newton wrote the famous hymn "Amazing Grace" after his years of involvement in the inhuman traffic—and others were clearly published with abolition of the trade in mind. But in the 1970s a group of economists and historians began examining statistical data to provide evidence for the trader's conclusions on the voyage between Africa and America. Herbert S. Klein's *The Middle Passage: Comparative Studies in the Atlantic Slave Trade* (1978) is a fascinating volume that compares a host of aspects of the trade of different nations, and articles by David Eltis and David Richardson ("West Africa and the Transatlantic Slave Trade: New Evidence of Long-Run Trends") and Klein and Stanley L. Engerman ("Long-Term Trends in African Mortality in the Transatlantic Slave Trade") in *Routes to Slavery* provide the latest thinking on their particular topics. A fine study of disease environments, epidemics, and medical practices as they relate to the middle passage is Richard B. Sheridan's *Doctors and Slaves: A Medical and Demographic History of Slavery in the British West Indies, 1680–1834* (1985). Joseph C. Miller argues that factors in Africa—drought or cycles of harvest, for example—affected mortality in the middle passage in his "Mortality in the Atlantic Slave Trade: Evidence on Causality," *Journal of Interdisciplinary History* (1981). Raymond L. Cohn and Richard A. Jensen in "The Determinants of Slave Mortality Rates on the Middle Passage," *Explorations in Economic History*, 19 (1982), argue that "profit-maximizing behavior" on the part of shipowners and captains made mortality rates higher on slaving voyages than others. David Eltis's "Free and Coerced Migrants: Some Comparisons," *American Historical Review*, 88 (1983), stresses similarities between the treatment of slaves on the one hand and soldiers and servants on the other. Eltis and Engerman offer explanations of why the middle passage carried twice as many men as women in "Was the Slave Trade Dominated by Men?" *Journal of Interdisciplinary History*, 23 (1992) and "Fluctuations in Sex and Age Ratios in the Transatlantic Slave Trade, 1663–1864," *Economic History Review*, 46 (1993). *The Atlantic Slave Trade: Effects on Economies, Societies, and Peoples in Africa, the Americas, and Europe* (1992), edited by Joseph E. Inikori and Stanley L. Engerman, consists of papers presented at a 1988 University of Rochester conference, several of which deal with issues relevant to transporting slaves to the New World.

Among the rare, first-hand accounts of African slaves are those of two kidnapping victims and one person captured by an enemy army, all from the eighteenth century. These are Olaudah Equiano's *Interesting Narrative of the Life of Olaudah Equiano, or Gustavus Vassa, the African, Written by Himself* (1789), edited by Paul Edwards (1967); Ayuba Suleiman Diallo's *Some Memories of the Life of Job, the Son of Solomon the High Priest of Boonda in Africa* (1734), treated recently in Douglas Grant, *The Fortunate Slave: An Illustration of African Slavery in the Eighteenth Century* (1968); and Venture Smith, *A Narrative of the Life and Adventures of Venture, A Native of Africa but Resident about Sixty Years in the United States of America* (1798). The first two of these receive excellent treatment in Philip D. Curtin's *Africa Remembered: Narratives of West Africans from the Era of the Slave Trade* (1967).

Control of economic power and resources in the English mainland colonies affected sale of slaves there. Thus, the clearest discussions of sale and transportation of slaves are in studies that deal with colonial society and slavery. The best of these studies are discussed in the next section, below. A good overview is Steven Deyle, "'By Far the Most Profitable Trade': Slave Trading in British Colonial North America," *Slavery and Abolition*, 10 (1989). Studies of particular colonial ports and importing regions are especially useful. For Charleston, where more slaves entered than at any other port, compare W. Robert Higgins's "Charleston: Terminus and Entrepôt of the Colonial Slave Trade" in *The African Diaspora* with Elizabeth Donnan's "The Slave Trade into South Carolina Before the Revolution," *American Historical Review*, 33 (1928) and Daniel C. Littlefield's, "Charleston and Internal Slave Redistribution," *South Carolina Historical Magazine* (1986). For other areas see Darold D. Wax's "Black Immigrants: The Slave Trade in Colonial Maryland," *Maryland History Magazine*, 73 (1978); Wax's "Africans on the Delaware: The Pennsylvania Slave Trade," *Pennsylvania History*, 50 (1983); and James G. Lyndon's "New York and the Slave Trade, 1700–1774," *William and Mary Quarterly*, 3rd series, 35 (1978).

Development of Slavery in Mainland North America

Ira Berlin's *Many Thousands Gone: The First Two Centuries of Slavery in North America* (1998) is a masterful synthesis of slavery's origin and development in lands that would become the United States. This book significantly broadens understanding of the issues and connects the development of slavery to African-American ways of life and black culture. Against Berlin's work, future studies of the subject will be measured. *How Did American Slavery Begin?* (1999), with readings selected and introduced by Edward Countryman, is a volume in Bedford/St. Martin's Historians at Work series, which is designed primarily for classroom use.

Because slavery on the North American mainland was so thoroughly involved with the economic situation of the colonies and their quest for laborers to produce exports, those wanting to study the origins of slavery and racism in America might turn early to *The Economy of British America, 1607–1789* (1985) by John J. McCusker and Russell R. Menard. The latter is a student of slavery in colonial Maryland, and, among other things, the book reflects his interest in and knowledge about early slavery in the colonies. James Horn's *Adapting to a New World: English Society in the Seventeenth-Century Chesapeake* (1994) is not so much about slaves as it is about "the degree to which English attitudes, values, and traditions shaped settlers' adaptation to the New World during the seventeenth century," but Horn's descriptions of the landscapes, the economic situation, and the "social web" of the English around the Chesapeake are excellent background for understanding how slavery grew there. Philip D. Morgan's "British Encounters with Africans and African-Americans, circa 1600–1780" in *Strangers Within the Realm: Cultural Margins of the First British Empire* (1991), edited by Bernard Bailyn and Philip D. Morgan, deals with a variety of "first encounter" issues. Other good beginnings are the examination of the development of colonial society in Gary B. Nash's excellent synthesis, *Red, White, and Black: The Peoples of Early America*, 2nd ed. (1982); and Wesley F. Craven's essays in *White, Red, and Black: The Seventeenth-Century Virginian* (1971). Raymond Starr's bibliographic essay on the subject, "History and the Origins of British North American Slavery," *Historian*, 36 (1973), is good, if now dated; Sylvia R. Frey's "In Search of Roots: The Colonial Antecedents of Slavery in the Plantation Colonies," *The Georgia Historical Quarterly,* 68 (1984) covers more recent work.

Modern studies of the origin of slavery in the English mainland colonies often trace their roots to an article by Oscar and Mary Handlin, "Origins of the Southern Labor System," *William and Mary Quarterly*, 3rd series, 7 (1950). The authors argue that black slavery evolved over the seventeenth century because of labor needs that the colonists could not otherwise meet. According to the Handlins, black and white servants in the colonies received similar treatment and were unconcerned with people's color. Racial prejudice came after, and as a result of, enslavement. This argument appeared at a fortunate time for interest in black American history. Kenneth Stampp made the Handlins' interpretation popular in his widely read *The Peculiar Institution: Slaves in the Ante-Bellum South* (1956). Soon, however, a counter argument appeared. In "Slavery and the Genesis of American Race Prejudice," *Comparative Studies of History and Society*, 2 (1959), Carl N. Degler suggests that racist ideologies preceded and played a major role in bringing about slavery in the English North American colonies. As the legal system of slavery evolved in the Chesapeake, Degler writes, "it reflected and included as part of its essence, the same discrimination which white men had practiced against the Negro all along." Thomas F. Gossett strengthened Degler's arguments in *Race: A History of an Idea in America* (1963). It remained for Winthrop D. Jordan to attempt resolution of the debate in *White Over Black: American Attitudes Toward the Negro, 1550–1812* (1968). Jordan calls the move to black slavery an "unthinking decision" and suggests "cause and effect" for the relationship between slavery and racism. More recently, Betty Wood in *The Origins of American Slavery: Freedom and Bondage in the English Colonies* (1997) reinforces Jordan's theme. "The economic argument must loom large," writes Wood, but "from the outset American slavery was characterized by an awareness of ethnic difference that over the course of a century hardened into . . . a racial contempt and hatred that was deliberately cultivated by those who stood to gain financially from the employment of enslaved Africans." Nash summarizes many of the arguments clearly in "Red, White, and Black: The Origins of Racism in Colonial America," in *The Great Fear: Race in the Mind of America* (1970), edited by Nash and Richard Weiss. Alden T. Vaughan and Virginia Mason Vaughan add to Jordan's argument about preexisting racial stereotypes of Africans in England in "Before *Othello*: Elizabethan Representation of Sub-Saharan Africans," *William and Mary Quarterly*, 3rd series, 54 (1997). African historian and linguist P. E. H. Hair raises interesting questions about Jordan's and others' acceptance of the existence of an English stereotype of blacks prior to 1650 in "Attitudes to Africans in English Primary Sources on Guinea up to 1650," *History in Africa: A Journal of Method*, 26 (1999).

Nearly two decades of focus on the issues, reinforced by national attention on civil rights toward the end of the 1960s, stimulated further investigation into colonial slavery and the early development of the institution. Many studies focused naturally on the Chesapeake, where slavery first appeared and became most thoroughly established through the first century of English rule of the North American mainland. Thad W. Tate's "The Seventeenth-Century Chesapeake and Its Modern Historians" in *The Chesapeake in the Seventeenth Century: Essays on Anglo-American Society* (1979), edited by Thad W. Tate and David L. Ammerman, surveys this literature; Anita H. Rutman's "Still Planting the Seeds of Hope: The Recent Literature of the Early Chesapeake Region," *The Virginia Magazine of History and Biography*, 95 (1987) is a critical examination of more current work. Engel Sluiter's "New Light on the '20. and Odd Negroes' Arriving in Virginia, August 1619," *William and Mary Quarterly*, 3rd series, (1997) and John Thornton's "The African Experience of the '20. and Odd Negroes' Arriving in Virginia in 1619," *William and Mary Quarterly*, 3rd series, 55 (1998) are the articles telling us so much more than we ever thought we would know about the first persons from Africa sold to English settlers in mainland North America.

One of the freshest approaches to appear in the 1970s was Edmund S. Morgan's *American Slavery, American Freedom: The Ordeal of Colonial Virginia* (1975). Morgan regards as especially important the need in the last third of the seventeenth century for control of unruly, armed, freed white servants. Slaves could never be freed, could be more carefully controlled, and were thus preferable to white servants. Russell R. Menard takes issue with Morgan in "From Servants to Slaves: The Transformation of the Chesapeake Labor System," *Southern Studies*, 16 (1977). Basing his study on work conducted for his University of Iowa doctoral thesis, eventually published as *Economy and Society in Early Colonial Maryland* (1985), Menard argues that the rise of black slavery was due principally to the change in white servant migration patterns after 1660 and the high cost of servants in comparison with the low cost of slaves. "Chesapeake planters did not abandon indentured servitude," Menard writes. "It abandoned them." Farley Grubb and Tony Stitt support Menard's statement in "The Liverpool Emigrant Servant Trade and the Transition to Slave Labor in the Chesapeake, 1697–1707," *Explorations in Economic History*, 31 (1994), arguing that "the large and protracted wars of King William III (1688–1697) and of Queen Anne (1702–1713) produced dramatic declines in servant supplies which explain the exact timing of the transition from servants to slaves in the Chesapeake." Kathleen M. Brown's *Good Wives, Nasty Wenches, and Anxious Patriarchs: Gender, Race, and Power in Colonial Virginia* (1996) adds patriarchy and gender to the mix, pointing out that as Virginia males moved toward greater control of black slaves following Bacon's Rebellion, they removed women from labor in the field and into even more subordinate positions.

More recent studies add evidence for standard arguments about slavery's beginnings in America, but a number of them include thorough study of black society and slave culture in the Chesapeake. Gloria L. Main supports the idea that opting for slavery was a rational economic choice in *Tobacco Colony: Life in Early Maryland, 1650–1720* (1982). Main documents the social life and material culture of all classes of early Marylanders with study in probate records from six different counties. She shows that slavery's institutionalization hastened permanent inequality in the colony. This last point is one Allan Kulikoff makes in *Tobacco and Slaves: The Development of Southern Culture in the Chesapeake, 1680–1800* (1986). Guided by interest in class formation, Kulikoff focuses on the rise of a Chesapeake gentry and its co-optation of a yeoman class to solidify white control over economy, society, and government. Once whites united under leadership of the gentry, Kulikoff argues, the status of blacks as a permanent underclass, with slavery as its outward manifestation, was established as the basis of southern culture. Marvin L. Michael Kay and Lorin Lee Cary's *Slavery in North Carolina, 1748–1775* (1995) shows how different slavery was in this colony because of its late-maturing, slave-based economy and the diversity of its exports. Because such a proportion of North Carolina slaves were Africans (as opposed to creoles) so late in the colonial period (two-thirds in 1750), the authors argue that these men and women relied more than others at the time on tools and ideas that stemmed from their African heritage to comprehend, react to, and cope with their situation.

Other recent studies use some of the same kinds of sources to reach different conclusions. T. H. Breen and Stephen Innes's *'Myne Owne Ground': Race and Freedom on Virginia's Eastern Shore, 1640–1676* (1980) focuses on successful free blacks and their broad social and economic relations. The authors conclude that the loss of property rights moved blacks swiftly toward a more permanent position of slavery. J. Douglas Deal's *Race and Class in Colonial Virginia: Indians, Englishmen, and Africans on the Eastern Shore during the Seventeenth Century* (1993) takes a broader look at the same topic. Paul G. E. Clemens's *Atlantic Economy and Colonial Maryland's Eastern Shore: From Tobacco to Grain* (1980) looks to the effect of wheat production after 1713 on the changing social order. Darrett B. Rutman and Anita H. Rutman's *A Place in Time: Middlesex County, Virginia, 1650–1750* (1984) analyzes everything from child-naming patterns to literacy and slaves' living conditions in a single Virginia population. For the beginnings of slavery the Rutmans conclude that, on the local level, individual choice and good or bad fortune played surprisingly important roles.

If early slavery in South Carolina and the Georgia Low Country has not commanded a quantity of attention equal to that in the Chesapeake, those books that have focused on the subject have been of considerable quality—and the gap in quantity is narrowing. For South Carolina, Peter H. Wood's *Black Majority: Negroes in Colonial South Carolina, from 1670 through the Stono Rebellion* (1974) treats origins and development of slavery as well as the formation of black culture in the colony. Everything from black pioneers in the early eighteenth century to the evolution of Gullah speech comes under Wood's scrutiny. Daniel Littlefield's *Rice and Slaves: Ethnicity and the Slave Trade in Colonial South*

Carolina (1981) is a different kind of book, examining rice production in particular and the African ethnic mix that provided much to white South Carolina as it formed its own, separate subculture. An article by John S. Otto and Nain E. Anderson, "The Origins of Southern Cattle-Grazing: A Problem in West Indian History," *Journal of Caribbean History*, 21 (1988), argues that decades of cultural interchange among Africans, Hispanics, and Britons brought about the special techniques of cattle grazing in colonial South Carolina that later spread throughout the South, and one by Judith A. Carney, "From Hands to Tutors: African Expertise in South Carolina Rice Economy, *Agricultural History*, 67 (1993), lends further support for Wood's and Littlefield's contention that West African slaves, in Carney's words, "tutored planters in the requisite skills and technologies to create one of the New World's most lucrative plantation economies." Other books and articles treating the earliest years of slavery in South Carolina include Peter Coclanis, *The Shadow of a Dream: Economic Life and Death in the South Carolina Low Country, 1670–1920* (1988); Converse D. Clowse, *Economic Beginnings in Colonial South Carolina, 1670–1730* (1971); and Russell R. Menard's "The Africanization of the Lowcountry Labor Force, 1670–1730" in *Race and Family in the Colonial South*, edited by Winthrop D. Jordan and Sheila L. Skemp (1987). Edward Ball's *Slaves in the Family* (1998) is far from a typical historical monograph, being the story of Ball's efforts to trace his ancestors, white and black, back through their lives in slavery on the family's rice plantations in South Carolina. The book shows that the lives of men and women in and out of slavery were woven together in just about every way. Robert Olwell's *Masters, Slaves, and Subjects: The Culture of Power in the South Carolina Low Country, 1740–1790* (1998) describes the "culture of power" in which Low-Country slaves had to operate. As James Horn does for the Chesapeake in *Adapting to a New World*, Olwell shows how so much of what became the slave society of the Low Country had a basis in English legal and social precedent.

The movement of planters with slaves to the South Carolina backcountry has gotten considerable interest in recent years.

Works dealing with this topic include Rachel N. Klein's *Unification of a Slave State: The Rise of the Planter Class in the South Carolina Backcountry, 1760–1808* (1990); Alan Gallay's *The Formation of a Planter Elite: Jonathan Bryant and the Southern Colonial Frontier* (1988); George Lloyd Johnson, Jr.'s *The Frontier in the Colonial South: South Carolina Backcountry, 1736–1800* (1997); Joyce E. Chaplin's *An Anxious Pursuit: Agricultural Innovation and Modernity in the Lower South, 1730–1815* (1993), in which she argues that Lower South planters were always innovators and "overtly commercial," making them eager to borrow new technology and plantation models that promised improvement of their slave-based production system; and Russell R. Menard's "Slavery, Economic Growth, and Revolutionary Ideology in the South Carolina Backcountry" in *The Economy of Early America: The Revolutionary Period, 1763–1790* (1988), edited by Ronald Hoffman.

Two studies dominate work on blacks in colonial Georgia. Betty Wood's *Slavery in Colonial Georgia, 1730–1770* (1984) is especially good for the period of the colony's social experiment, when planter pressures brought about the demise of the ideal colony. Wood devotes the second half of the book to the form of slavery that came to exist in Georgia up to the time of the Revolution, with good chapters on the public and private lives of slaves. Julia Floyd Smith's *Slavery and Rice Culture in Low Country Georgia, 1750–1860* (1985) is interesting for its perspective. Smith believes slavery on rice plantations in Georgia was different from other manifestations of the institution in America. Rice production had its own requirements for labor, in particular a task system for fieldwork. This setting, Smith argues, enabled Low-Country blacks to develop a culture with more African elements in the mix and to enjoy physical well-being and general treatment that was better than slaves experienced elsewhere.

Study of blacks in Spanish East Florida is dominated by work over the last decade of Jane Landers, much of which is summarized in her new, thorough, *Black Society in Spanish Florida* (1999). Leslie B. Rout, Jr.'s *The African Experience in Spanish America: 1502 to the Present Day* (1976) places the Florida experience in the broader Spanish perspective, and Landers examines some of the earliest Africans on the mainland in "Africans in the Land of Ayllón: The Exploration and Settlement of the Southeast" in *Columbus in the Land of Ayllón*, edited by Jeannine Cook (1992).

The 1990s has witnessed a relative explosion of solid works on African Americans in the lower Mississippi Valley during colonial times, which add detail and interpretation to Joe Gray Taylor's *Negro Slavery in Louisiana* (1963). Each of the recent books has a different focus. Daniel H. Usner, Jr.'s *Indians, Settlers, and Slaves in a Frontier Exchange Economy: The Lower Mississippi Valley Before 1783* (1992) highlights how blacks had economic and social relations across race and class lines in the fluid setting of Louisiana and West Florida; Gwendolyn Midlo Hall's *Africans in Colonial Louisiana: The Development of Afro-Creole Culture in the Eighteenth Century* (1992) emphasizes that Africans in general, and Bambara slaves from Senegambia in particular, played a major role in shaping Louisiana creole culture; Thomas N. Ingersoll's *Mammon and Manon in Early New Orleans: The First Slave Society in the Deep South* (1999) argues that the development of slavery in the region's major city was not so different from other North American mainland slave societies; and Kimberly S. Hanger's *Bounded Lives, Bounded Places: Free Black Society in Colonial New Orleans, 1769–1803* (1997) shows how the period of Spanish control of New Orleans expanded opportunities for free African Americans, the basis of the city's more noted nineteenth-century creole population. Robert L. Jenkins's "Africans in Colonial and Territorial Mississippi," in *Ethnic Heritage in Mississippi*, edited by Barbara Carpenter (1992) deals with West Florida and Natchez.

Because of the relatively small number of blacks in New England and the Middle Colonies, and because states in the region terminated slavery around the time cotton production began to boom in the Deep South, historians in the field of slave studies have tended to overlook the area. But this is not to the same extent as it was a decade or more ago. A solid, general treatment of the topic is Edgar J. McManus's *Black Bondage in the North* (1973), which follows the story past Emancipation. Lorenzo J. Greene's *The Negro in Colonial New England* (1942) remains useful. Greene's book has a massive bibliography and useful appendices with population figures for each colony. A refreshing newer study of blacks in New England is William D. Piersen's *Black Yankees: The Development of an Afro-American Subculture in Eighteenth-Century New England* (1988), which focuses less on the institution of slavery and more on "what it was like to be an African immigrant in colonial New England." Piersen examines African-American religion, rituals, arts and crafts, folklore, social mores, and daily behavior, concluding that in spite of being "engulfed in a pervasive, narrow-minded Euro-American society that had no interest in fostering Afro-American autonomy," blacks in New England created a viable folk culture that maintained African values and gave blacks a positive identity. Robert P. Twombly and Robert H. Moore's "Black Puritan: The Negro in Seventeenth-Century Massachusetts," *William and Mary Quarterly*, 3rd series, 24 (1967) addresses the situation of blacks in the Puritan colony. The early pages of James O. Horton's and Lois E. Horton's *Black Bostonians: Family Life and Community Struggle in the Antebellum North*, rev. ed. (1999) provide the colonial background for that population. For Connecticut and Rhode Island, see Ber-nard Steiner's *History of Slavery in Connecticut* (1893) and Robert K. Fitts's *Inventing New England's Slave Paradise: Master/ Slave Relations in Eighteenth-Century Narragansett, Rhode Island* (1998).

Scholarly study of slavery in the Middle Colonies has fairly exploded in recent years. Edgar J. McManus's *A History of Negro Slavery in New York* (1960) and Roi Ottley's *The Negro in New York* (1967) remained authoritative on that topic until 1999 when Graham Russell Hodges published his thorough treatment, *Root and Branch: African Americans in New York and East Jersey, 1613–1863* (1999). Shane White's *Somewhat More Independent: The End of Slavery in New York City, 1770–1810* (1991) adds excellent treatment of the last decades of slavery in the city; Joyce D. Goodfriend's *Before the Melting Pot: Society and Culture in Colonial New York City, 1664–1730* (1992) has a useful section on

African-American culture; Richard Shannon Moss's *Slavery on Long Island: A Study in Local Institutional and Early African-American Communal Life* (1993) treats a particular, small portion of New York's slave population; and Robert J. Swann's "The Other Fort Amsterdam: New Light on Aspects of Slavery in New Netherland," *Afro-Americans in New York Life and History*, 22 (1998) touches on slavery's earliest years.

Similarly, for slavery in colonial Pennsylvania, one formerly had to rely on two dated books, Edward J. Turner's *The Negro in Pennsylvania: Slavery—Servitude—Freedom* (1911) and Thomas E. Drake's *Quakers and Slavery in America* (1950), and a few good articles, including Allan Tully's "Patterns of Slaveholding in Colonial Pennsylvania: Chester and Lancaster Counties, 1729–1758," *Journal of Social History*, 6 (1973) and two by Darold D. Wax in *Pennsylvania History*, "Negro Imports into Pennsylvania, 1720–1766," 32 (1965), and "The Demand for Slave Labor in Colonial Pennsylvania," 32 (1967). This situation was relieved by the publication of books by Jean R. Soderlund and Gary B. Nash: Soderlund's *Quakers and Slavery: A Divided Spirit,* which appeared in 1985, and Nash's *Forging Freedom: The Formation of Philadelphia's Black Community, 1720–1840,* which came out in 1988. Then the two authors combined to write the excellent *Freedom by Degrees: Emancipation in Pennsylvania and Its Aftermath* (1991). All three works show that even the presence of strong abolitionist sentiment among some Quakers and others in the city had little effect when Philadelphia residents wanted slave labor. For New Jersey, Graham Russell Hodges's *Slavery and Freedom in the Rural North: African Americans in Monmouth County, New Jersey, 1665–1865* (1997) supersedes Henry S. Cooley's *A Study of Slavery in New Jersey* (1896). Delaware did not fit many schematics in regard to slavery. Two solid, new studies of the topic are Patience Essah's *A House Divided: Slavery and Emancipation in Delaware, 1638–1865* (1996) and William H. Williams's *Slavery and Freedom in Delaware, 1639–1865* (1996).

Study of the legal basis of American slavery, developed in the colonial period, has surged forward in recent years with publication of several excellent books. The broadest in sweep include two by A. Leon Higginbotham, *In the Matter of Color: Race and the American Legal Process, I: The Colonial Period* (1978), and *Shades of Freedom: Racial Politics and Presumptions of the American Legal Process, II: Race and the American Legal Process* (1996), the latter of which traces in American law the "precept" to "presume, preserve, protect, and defend the ideal of the superiority of whites and the inferiority of blacks," and Thomas D. Morris's *Southern Slavery and the Law, 1619–1860* (1996), which has greater emphasis on the Antebellum era. Two good books by Philip J. Schwarz focus on the legal basis of slavery in Virginia: *Twice Condemned: Slaves and the Criminal Laws of Virginia, 1705–1865* (1988), which examines trials of slaves to prove how conflict and brutality were so much at the heart of the relationship between white and black in colonial Virginia, and *Slave Laws in Virginia* (1996).

African-American Culture

Philip D. Morgan's long-awaited, massive, and greatly detailed *Slave Counterpoint: Black Culture in the Eighteenth-Century Chesapeake and Lowcountry* (1998) is the best study of African-American culture in the regions where slavery dominated. One finishes Morgan's book with an appreciation for how complex the situations were for Africans in America and how African-American life differed according to time and place. This corresponds with the theme of Berlin's *Many Thousands Gone,* which echoes a point he made much earlier in "Time, Space, and the Evolution of Afro-American Society on British Mainland North America," *American Historical Review,* 85 (1980). In emphasizing the importance of place and an evolutionary process in African acculturation, Morgan and Berlin complete the dislodging of historians from any idea that colonial black culture was mostly uniform and static. T. H. Breen's "Creative Adaptations: Peoples and Cultures" and Gary B. Nash's "Social Development" in *Colonial British America: Essays in the New History of the Early Modern Era* (1984), edited by Jack P. Greene and J. R. Pole, and Greene's *Pursuits of Happiness: The Social Development of Early Modern British Colonies and the Formation of American Culture*

(1988) are good introductions to the culture change that took place on the North American mainland.

The best studies of African-American acculturation in the New World have been anthropological works focusing on slave societies in the Caribbean. What they say about how the process takes place is instructive for colonial America. Melville Herskovits's *The Myth of the Negro Past* (1941) is the classic study of "creolization"; Sidney W. Mintz's *Caribbean Transformations* (1974); Mintz and Richard Price's *An Anthropological Approach to the Afro-American Past: A Caribbean Perspective* (1976), and the same two authors' *The Birth of African-American Culture: An Anthropological Perspective* (1992) offer valuable ideas about the joining of cultures. Lorena S. Walsh's *From Calabar to Carter's Grove: The History of a Virginia Slave Community* (1997) follows generations of slaves, from their African origins to the Virginia tidewater and piedmont, showing clearly that even where large numbers of slaves shared the same African regional heritage, their ways changed rapidly in America and their culture was indeed something new. Walsh notes the kinds of things one can tell about individuals and group culture in such things as names in "A 'Place in Time' Regained: A Fuller History of Colonial Chesapeake Slavery through Group Biography" in *Working Toward Freedom: Slave Society and the Domestic Economy in the American South* (1994), edited by Larry E. Hudson, Jr.

Although most books on slave community and culture focus on the antebellum period, a good introduction to the topic is in the early chapters of Peter Kolchin's *American Slavery, 1619–1877* (1993). Relevant books that have references to colonial times include Lawrence W. Levine's *Black Culture and Black Consciousness: Afro-American Folk Thought from Slavery to Freedom* (1977); Eugene D. Genovese's *Roll, Jordan, Roll: The World the Slaves Made* (1972); and John W. Blassingame's *The Slave Community: Plantation Life in the Antebellum South*, rev. ed. (1977). The studies of blacks in specific regions of colonial America noted above—particularly those by Gloria Main, Allan Kulikoff, Darrett and Anita Rutman, Peter Wood, Daniel Littlefield, Betty Wood, Julia Floyd Smith, Lorenzo Green, and William Piersen—have useful parts on black community and culture.

Kulikoff's book emphasizes the role demographics played in black family and community formation and shows how these institutions were the prerequisites for stable black culture in the Chesapeake. Agreeing generally with Kulikoff's demographic analysis is Russell R. Menard's "The Maryland Slave Population: A Demographic Profile of Blacks in Four Counties," *William and Mary Quarterly*, 3rd series, 32 (1975). Jean Butendoff Lee's "The Problem of Slave Community in the Eighteenth-Century Chesapeake," *William and Mary Quarterly*, 3rd series, 43 (1986) questions assumptions about the existence of a stable African-American community by the time of the Revolutionary era. She recognizes the broad attempts of slaves to achieve communal lives, but emphasizes that these efforts were more difficult and often less successful than many historians believe. *The Diary of Landon Carter of Sabine Hall, 1752–1778*, 2 vols. (1965), edited by Jack P. Greene, contains insight into the way one not altogether typical planter thought of and related to his slaves.

A handful of books bring refreshing perspective to one or another aspect of colonial black culture. James Sidbury's *Ploughshares into Swords: Race, Rebellion, and Identity in Gabriel's Virginia, 1730–1810* (1997) traces African-American culture formation in eighteenth-century Virginia before emphasizing how many forces and experiences came to bear on individual and group identity—and thus cultural formation—in Richmond at the end of the century. Douglas R. Egerton's *Gabriel's Rebellion: The Virginia Slave Conspiracies of 1800 and 1802* (1993) places blacks in the context of Richmond's late-eighteenth-century working class and shows how such individuals were buffeted by the political and social winds of the times. W. Jeffrey Bolster's *Black Jacks: African American Seamen in the Age of Sail* (1997) shows the African roots to black seafaring in America and, more generally, how from the 1740s "seafaring men of color stirred black society and shaped Atlantic maritime culture." Mart A. Stewart's *"What Nature Suffers to Groe": Life, Labor, and Landscape on the Georgia Coast, 1680–1920* (1996) is a fascinating examination of the ecosystem of the Georgia Low Country and the effects it had on African-American lives—and vice versa. Mark

M. Smith's *Mastered by the Clock: Time, Slavery, and Freedom in the American South (1997)* contains discussion of African concepts of time and shows that slaves' and masters' ideas about time were not so far apart through the colonial period. In *The World They Made Together: Black and White Values in Eighteenth-Century Virginia* (1987), Mechal Sobel examines religious and secular worlds and finds that black and white values and perceptions had considerable effect on one another's group culture. Sobel ventures into the fascinating realm of black and white concepts of space, time, home, the afterlife, and more to suggest that neither group developed its culture alone, but that indeed they made their worlds together. Piersen's *Black Yankees* makes a similar argument, concluding that blacks helped "mellow those rather puritanical" white Yankees, and his *Black Legacy: America's Hidden Heritage* (1993) makes the broadest case yet for southern white culture having "strong African blood-lines."

When considering influences of particular African groups on African-American and American culture, some authors contend that a limited number of African "nations" or "cultural units" dominated the Atlantic trade to specific regions of the Americas and thus were able to maintain many of their largely unified ways and affect American culture in those particular ways far more than previously considered. Thornton in *Africa and Africans in the Making of the Atlantic World* and Hall in *Africans in Colonial Louisiana* make such arguments, and Douglas B. Chambers lends support in "'My own nation': Igbo Exiles in the Diaspora," in *Routes to Slavery*, and "'He is African But Speaks Plain': Historical Creolization in Eighteenth-Century Virginia," in *Africa and the African Diaspora*, edited by Alusine Jalloh and Stephen Maizlish (1996). Probably the broadest and most ambitious effort of them all is Michael A. Gomez's *Exchanging Our Country Marks: The Transformation of African Identities in the Colonial and Antebellum South* (1998), which brings together and advances arguments about how particular West and West-Central African cultures affected African-American ways in seventeenth- and eighteenth-century British mainland North America. Philip D. Morgan provides a strong counterargument in "The Cultural Implications of the Atlantic Slave Trade: African Regional Origins, American Destinations and New World Development," in *Routes to Slavery*. Examining issues from "the broadest transoceanic framework," Morgan argues, "the homogenizing tendency of stressing cultural unity in Africa, of emphasizing the nonrandom character of the slave trade, and of seeing the dominance of particular African coastal regions or ethnicities in most American settings, is at variance with the central forces shaping the early modern Atlantic world." Peter Caron's "'Of a nation which the others do not Understand': Bambara Slaves and African Ethnicity in Colonial Louisiana, 1718–60," in *Routes to Slavery*, supports the heterogeneity model and argues against Hall's emphasis on the existence of powerful, ethnic Bambara influences in eighteenth-century Louisiana. Useful to read in this context is William S. Pollitzer's study of those African Americans, on the Sea Islands off South Carolina and Georgia, who retained African elements in their language and culture as long as any: *The Gullah People and Their African Heritage* (1999).

If work dominated the daily lives of African Americans in the colonial period, blacks dominated the colonial American world of work—for whites as well as blacks. One gets this strong impression from reading a number of studies noted earlier, none more so than in Sobel's *The World They Made Together*. Separate articles in *Cultivation and Culture: Labor and the Shaping of Slave Life in the Americas* (1993) deal with the various forms of slave labor and its effect on how people lived in various parts of the New World. The best short introduction to slaves' work in all the British mainland colonies is Richard S. Dunn's "Servants and Slaves: The Recruitment and Employment of Labor" in *Colonial British America*. Studies of specific kinds of African-American workers include Philip D. Morgan's "Work and Culture: The Task System and the World of Lowcountry Blacks, 1700–1880," *William and Mary Quarterly*, 3rd series, 40 (1982), which shows how greatly the task system affected the black and white worlds of the South Carolina and Georgia Low Country; Morgan's "Black Life in Eighteenth-Century Charleston," *Perspectives in American History*, new series, 1 (1984), a detailed description of living and working conditions of urban slaves; Thad W. Tate's *The Negro in Eighteenth-Century Williamsburg* (1965), for a glimpse at the lives of, and kinds of work peformed by, African Americans in the town setting; Sarah S. Hughes's, "Slaves for Hire: The Allocation of Black Labor in Elizabeth City County, Virginia, 1787–1810," *William and Mary Quarterly*, 3rd series, 35 (1978); and Ronald L. Lewis's *Coal, Iron, and Slaves: Industrial Slavery in Maryland and Virginia, 1715–1865* (1979).

That black women slaves had especially full lives of hard work is evident in Joan Rezner Gundersen's "The Double Bonds of Race and Sex: Black and White Women in a Colonial Virginia Parish," *Journal of Southern History*, 52 (1986). Gundersen reminds readers that black women on small farms often had to do their own domestic work after the fieldwork was finally finished. She shows also that in part of Virginia women were hired out more frequently than were men. Two collections, *Discovering the Women in Slavery: Emancipating Perspectives on the American Past*, edited by Patricia Morton (1996) and *More Than Chattel: Black Women and Slavery in the Americas*, edited by David Barry Gaspar and Darlene Clark Hine (1996), have articles on women in the colonial period. In the latter book, Cheryll Ann Cody makes an interesting point in "Cycles of Work and Childbearing: Seasonality in Women's Lives on Low Country Plantations" that on some plantations women tended to have the most children during times of heaviest labor demand, and Richard Steckel summarizes his findings on "Women, Work, and Health under Plantation Slavery in the United States." Deborah Gray White's *Ar'n't I a Woman? Female Slaves in the Plantation South* (1985) contains a description of the mythology of female slavery as well as select information on black women in the colonial period. Other studies of women in slavery focus heavily on the antebellum South, but see Angela Davis's "Reflections on the Black Woman's Role in the Community of Slaves," *The Black Scholar*, 3 (1971) for a theoretical approach; Catherine Clinton's *The Plantation Mistress: Woman's World in the Old South* (1982), which is especially good for "the sexual dynamics of slavery"; and Suzanne Lebsock's *The Free Women of Petersburg: Status and Culture in a Southern*

Town, 1784–1860 (1984) for the chapter on "Free Women of Color."

E. Franklin Frazier's *The Negro Family in the United States* (1939), which emphasizes the damage slavery did to the black family, was a standard work on the subject. However, Herbert G. Gutman's *The Black Family in Slavery and Freedom, 1750–1925* (1976) altered ideas that slavery brought disorganization and instability to black families. Gutman draws attention to the remarkable adaptive capacities of African Americans, and he credits the black family with preserving cultural traditions and the double-headed household. Most of Gutman's evidence is from the antebellum period and after, but he has a chapter on the family in the eighteenth century in which he deals with African-American marriage and broadening kinship ties. Allan Kulikoff's "The Beginnings of the Afro-American Family in Maryland" in *Law, Society, and Politics in Early Maryland: Essays in Honor of Morris Leon Radoff* (1976), edited by Aubrey C. Land, Lois Green Carr, and Edward C. Papenfuse, summarizes Kulikoff's thoughts on demographic considerations and the formation of colonial black families. Mary Beth Norton, Herbert G. Gutman, and Ira Berlin in "The Afro-American Family in the Age of Revolution" in *Slavery and Freedom in the Age of the American Revolution* (1983), edited by Berlin and Ronald Hoffman, examine the workings of slave families in the Chesapeake and the Carolinas in a more mature African-American society.

Because many agree with Michael R. Bradley's assessment in "The Role of the Black Church in Colonial Slave Society," *Louisiana Studies*, 14 (1975), "that the formation of the Negro church is the key to the beginning of Afro-American community and culture," a number of studies have focused on the early years of black religion in America. Several noted historians have written good books on African-American religion. These include Carter G. Woodson's *History of the Negro Church* (1921); Benjamin E. Mays and Joseph W. Nicholson's *The Negro's Church* (1933); and E. Franklin Frazier's shorter *The Negro Church in America* (1963). Lester B. Scherer's *Slavery and the Churches in Early America, 1619–1819* (1975) treats the colonial period more thoroughly;

David M. Reimers's *White Protestantism and the Negro* (1965) has a portion on conversion and church origins. Sylvia R. Frey and Betty Wood in *Come Shouting to Zion: African American Protestantism in the American South and British Caribbean to 1830* (1999) argue that through most of the colonial period American blacks rejected Christianity because it was not adaptable to their African world view and social customs, and that only with the more flexible push of the Baptist and Methodist faiths did blacks begin converting in large numbers—in the 1780s, but still more after 1800. Wood adds an interesting note in "Never on a Sunday? Slavery and the Sabbath in Low-Country Georgia, 1750–1830" in *From Chattel Slaves to Wage Slaves*, edited by Mary Turner (1995). Hodges's *Root and Branch*, noted above, charts the relations of blacks with various branches of Christianity through the colonial period and beyond in New York and East Jersey. Various essays in *African-American Religion: Interpretive Essays in History and Culture*, edited by Timothy E. Fulop and Albert J. Raboteau (1996), pertain to early slave religion.

Works that deal with particular denominations and blacks in early America include Donald G. Mathews, *Slavery and Methodism: A Chapter in American Morality, 1780–1845* (1965); T. Erskine Clark, "An Experiment in Paternalism: Presbyterians and Slaves in Charleston, South Carolina," *Journal of Presbyterian History*, 53 (1975); and Denzil T. Clifton, "Anglicanism and Negro Slavery in Colonial America," *Historical Magazine of the Protestant Episcopal Church*, 39 (1970). Harold E. Davis's *The Fledgling Province: Social and Cultural Life in Colonial Georgia, 1733–1776* (1976) argues that Quakers and Moravians wanted their slaves to become literate so they could experience Christianity more fully. Davis maintains that churches in colonial Georgia were more integrated than previously believed. Jon F. Sensbach's *A Separate Canaan: The Making of an Afro-Moravian World in North Carolina, 1763–1840* (1998) shows how even Moravians, who believed in the universality of salvation and included slaves in biracial worship, moved toward separate services as race became increasingly important in North Carolina's slave society. Mechal Sobel's *Travelin' On: The Slave Journey to*

232 BIBLIOGRAPHICAL ESSAY

an Afro-Baptist Faith (1979) includes ideas on acculturation as they pertain to the formation of African-American religions. Sobel's is the most thorough treatment of the "African Sacred Cosmos" and of how such African concepts as spiritual force, visions, travels to meet the Lord, and rebirth entered into the African-American Christian world view. Leonard Barrett's *Soul Force: African Heritage in Afro-American Religion* (1974) shows how other Africanisms mingled with European Christianity in the formative years of black religion in America. Alan Gallay's "Planters and Slaves in the Great Awakening" in *Masters and Slaves in the House of the Lord: Race and Religion in the American South, 1740–1870* (1988), edited by John B. Boles, argues that the Great Awakening had more effect on slave society, especially in South Carolina and Georgia after the 1740s, than previously thought. Carol V. R. George offers a modern treatment of Richard Allen and the birth of the Bethel African Methodist Episcopal Church in *Segregated Sabbaths: Richard Allen and the Emergence of Independent Black Churches* (1973).

Herbert Aptheker's *American Negro Slave Revolts*, rev. ed. (1969) remains the most thorough compilation of information on the subject. Peter H. Wood surveys the topic from a more recent perspective in "Slave Resistance" in Volume 2 of the *Encyclopedia of the North American Colonies*. An analysis of how and why slaves resisted, ran away, or rebelled is Gerald W. Mullin's *Flight and Rebellion: Slave Resistance in Eighteenth-Century Virginia* (1972). Mullin establishes the relationship between level of acculturation and methods of resistance that seemed to apply throughout the colonial period. In a subsequent book, *Africa in America: Slave Acculturation and Resistance in the American South and the British Caribbean, 1736–1831* (1992), Mullin uses a comparative perspective to answer questions relating to why, in his analysis, rebellions in British North American colonies tended to be African-led through the 1760s and then creole-led thereafter. Studies of particular topics related to resistance or rebellion include John Thornton's "African Dimensions of the Stono Rebellion," *American Historical Review*, 96 (1991), which brings up the possibility that soldiers from the Kingdom of Kongo formed the core of the Stono uprising and used their knowledge of firearms and military tactics to their temporary advantage; Thomas J. Davis's *A Rumor of Revolt: The "Great Negro Plot" in Colonial New York* (1985), which argues the plot was more than rumor and that "slaves in New York City during 1741 clearly talked of doing damage to the society enslaving them"; John J. TePaske's "The Fugitive Slave: Intercolonial Rivalry and Spanish Slave Policy, 1686–1764" in *Eighteenth-Century Florida and Its Borderlands* (1975), edited by Samuel Proctor; Alan D. Watson's "Impulse toward Independence: Resistance and Rebellion among North Carolina Slaves, 1750–1775, *Journal of Negro History*, 63 (1978); Jeffery J. Crow's "Slave Rebelliousness and Social Conflict in North Carolina, 1775–1802," *William and Mary Quarterly*, 3rd series, 37 (1980); and Darold D. Wax's "Negro Resistance to the Early American Slave Trade," *Journal of Negro History*, 46 (1961). Peter Linebaugh and Marcus Rediker's "The Many-Headed Hydra: Sailors, Slaves, and the Atlantic Working Class in the Eighteenth Century," *Journal of Historical Sociology*, 3 (1990) makes the important point that no small part of the restiveness and rebellion in which African Americans became engaged was multi-racial and multi-ethnic, having a basis in grievances of an international working class.

Historians of African Americans increasingly are relying on the work of archaeologists for study of the material culture of pre-Revolutionary slaves. Summarizing relevant archaeological work since the 1960s are *"I, Too, Am America": Archaeological Study of African-American Life,* edited by Theresa A. Singleton (1999) and Leland Ferguson's *Uncommon Ground: Archaeology and Early African America, 1650–1800* (1992). The most interesting archaeological discovery in the North in recent years is a black burial ground in New York City, which is described in Joyce Hansen and Gary McGowan's *Breaking Ground, Breaking Silence: The Story of New York's African Burial Ground* (1998). Studies of archaeological work from the Chesapeake region include William M. Kelso's *Kingsmill Plantations, 1619–1800: Archaeology of Country Life in Colonial Virginia* (1984), which provides details of slave quarters, gardens, wells, pots, root cellars, and garbage pits, from which the author draws inferences about slave living conditions, and Anne E. Yentsch's *A Chesapeake Family and Their Slaves: A Study in Historical Archaeology* (1994). Two additional works by Singleton are useful to colonial historians: *Archaeology of Slavery and Plantation Life* (1985) and "Breaking New Ground," *Southern Exposure*, 15 (1988). Kathleen Deagan and Darcie McMahon's *Fort Mose: Colonial America's Black Fortress of Freedom* (1995) is an award-winning catalogue that accompanied the nationally touring Fort Mose exhibit. Elizabeth J. Reitz, the zooarchaeologist who analyzed the diet of blacks at Fort Mose, determined that they ate much as did the neighboring Indians—and Spaniards—in "Zooarchaeological Analysis of a Free African American Community: Gracia Real de Santa Teresa de Mose," *Historical Archaeology*, 28 (1994).

A particularly enlightening body of work considers health, nutrition, disease, and medical practice in the slave community, of which Kenneth F. Kiple and Virginia Himmelsteib King's *Another Dimension of the Black Diaspora: Diet, Disease, and Racism* (1981) is the most valuable for the colonial period. The authors discuss African immunities, New World epidemics related to the Atlantic trade, blacks' particular susceptibility to disease because of nutritional deficiencies and special problems experienced by transplanted tropical Africans. Todd L. Savitt's *Medicine and Slavery: The Diseases and Health Care of Blacks in Antebellum Virginia* (1978) reinforces many of Kiple and King's conclusions with a clearer nineteenth-century focus. Tom W. Shick's "Healing and Race in the Carolina Low Country" in *Africans in Bondage: Studies in Slavery and the Slave Trade* (1986), edited by Paul E. Lovejoy, describes black "root doctors" and their holistic approach to healing. Gary Puckrein's "Climate, Health, and Black Labor in English America," *Journal of American Studies*, 13 (1979) argues that the white notion that African Americans could live longer under conditions of hard labor in tropical climes—in spite of there being no clear evidence to support the supposition—was a factor in landowners' decisions to turn to Africa for slave labor.

There is not a deep literature on the more personal aspects of the folk culture of slaves and free blacks during the colonial period.

But Shane White and Graham White do crack open the world of black expression in *Stylin': African American Expressive Culture from Its Beginnings to the Zoot Suit* (1998), writing elegantly about such matters as "the ways in which African Americans have clothed themselves, styled their hair, and communicated meaning through gesture, dance, and other forms of bodily display," some of it from colonial times. Philip D. Morgan addresses song, dance, and play in the last chapter of *Slave Counterpoint*. One can supplement this with the second chapter of Eileen Southern's *The Music of Black Americans: A History*, 2nd ed. (1983); portions of John Lovell, Jr.'s *Black Song: The Forge and the Flame* (1972); and Michael J. Morgan's improbably titled "Rock and Roll Unplugged: African-American Music in Eighteenth-Century America, *Eighteenth-Century Studies*, 27 (1994).

African Americans in the Revolutionary Era

For more than a quarter century following its 1961 publication, Benjamin Quarles's *The Negro in the American Revolution* (2nd ed., 1996) was the standard work not only on African-American participation in the revolutionary struggle but on its effect on black lives. Written at a time of hope for progress in American race relations, the book rests on Quarles's view that "the colored people of America benefited from the irreversible commitment of the new nation to the principles of liberty and equality." The bicentennial of the Revolution brought renewed interest in the subject; Ira Berlin's "The Revolution in Black Life" in *The American Revolution: Explorations in the History of American Radicalism* (1976), edited by Alfred F. Young, and essays by various authorities in *Slavery and Freedom in the Age of the American Revolution* (1983), edited by Berlin and Ronald Hoffman, pointed toward new directions in scholarship relating to the topic. More recently, a number of studies have questioned Quarles's optimistic view of the Revolution's effect on black lives. A thoughtful review of some of the most important of the newest books, with reference to many more, is Douglas R. Egerton's "Black Independence Struggles and the Tale of Two Revolutions:

A Review Essay," *Journal of Southern History,* 64 (1998). Among the newer books, the most broadly useful in presenting the more critical assessment of the revolution's effects on African Americans may be Sylvia R. Frey's *Water from the Rock: Black Resistance in a Revolutionary Age* (1991). Frey sees blacks during the Revolution as persons struggling with two warring groups of determined slaveholders to gain greater freedom. The early chapters of Egerton's *They Shall Go Out Free: The Lives of Denmark Vesey* (1999) show how much people of African descent in North America were tied into an Atlantic world of spreading revolutionary ideas.

Two books by David B. Davis, *The Problem of Slavery in Western Culture* (1966) and *The Problem of Slavery in the Age of Revolution, 1770–1823* (1975) are standard treatments of the broad range of issues connecting slavery with Western and libertarian ideology. Jordan's *White Over Black* is a thorough consideration of some of the same topics. *The Journal of John Woolman* (1775) is good for understanding the strong Quaker sentiment against slavery. Paul Finkelman's *Slavery and the Founders: Race and Liberty in the Age of Jefferson* (1996) brings the focus to the first generation of leaders of the United States, examining critically how they dealt with slavery in such documents as the Declaration of Independence, the Northwest Ordinance, and the Constitution. Also useful is Donald L. Robinson's *Slavery and the Struggle for American Politics, 1765–1820* (1971).

Where slavery fit into Thomas Jefferson's thinking is the subject of two good, if now dated, books: John C. Miller's *The Wolf by the Ears: Thomas Jefferson and Slavery* (1977) and Robert McColley's *Slavery and Jeffersonian Virginia,* 2nd ed. (1973). More recent thinking on the matter, reflecting greater knowledge of Jefferson's relationship with his slave Sally Hemings, and other of his relatives whom he kept in bondage, is reflected in Finkelman's *Slavery and the Founders.* A 1999 update of Annette Gordon-Reed's analytical *Thomas Jefferson and Sally Hemings: An American Controversy* (1997, 1999) has a new preface, written with the recent DNA findings in mind, and further argument on the issue is in *Sally Hemings and Thomas Jefferson: History, Memory, and Civil Culture*, edited by Jan Ellen Lewis and Peter S. Onuf. One can supplement these with Fawn Brodie's *Thomas Jefferson: An Intimate History* (1974); David Brion Davis's *Was Thomas Jefferson an Authentic Enemy of Slavery?* (1970); Joseph J. Ellis's *American Sphinx: The Character of Thomas Jefferson* (1997); Lucia Stanton's "'Those Who Labor for My Happiness': Thomas Jefferson and His Slaves" in *Jeffersonian Legacies*, edited by Peter S. Onuf (1993); and William Cohen's "Thomas Jefferson and the Problem of Slavery," *Journal of American History*, 56 (1969). Douglas R. Egerton's "Thomas Jefferson and the Hemings Family: A Matter of Blood," *The Historian*, 60 (1997), reviews some of the literature on the matter from a critical perspective. Interesting for the sake of comparison with Jefferson's actions and views on slavery is Fritz Hirschfeld's *George Washington and Slavery: A Documentary History* (1997).

Arthur Zilversmit's *The First Emancipation: The Abolition of Slavery in the North* (1967) argues that idealism prevailed over economic interest to end slavery north of Maryland. Gary B. Nash in *Race and Revolution* (1990) tends to agree, noting how close the Revolutionary generation came to abolishing slavery and how quickly abolitionist sentiment waned in the new country. Joanne Pope Melish's *Disowning Slavery: Gradual Emancipation and "Race" in New England, 1780–1860* (1998) complements Nash on the speed of the decline of any Revolutionary idealism behind abolition: she brings to light how frequently and in what ways New England slave owners ignored or abused the gradual abolition laws. One can supplement these with Robin Blackburn's much more broadly focused *The Overthrow of Colonial Slavery, 1776–1848* (1988). T. H. Breen's "Making History: The Force of Public Opinion and the Last Years of Slavery in Revolutionary Massachusetts" in *Through a Glass Darkly: Reflections on Personal Identity in Early America*, edited by Ronald Hoffman, Mechal Sobel, and Fredrika J. Teute (1997), places Quock Walker's suit to gain his freedom in the context of two previous slave executions and their effect on public opinion in Massachusetts. Robert W. Fogel and Stanley L. Engerman's "Philanthropy at

Bargain Prices: Notes on the Economics of Gradual Emancipation," *Journal of Legal Studies*, 13 (1974) shows how arrival of white immigrants provided northern states an adequate labor supply and made adherence to ideals and gradual emancipation possible. T. Stephen Whitman's *The Price of Freedom: Slavery and Manumission in Baltimore and Early National Maryland* (1997) explains how Baltimore could have such a high rate of manumission and yet still have so many slaves, arguing that slave owners used the promise of freedom as an incentive to gain work from their slaves, eventually did indeed free them, and then purchased more slaves with profits derived from the recently emancipated men and women.

Books that focus more specifically on the effects of freedom on the free black population, as opposed to how its constituents became free, include James Oliver Horton and Lois E. Horton's *In Hope of Liberty: Culture, Community and Protest Among Northern Free Blacks, 1700–1860* (1997), for the North, and Ira Berlin's *Slaves Without Masters: The Free Negro in the Antebellum South* (1974), for the Upper South. A number of good works deal with free African Americans in particular places in colonial America. Articles by Jane G. Landers, Daniel Schafer, Paul Lachance, Kimberly Hanger, and Robert Olwell in *Against the Odds: Free Blacks in the Slave Societies of the Americas*, edited by Landers (1996), examine free black communities in Spanish Florida, Spanish Louisiana, and South Carolina. John Hope Franklin's *The Free Negro in North Carolina, 1790–1860* (1943) is a detailed study of the "unwanted people" in that state. Shane White's *Somewhat More Independent* and Nash and Soderlund's *Freedom by Degrees*, both noted above, show how long it took freedom to come in those states and how marginal remained the existence of former slaves. Nash treats the subject more broadly in "Forging Freedom: The Emancipation Experience in the Northern Seaport Cities, 1775–1820," in *Slavery and Freedom in the Age of the American Revolution.* Sidney Kaplan's *The Black Presence in the Era of the American Revolution* (1973) includes treatment of a number of individual free blacks whose accomplishments were extraordinary.

The most thorough study of black participation in the Revolutionary struggle is Quarles's *The Negro in the American Revolution*. Woody Holton's *Forced Founders: Indians, Debtors, Slaves, and the Making of the American Revolution in Virginia* (1999) suggests that African Americans played a bigger role in bringing Virginia aristocrats to sever ties with England than previously thought. Sylvia R. Frey's "Between Slavery and Freedom: Virginia Blacks in the American Revolution," *Journal of Southern History*, 49 (1983) covers British attempts to lure away Virginia slaves, showing the strength of the British appeal and the unhealthy living conditions for those who escaped to British armies. Peter H. Wood's "'Liberty is Sweet': African-American Freedom Struggles in the Years before White Independence" in *Beyond the American Revolution: Explorations in the History of American Radicalism*, edited by Alfred F. Young (1993), is an examination of the wave of hope and discontent that welled up among African Americans between 1765 and 1776. American blacks manifested these feelings in serious efforts of resistance and a struggle to free themselves from slavery that culminated in death and disappointment in 1775–76. Good supplements are Luther P. Jackson's "Virginia Negro Soldiers and Seamen in the American Revolution," *Journal of Negro History*, 27 (1942); Pete Maslowski's "National Policy Toward Use of Black Troops in the Revolution," *South Carolina Historical Magazine*, 73 (1972); and chapters on "Violence and Religion in the Black American Revolution" and "Black Revolt in New York City and the Neutral Zone, 1775–1783" in Graham Russell Hodges's *Slavery, Freedom, and Culture among Early American Workers* (1998). For the fate of blacks who left with the British see James W. Walker's *The Black Loyalists: The Search for a Promised Land in Nova Scotia and Sierra Leone, 1783–1870* (1976) or Ellen Gibson Wilson's *The Loyal Blacks* (1976).

Articles by Gary B. Nash, Richard S. Dunn, Philip D. Morgan, and Allan Kulikoff in *Slavery and Freedom in the Age of the American Revolution*, which trace changes in black society in various regions through the period, spawned debate, further study, and some disagreement. Betty Wood's *Women's Work, Men's*

Work: The Informal Slave Economies of Lowcountry Georgia (1995) stresses the role played by the disruption of Revolutionary times in the broadening of slave autonomy and black participation in the region's informal economy. Gary B. Nash and Peter Coclanis in review essays in the *Georgia Historical Quarterly*— Nash's in Volume 77, 1993 ("Review Essay: Slavery, Black Resistance, and the American Revolution") and Coclanis's in Volume 79, 1995 ("Review Essay: Slavery, African-American Agency, and the World We Have Lost")—and Michael Mullin in *Africa in America*, disagree with Wood, arguing that no thriving informal economy could have existed given the master's over-whelming control and the difficult work regime of Low-Country slaves. Kulikoff's *Tobacco and Slaves* is good to read with Dunn's article for social change in the Chesapeake and for implications of this change in the antebellum period. Likewise, Olwell's "Revolutions Achieved and Denied: Charles Town and the Low Country, 1775–1782," in his *Masters, Slaves, and Subjects,* shows how some slaves gained temporary autonomy during the Revolutionary fighting, but in the end had to come to terms with the "culture of power" in which they were forced to live. Studies in David Colin Crass, Steven D. Smith, and Martha Zierden, eds., *The Southern Colonial Backcountry: Interdisciplinary Perspectives on Frontier Communities* (1998) touch on the effects on slaves of the movement into the interiors of South Carolina, North Carolina, Virginia, and Tennessee following the Revolution.

Duncan J. MacLeod's *Slavery, Race and the American Revolution* (1974) argues the importance of the Revolutionary era for the establishment of racism in America. Staughton Lynd's *Class Conflict, Slavery, and the United States Constitution* (1967); Edmund S. Morgan's "Conflict and Consensus in the American Revolution" in *Essays on the American Revolution* (1973), edited by Stephen G. Katz and James H. Hutson; and Richard R. Beeman's *The Evolution of the Southern Backcountry: A Case Study of Lunenburg County, Virginia, 1746–1832* (1984) are provocative studies that relate the revolution to heightened racism. Fredrika Teute Schmidt and Barbara Ripel Wilhelm's "Early Proslavery Petitions in Virginia," *William and Mary Quarterly*, 3rd series, 30

(1973), shows the strength of proslavery sentiment in Virginia through times when there was a push for manumission. F. Nwabueze Okoye's "Chattel Slavery as the Nightmare of the American Revolutionaries," *William and Mary Quarterly*, 3rd series, 37 (1980) is critical of the "establishment historians" who have underplayed the importance of race and slavery to the colonial pamphleteers. William W. Freehling's "The Founding Fathers and Slavery," *American Historical Review*, 77 (1972) argues that the founders had the long-term demise of slavery in mind in the 1780s.

More specific studies that relate to the topic include Jeffrey J. Crow's *The Black Experience in Revolutionary North Carolina* (1977); and Frances D. Pingeon's "Slavery in New Jersey on the Eve of the Revolution" in *New Jersey in the American Revolution*, rev. ed. (1974), edited by William C. Wright; as well as chapters by Mary Beth Norton on southern women in the Revolution, Michael Mullin on British Caribbean and mainland slaves through the war, and Peter H. Wood on republicanism and slave society in South Carolina in *The Southern Experience in the American Revolution*, edited by Jeffrey J. Crow and Larry E. Tise (1978). Jacqueline Jones's "Race, Sex, and Self-Evident Truths: The Status of Slave Women during the Era of the American Revolution" in *Women in the Age of the American Revolution*, edited by Ronald Hoffman and Peter J. Albert (1989), has a broader focus— on enslaved women over the eighteenth century—than its title indicates. Mark E. Brandon's *Free in the World: American Slavery and Constitutional Failure* (1998) is a detailed examination, from the point of view of constitutional theory, of the flaws in the Constitution that enabled slavery to exist and thrive.

INDEX

African Americans in the Colonial Era: From African Origins through the American Revolution, Second Edition
Developmental editor and copy editor: Andrew J. Davidson
Production editor: Lucy Herz
Proofreader: Claudia Siler
Cartographers: James Bier, Jane Domier
Printer: Versa Press, Inc.